The Novels of D. H. Lawrence

The Novels of D. H. Lawrence

A SEARCH FOR INTEGRATION

John E. Stoll

University of Missouri Press

Columbia

Excerpts from the writings of D.H. Lawrence are reproduced in this book with the permission of the copyright holders, as follows:

From *The Collected Letters of D.H. Lawrence*, edited by Harry T. Moore, copyright 1932 by The Estate of D.H. Lawrence and 1934 by Frieda Lawrence, © 1933, 1948, 1953, 1954 and each year 1956–1962 by Angelo Ravagli & C. Montague Weekley, Executors of the Estate of Frieda Lawrence Ravagli. Reprinted by permission of The Viking Press, Inc.

From *Aaron's Rod* by D.H. Lawrence, copyright 1922 by Thomas Seltzer, Inc., renewed 1950 by Frieda Lawrence. Reprinted by permission of The Viking Press, Inc.

From *Sons and Lovers* by D.H. Lawrence, copyright 1913 by Thomas Seltzer, Inc. All Rights Reserved. Reprinted by permission of The Viking Press, Inc.

From *Women in Love* by D.H. Lawrence, copyright 1920, 1922 by David Herbert Lawrence, renewed 1948, 1950 by Frieda Lawrence. Reprinted by permission of The Viking Press, Inc.

From *Kangaroo* by D.H. Lawrence, copyright 1923, renewed 1951 by Frieda Lawrence. Reprinted by permission of The Viking Press, Inc.

From *The Rainbow* by D.H. Lawrence, copyright 1915, renewed 1943 by Frieda Lawrence. Reprinted by permission of The Viking Press, Inc.

From *Studies in Classic American Literature* by D.H. Lawrence, copyright 1923, renewed 1951 by Frieda Lawrence. Reprinted by permission of The Viking Press, Inc.

From *The Plumed Serpent* by D.H. Lawrence, by permission of Alfred A. Knopf, Inc.

From *The White Peacock* by D.H. Lawrence, by permission of Laurence Pollinger, Ltd., and the Estate of the late Mrs. Frieda Lawrence.

From *The Trespasser* by D.H. Lawrence, by permission of Laurence Pollinger, Ltd., and the Estate of the late Mrs. Frieda Lawrence.

From *Lady Chatterley's Lover* by D.H. Lawrence, by permission of Laurence Pollinger, Ltd., and the Estate of the late Mrs. Frieda Lawrence.

Materials from *The Deed of Life: The Novels and Tales of D.H. Lawrence* by Julian Moynahan, copyright © 1963 by Princeton University Press, have been quoted by permission of the Princeton University Press.

Materials from "On *Lady Chatterley's Lover*" by Mark Schorer, which was published in *Evergreen*, I:1, pages 149–78, and as the Introduction to the Grove Press edition of *Lady Chatterley's Lover*, copyright © 1957 by Grove Press, Inc., are reprinted by permission of Grove Press, Inc.

For Alice Bertilson Stoll
and Joseph Prescott

Acknowledgments

It is a pleasure to acknowledge my indebtedness to Moody Prior, Richard Ellmann, and Meno Spann, my teachers early and late, and to Wallace Douglas, that committed man.

One chapter of this book has appeared in the *Ball State University Monograph Series* and parts of two others in *Ball State Forum*.

J.E.S.
Ethridge, Tennessee
June, 1971

Contents

/

The Argument

Lawrence's imagery—its peculiar intensity and specific contextual meanings—has often been discussed but never related to the theory of consciousness that shapes all the novels. A manifestation at once of the author's self-division and his attempt to overcome duality through art, the theory is the cornerstone of Lawrence's psychology. It is implicit in his literary criticism: "The artist usually sets out—or used to—to point a moral and adorn a tale. The tale, however, points the other way, as a rule. Two blankly opposing morals, the artist's and the tale's. Never trust the artist. Trust the tale. The proper function of a critic is to save the tale from the artist who created it."[1] Clearly, Lawrence's romantic view of art rests upon the artist's personality; if it is not unified, his work will not be. The conscious intention of the writer may conflict with the emotional experience the work of art conveys, unconsciously or by the "duplicitous cunning" of the artist. My point is that Lawrence's criticism applies specifically to his own work and that the very means he uses to overcome duality— the theory of consciousness—perpetuates the disproportion in the novels between idea and form, intention and performance. Succeeding chapters will show how implicit Lawrence's theory is in the light imagery of *The White Peacock* and how it develops progressively thereafter to include several rather startling assumptions, all of which depend to some extent upon the biographical connection between the artist and his work.

Now, however, it is important to uncover the foun-

---

1. D. H. Lawrence, *Studies in Classic American Literature*, p. 2.

dations upon which Lawrence gradually constructed the elaborate symbolic system that embodies his views of psychic processes and, correlative with this discovery, to know why neither of the two mutually exclusive schools of Lawrence criticism, the Freudian and the "vitalist" (Jungian), can adequately explain the baffling critical problem the novels present. The Freudians, with whose view of the man and several aspects of the work I sympathize, with some reservations, inevitably reduce the novels to a series of case studies that violate the objectivity of the art and befoul the already impure aesthetic principles it reflects. Lawrence abhorred Freud and all (for Lawrence) Freud represented—the reduction of the vital self to a mere appendage of the socially conditioned id and the advocacy of incest as a means of curing that malady. The vitalists, with whom I agree concerning the general merit of Jungian psychology, constantly misapply Jung to Lawrence and do injustice to them both. Lawrence would also have abhorred a Jungian view of his work, for he rejected the reconciliation of psychic opposites as a distasteful example of incestuous merging, a perverse product of the modern age. To approach the novels rightly, one must grant Lawrence his initial attitudes and premises and find a way to the work that will take advantage of previous critical insight without binding the author to any single school. This "way," the basis of my reasoning, depends upon several definitions and distinctions that will clarify my approach to the novels.

The cornerstone of Lawrence's theory of consciousness rests initially upon his view of the individual in relation to the family unit and the social environment. *Consciousness* is that which is received from the outside —the values and mores that comprise the social milieu and reduce the family to little more than moral automatons. In deliberately or subliminally passing on these social values to the child, the mother, or "culture carrier,"[2] in effect cuts him off from vast areas of deeper experience and being—from his vital self. As a result, even if he is fortunate enough to recognize his predicament, the child is permanently scarred and self-divided. If he does not become aware of this social and maternal conditioning, he survives in a stunted, half-human state, a piece of clay ready to be molded by whoever will. Lawrence the artist and Lawrence the man are inseparable in that both are determined not to be clay, not to be permanently self-divided, not to be victims of the social order. And both reject the mother, society, and blunted behavioristic responses as different aspects of the same threat to individual integrity, the right of the person to respond freely to his world and to himself. Because of the similarity of their effects upon him, Lawrence comes to regard the maternal mind, the social milieu, and the individual consciousness as synonymous and interchangeable. The first two fix themselves to the psyche and rob the individual of a personal and private identity by compelling him to mirror them.

As Lawrence perceives consciousness, then, it is much more than reason or intellect, the instruments it evolves to justify itself and that which it includes. Consciousness is imposed from without but becomes internalized, a psychological process as well as a social product so powerful and threatening that it would smother the role of the unconscious in the reintegrative process and would usurp its place if any attempt were made to reconcile the two. For Lawrence, consciousness as a social product poisons the spontaneous wellsprings of existence and must therefore be destroyed in order to guarantee the integrity of the passions and the individual psyche it infects. Only after the poison is extracted, that is, only after social consciousness has been obliterated, will the unconscious be free to develop its

2. Ernest W. Tedlock, Jr., *D. H. Lawrence, Artist and Rebel*, p. 67.

own kind of awareness to directly reflect and obey its dictates rather than merely to usurp and meddle with the processes of existence. In this way a vital, growing, and fulfilled personality or self will be assured, psychic opposites will be reconciled, and human completeness and community will result—the goal of Lawrence's quest through all his novels.

Nevertheless, even though what may be considered to be Lawrence's own conception of psychic integration is at the end of the quest, the means to the end are Blakean and apocalyptic. If the lion is, ultimately, to lie down with the lamb, it will be only after the lamb has been entirely refashioned in the lion's image; for this alteration to take place, according to Lawrence, both the psyche as we know it and the social order must be destroyed in order to be restructured. Complete reduction or complete self-transformation tend to be the only alternatives in modern life because the collective consciousness permeates and seeks to control all psychic processes, uproots the impulses from which individual differences and identities stem, and creates mass man. In this sense the child is indeed father to the man, for the consequence of living in the industrial state merely intensifies and realizes the reductive process begun at birth—or before birth, in the womb.

As I hope to show, anything less than complete transformation would, in Lawrence's thinking, be regressive and in fact incestuous. Since incestuous desire is the product of the socially conditioned mind alone, it is really the measure of the male's assimilation to that mind, of his longing to be reduced to an adjunct of possessive womanhood (the mother, mother surrogate, or predatory woman as Lawrence comes to call her), and, by extension, to the social milieu. The early novels, *The White Peacock*, *The Trespasser*, and *Sons and Lovers*, reveal the first stage of this process: the attempt of the mother surrogate to assimilate the passive male to her, Lawrence's repudiation of mental (as distinct from social) consciousness as incestuous, and his rejection of the victimized male. Beginning with *The Rainbow*, Lawrence extends his view of consciousness and incest from the man–woman relationship to the social order as a whole. In that novel, psychological reintegration, seen as the reconciliation of the demands of consciousness (right reason, superego, social mores) with those of the unconscious (the id, the feelings, the Adamic), is explicitly rejected because the harmonizing of psychic opposites, of social or mental consciousness and the vital self, leads not to human wholeness but to the complete loss of male identity. Only when the submerged psyche takes on its own identity apart from consciousness will individual wholeness ensue and the vital self emerge.

Lawrence's discovery of this vital self is gradual. First comes his description of consciousness, in the light imagery of *The White Peacock*, as implicitly incestuous, and from *The Trespasser* on, he explicitly identifies this consciousness with the loss of maleness and with enclosure in the womb—again through use of light imagery. Beginning with *Sons and Lovers*, a pattern of light and dark imagery appears in the novels, a manifestation of the increasing struggle between opposed psychic forces. A movement toward resolving the conflict by obliterating mental (or social) consciousness becomes increasingly evident in *The Rainbow*, *Women in Love*, *Aaron's Rod*, *Kangaroo*, *The Plumed Serpent*, and *Lady Chatterley's Lover*. The result in each of these works, however, is a "broken circuit"[3] or gap between the nature of the experience presented and the author's conceptualizations of it, between intention and achievement. Lawrence never shows how (social) consciousness, which up to this time has conditioned, if not determined, the entire psychic life of his heroes, can be uprooted without destroying the entire organism.

His insistence that this destruction is possible and that it will lead to human wholeness is the source, I

3. Richard Chase, *The American Novel and Its Tradition*, p. 1.

believe, of much of the emotional stridence in the work, the sense he projects of a baffling incompleteness and incongruity. While his goal is the restored human relation and a self in which all psychic forces are in harmony and play equal parts, the means or process of the quest involves Lawrence in a dangerous commitment to the irrational. If he does not ultimately advocate destruction for its own sake, his conception of the vital self often makes him appear to do so. For, in attributing to consciousness most of the characteristics usually associated with the Freudian id in a state of neurosis, Lawrence in effect denies the existence of the id as an unconscious principle that motivates our behavior while at the same time unwittingly incorporating many of its qualities into his conception of the vital self. Thus, the claims he makes for the vital self are in some measure contradicted by his handling of the idea in the novels—the result, I suggest, of his view of the mental life as a principle antagonistic to the vital self. It is this contradiction between means and ends that disturbs so many readers of Lawrence and that creates the aesthetic imbalance in his work.

In a more immediate sense, the raw materials for the art do not seem to be altogether transmuted by the art, as Freudian critics and moralists such as Eliseo Vivas have been so ready to point out. Still, while it is true that the artist is indeed omnipresent and constantly interferes with the tale, the thrust of such criticism is unnecessarily reductive. The art all too often disappears in case studies and ethical arguments, and the artist's intention seems to be totally opposed to his achievement. The problem of the novels will never be fairly met or their value clearly demonstrated until Lawrence's special relation to his work is accounted for through the symbolic techniques he employed. He is much more detached and the art more fully unified than his critics have perceived, though much less so than his doctrinaire supporters have asserted. To make this point absolutely clear, the critic has no right to account for the work through the personality of the artist except when the artist leaves him no choice, and though a superior artist, Lawrence does not always leave such a choice.

The question of homosexuality must of necessity loom large in any consideration of Lawrence's view of psychic processes. The Freudians and some moralists are entirely correct in pointing to the homosexuality apparent in the novels, but they have not sought to connect it to recognizable and developed themes in the art. I suggest that homosexuality comes to be a deliberately handled theme in Lawrence's works and that it is a manifestation, not the source, of the critical problem the novels present. The primary difficulty concerns the author's view of homosexuality as a product of (social) consciousness alone, unrelated to any other source or influence. The Freudians are right in noticing an unrecognized deviance in the man himself, which may qualify and in part negate in any categorical sense his theory of its source. But the Freudians are wrong in maintaining that Lawrence is unaware of perversity in his own work. Not only does he consider the fact of perversity, but he weighs its significance as well. For Lawrence, the relation between superimposed consciousness and what others would consider the id is a dynamic, intermingling one. Consciousness creates the id and is at times in the novels synonymous with it; to penetrate the id to the vital self beyond involves the destruction of the socially conditioned mind, which is the principle that structures and molds the unconscious to its image.

Nevertheless, by regarding homosexuality only as a product of the mental life and by advocating the destruction of consciousness, Lawrence is overresponding to the threat deviance posed for him. And this response is evident in the emotional dogmatism in the work, in the author's underlying insistence that he is right, the

7

intellectual tentativeness of many of his thematic statements notwithstanding, when there is nothing in the
work to justify such a response. His manner of handling
consciousness, I believe, involves a rationalizing process
that enables him to deny any relationship between deviance and the vital self, and to identify consciousness,
the social order, and Christianity as obstacles to be destroyed in the quest for self-fulfillment.

At the same time, Lawrence incorporates this rationalization so firmly into a symbolic pattern that it becomes
an almost completely realized aesthetic objectification
within the work. The almost successful nature of this
attempt is the basis of my approach to the novels and
distinguishes my viewpoint from that of the Freudians
and moralists. Mark Spilka, Julian Moynahan, and other
vitalist critics, to be sure, would deny this view of Lawrence altogether. They emphasize the integrative ends
of the quest only, not the apocalyptic and contradictory
means to the end, although their insights are in other
respects illuminating. The critical reasons for this judgment and for the differences among the Freudian, vitalist,
and my own point of view will be discussed in the chapter on *Sons and Lovers.*

Since references to "Lawrentian," "Freudian," "Jungian," and to the psychic processes they include occur
throughout this study, Lawrence's agreements and dis-
agreements with Freud and Jung ought to be established
as clearly as possible. In general, he differs most widely
from Freud in emphasizing the dynamic interrelation-
ship (and ultimate identity) between the social order,
Christianity, and individual consciousness, the threat
they pose to the unconscious, and his rejection of the id
as a principle of the unconscious. For Freud, who was
thoroughly Victorian and, to the present generation, old-
fashioned in this respect, the connection between consciousness and the unconscious (the id) scarcely involved
the social context at all. On the one hand, Lawrence

would agree with Freud that neurosis is caused by the repression of formerly "known" or experienced impulses and awarenesses. But he would not agree that the unconscious is originally a clear and empty slate, that it is a mechanism determined by environment and heredity, and that it is affected by or is the source of neurosis. For Lawrence, the essential unconscious, the vital self, is pure and pristine, collective, archetypal, dynamic, beyond and uncorrupted by environment (if not heredity), and not affected by neurosis. In this respect, Lawrence not only opposes Freud's view of the unconscious, but stands Freud on his head by insisting that repressed materials are not deposited in the vital self at all.[4] Neurosis—and when Lawrence speaks of neurosis he most often means incest—is strictly a product of conscious merging, entirely dissociated from the vital self.[5]

It is not my purpose to agree with Lawrence or with Freud per se, but simply to suggest that in setting himself at odds with Freud and in using him as a frame of reference, Lawrence places himself in relation to a Freudian context. Of course, if one approaches Lawrence's idea of neurosis from a Freudian viewpoint, he must consider it a wrong-headed inversion of Freud's incest hypothesis. Although both would agree that consciousness plays a role in neurosis, only Lawrence would assert that the cause of neurosis is consciousness and that neurosis remains in consciousness as its product. With the novels as evidence, the matter resolves into the single relevant question of whether, given his view of psychic processes, the artist adequately transforms and objectifies the raw materials for his theory into art. I will attempt to show that Lawrence is only partially

4. Frederick J. Hoffman, "Lawrence's Quarrel with Freud," in Frederick J. Hoffman and Harry T. Moore, eds., *The Achievement of D. H. Lawrence*, pp. 121–22.

5. Lawrence, *Studies*, p. 76.

successful, not because his ideas are artistically wrong, though I disagree with many of them, but because his emotional insistence that he is right helps to create an aesthetic imbalance in his work. The author's emotional dogmatism lends itself to pronouncements about the nature and the significance of human experience that deliberately preclude other possibilities implicit in the novels. These he refuses to encounter, and I believe that the source of the imbalance is in his theory of consciousness and his doctrine of the vital self.

Lawrence's differences with Jung seem less extensive at first glance. Both would consider the unconscious basically healthy and nondestructive; archetypal, creative, and evolving, rather than mechanical or determined; unconditioned by environment and, in this sense, collective. In addition, both would reject Freud's original view of art as a manifestation of neurotic wish fulfillment, and both would consider the "paradise within" to be the result of integration, of psychic opposites reconciled. Lawrence might assert that art is a way of shedding neurosis, but he would agree that art is also the attempt to recapture and to discover the archetypal experience or the essential self. His greatest difference with Jung—and a crucial one—involves the means he would employ to overcome psychic duality: the achievement of a rational, ordered goal through a destructive, irrational process. Lawrence's commitment to the destruction of consciousness and the entire society in order to begin the integrative process sets him in diametric opposition to Jung and suggests his fundamental kinship to Blake. Whether or not Lawrence's approach to psychic processes is acceptable, however, is again not directly to the point. The primary consideration is whether the artist successfully formulates his concepts from the experience he presents in the work.

As a manifestation of the psychological dissociation inherent in his theory of consciousness, the light and dark imagery in *Sons and Lovers* reflects the author's struggle to go beyond "normal" integration by initially doing away with one of the components essential to that process. Lawrence's view of masculine (dark) and feminine (light) is an offshoot of this attempt. It suggests the radical nature of the experience behind the theory and shows the importance of the symbolism as a way of describing his departure from Jung's integrative concept. The effects of this departure are most evident in the "leadership" novels, from *Aaron's Rod* through *The Plumed Serpent*. Lawrence's hope that darkness would extinguish light is embedded in the very means he chooses to convey it, and the results are artistically disastrous.

The connection between Lawrence's rejection of Freud's incest hypothesis and his departure from Jung is now evident. The disagreement with Freud permits him to consider incest the product of consciousness and to assert a causal relation, sometimes a symbolic identity, between them. By denying Jung's integrative concept, he can keep the unconscious pure. Since the imposed social consciousness is incestuous, any attempt at integration will only enlarge the area of blight and more immediately endanger the individual. This psychoanalytic context, I believe, can aid in evaluating the basis of Lawrence's thought, and my use of certain terms should be understood within such a context. Though definitely non-Freudian in their application here, references to the *known self* or *conscious self*, for example, cannot be grasped adequately apart from Freudian psychology. Lawrence saw himself in relation to Freud, and Freud's theories provide a convenient instrument to illuminate one part of his dialectic. The terms suggest both an evaluation and a description of one phase of the struggle waged in the art between psychic opposites. For like reasons, the terms *vital self* or *unknown self* are illuminated by Jung, and it is useful to keep that frame of reference in mind: Together, the known self and the vital self signify Lawrence's complete dialectic, the psychological duality in which the art develops.

Lawrence's estimate of Moby Dick captures this spirit of duality and its symbolism:

> What then is Moby Dick? He is the deepest blood-being of the white race; he is our deepest blood-nature.
>
> And he is hunted, hunted, hunted by the maniacal fanaticism of our white mental consciousness. We want to hunt him down. To subject him to our will. And in this maniacal conscious hunt of ourselves we get dark races and pale to help us, red, yellow, and black, east and west, Quaker and fire-worshipper, we get them all to help us in this ghastly maniacal hunt which is our doom and our suicide.
>
> The last phallic being of the white man. Hunted into the death of upper consciousness and the ideal will. Our blood-self subjected to our will. Our blood-consciousness sapped by a parasitic or ideal consciousness.
>
> Hot-blooded sea-born Moby Dick. Hunted by the monomaniacs of the idea.[6]

The attack against "the maniacal fanaticism of our white mental consciousness" implies the mutual exclusiveness of the known and vital selves and locates the source of my methodology in Lawrence. The known self is identical with "white mental consciousness," "ideal consciousness," and "ideal will," the pursuit of which ends in doom and suicide. The vital self, on the other hand, is explicitly associated with "phallic being," "blood-self," and "blood-consciousness," implicitly with life and wholeness of being, and obliquely with darkness. From many such instances in the essays and fiction, the hypothesis follows that Lawrence's art has its origins in an extreme split, a dissociation of upper and under consciousness, mental and passional, abstract and concrete, feminine and masculine.

As a response to the split, the novels as a whole are conditioned by a basic quest for wholeness of being.

6. Lawrence, *Studies*, p. 160.

The characters discover, encounter, and interpret the significance of their experiences in order to arrive at conceptions of themselves that are at once positive and in accord with reality. The quest begins with the recognition of psychological abnormality, leads to the rejection of the Jungian means to psychic integration as incestuous and regressive, and culminates in the attempt to arrive at the vital self, the pristine unconscious, and the consciousness evolving from it. As I have stated, Lawrence's attempt is not completely successful. In the novels beginning with *Sons and Lovers* a disproportion becomes apparent between what the Lawrentian hero asserts about his experience and the nature of the experience, between the hero's means and his ends, and between Lawrence's rational and tentative claims for the validity of his theses and the emotional dogmatism that governs them. Before *Sons and Lovers*, the formal problem appears primarily in the discrepancy between the characters' responses to experience and the ostensible causes of the responses, which suggests that the earlier work is much less conceptualized than the later. If *The White Peacock* and *The Trespasser* describe the basic experience, *Sons and Lovers* is the first concerted attempt to analyze it. Lawrence's novels, indeed the whole body of his work, can thus be systematically arranged according to the state of the psychic quest and the attending formal problems.

Reflected in the very structure of each novel, often in what critics have called an aesthetic imbalance between symbolism and realism, the quest involves two fundamentally opposed aims. The first is to explore the known self and to state what exists. Compared with the rest of the novels, *The White Peacock*, *The Trespasser*, and *Sons and Lovers* are more free of generalization and make a progressive effort to ascertain the psychic facts. Technically, each is an improvement upon its predecessor in many ways: in the more objective relationship of the narrator to the work; in the increasing ability of the

author to involve himself in the material; in the developing cohesiveness between dramatic intent and dramatic
structure; in the growing sharpness and analytic precision of style; and in the increasing suitability of the
symbolism to realistic detail. In *The White Peacock* the
divided self is discovered and presented obliquely in
lyrical isolation; in *The Trespasser* the breach is wid-
ened, and the divided self is revealed more directly
through the psychic interaction of the two main characters; in *Sons and Lovers* both techniques are wedded
rather unsuccessfully to a dominant dramatic realism.
While he does not clearly enough perceive the reason for
Paul Morel's final casting off of Miriam, Lawrence for the
first time does come to grips with the problem of self.
The known self is encountered, the self-division admitted, the causes—as far as understood—duly noted,
and the struggle begun for dealing rationally with the
past as a means of finding hope for the future through
the pursuit of a new and undiscovered personality.

The second purpose is to show the vital self emerging from the old. This process commences in *Sons and
Lovers* and is much more evident in *The Rainbow*;
Women in Love reveals not so much the emergence of the
vital self as the necessity for it. Though the opposed aims
are for the most part held in balance in these most successful of Lawrence's novels, they are not as controlled in
Aaron's Rod, *Kangaroo*, and *The Plumed Serpent*. The
leadership works break into two unintegrated halves
that involve the hero in time and in transcending time,
and the hero as the old known self and as the new vital
self. Nor is Lawrence's aim there to show the means by
which the hero succeeds, but simply to assert dogmatically that he is successful or will be. The major flaw in
these novels, to repeat, is that experience and hypothesis
diverge: the independent existence of the vital self and
the validity of Lawrence's conception of it. Finally, in
Lady Chatterley's Lover Lawrence presents the main
characters as having come through, as having already

arrived at the rainbow, the psychic quest attained. In my view, the faults of this work reside in the evidence that Lawrence does not fully recognize and deal honestly with sexual materials; that he confuses the will to power with the vital self, perhaps deliberately; and that his rejection of mental consciousness and its role in the re-integrative process perpetuates disunity in the work.

In short, Lawrence's development as an artist, through his four major creative phases, stands revealed in his progressive mastery of the thematic and technical conflict between the known and the unknown self. Phase One includes *The White Peacock, The Trespasser,* and *Sons and Lovers;* Phase Two, *The Rainbow* and *Women in Love;* Phase Three, *The Lost Girl, Aaron's Rod, Kangaroo,* and *The Plumed Serpent;* and Phase Four, *Lady Chatterley's Lover.* It is also possible to arrange the shorter fiction within this scheme and to discuss it in relation to the novels. The virtue of this approach to Lawrence generally, I believe, is that the special relation of the author to his work can be taken into consideration without needless dabbling in psychological and bio-graphical criticism. With these conclusions, perceptive reading of his work moves easily from *The White Peacock* to *Lady Chatterley's Lover.* The following chapters apply the conclusions to show how the symbolism functions in each work and how it develops cumulatively into a patterned whole.

//

The Fabricated Personality
The White Peacock

The White Peacock reflects Lawrence's concern with the psychological processes of the self, and the critical problem of the novel results from a lack of fusion between the major themes. The incestuous tie between Lettie and Cyril—and ultimately between all the male and female characters—is not linked to the idea of manhood and the nature of the male relationships proposed. Thus, while the author more than adequately describes the qualities of the possessive woman, he never wholly accounts for the reasons for the passive male's bondage to her and thus blurs the dramatic structure of the novel. This ambiguity of form, which is apparent throughout Lawrence's fiction in his incomplete detachment from his characters, follows from the characters' unwillingness to confront themselves, from their rationalization, rejection, or overresponse to certain facets of experience. Formulated afterward as a theory of consciousness, the distortion of experience includes an assumed identity between the possessive woman, modern society, and Christianity as the agents responsible for the hero's plight. In *The White Peacock*, the rationalizing process is evident in the discrepancy between the characters' reactions to stimuli and the stated reasons for their reactions. The process is perceivable in the use Lawrence makes of natural background as a symbolic device to relate character, theme, and form—the successful embodiment of theme in the character(s) and/or their relationships.

The aesthetic of withdrawal, the vivid expression of emotion for emotion's sake, and the use of character and background to support a theme all mark *The White Peacock* as a product of the decadence, a *fleur du mal* of the Midlands. The work supports the hypothesis that the literary and historical milieu influences the form of the novel. Some of the art and creators Lawrence cites are "La Belle Dame Sans Merci," "The Lady of Shalott," "The Blessed Damozel," "The Raven," Burne-Jones, Aubrey Beardsley, Clausen, Wagner, Debussy, Strauss, Schopenhauer, Merimée, and Flaubert. Most of these references, of course, are not in themselves functional, merely decorative, but they do help to establish the tone of lush hypersensitivity, add a historical dimension to the novel, and suggest that at least in the beginning Lawrence saw himself in relation to his milieu.

Given the historical context, the reader can deter-mine more exactly what this relationship was and how it influenced the form of the novel. As a combination of the Blessed Damozel, Ligeia, and La Belle Dame, Lettie is a criticism of a particular society. Lawrence views the type of woman she is as basically possessive and predatory, a manifestation of male-betraying idealism. To this extent, *The White Peacock* is an attempt to an-alyze the times, not merely to describe them. The explicit rejection of the white peacock is at least an implicit re-jection of the age that glorified her type.

Cyril Beardsall, the narrator of the book, is also tied to this theme. He is a created persona, pale and abstract, not a character at all in any traditional sense. Overly sensitive, with a horror of ugliness that rivals Dorian Gray's, he is the effete embodiment of Schopenhauer's "world as will and idea." Completely negative, he sur-vives, not by exerting will but by rejecting it. Like Marius, also, Cyril wishes to transcend life by denying its validity outside the realm of sensation and to create from sensation a static, private world of self-contemplation. Together with the negation of self this evasion of reality implies, Cyril's rejection of will per-mits the reader to regard him as the historical male counterpart to the Pre-Raphaelite Lettie. Behind the brother–sister relationship, then, lies a symbolic one that links his feminine passivity, his homosexual attraction to George Saxton, and his ties with all the other characters to the concept of the possessive woman. In this work, Lawrence's first novel, the causes of Cyril's problems are related to incest.

To begin with, each of the male characters has significance only through his relation to the white peacock, whose meaning is determined primarily through Lawrence's use of background. As the guiding intelligence in the work, Cyril identifies the peacock symbolism with the characters, illuminates their interrelationships, and determines the reader's view of the characters and their views of each other. This organic connection between the background, Cyril, and the other characters is fixed at the very beginning: "I stood watching the shadowy fish slide through the gloom of the mill-pond. They were grey, descendants of the silvery things that had darted away from the monks, in the young days when the valley was lusty. The whole place was gathered in the musing of old age. The thick-piled trees on the far shore were too dark and sober to dally with the sun; the weeds stood crowded and motionless. Not even a little wind flickered the willows of the islets. The water lay softly, intensely still. Only the thin stream falling through the mill-race murmured to itself of the tumult of life which had once quickened the valley."[1] The tone of decay and despair, of life seeping away, not only establishes Cyril's mood and the dominant tone of the novel as a whole, but it is gradually transferred to the characters and psychologically restated. The causes of the decay are then sought in the characters themselves and expressed once more through the background. This process is deliberately and delicately accomplished.

Immediately afterward, Lawrence introduces a scene in which Cyril's friend, George Saxton, is destroying a bees' nest: " 'Leave them alone,' said I. . . . He persisted, however, and broke the wing of the next. 'Oh, dear—

1. D. H. Lawrence, *The White Peacock*, p. 1.

pity!' said he, and he crushed the little thing between his fingers" (p. 2). The original impression of sadness and decay jars against the sudden cruelty, but when the scene shifts to Lettie and George looking at "Hoeing," a painting by Clausen, the relationship between them is clear enough:

> "You [George] are a piano which will only play a dozen common notes. Sunset is nothing to you—it merely happens anywhere. Oh, but you make me feel as if I'd like to make you suffer. If you'd ever been sick; if you'd ever been born into a home where there was something oppressed you, and you couldn't understand; if ever you'd believed, or even doubted, you might have been a man by now. You never grow up, like bulbs which spend all summer getting fat and fleshy, but never wakening the germ of a flower. As for me, the flower is born in me, but it wants bringing forth. Things don't flower if they're overfed. You have to suffer before you blossom in this life. When death is just touching a plant, it forces it into a passion of flowering. You wonder how I have touched death. You don't know. There's always a sense of death in this home. I believe my mother hated my father before I was born. That was death in her veins for me before I was born. It makes a difference—" (P. 27)

Not only do the causes of Lettie's unhappiness point homeward; their outward manifestations—the emphasis on death, the sense of decay, the hatred and the cruelty —are now associated within a given character. In George a similar disaffection has taken place. It becomes apparent initially in his cruelty to the bees and gradually strengthens until it turns against him through his relation with Lettie. George's difficulty, however, is never tied explicitly to its cause, his hatred of his parents.

The joining of the themes, the possessive woman and the tormented male, is then once more projected into the background. It receives fullest expression in this garden scene: "The garden was not very productive, save of weeds, and perhaps, tremendous lank artichokes or swollen marrows. But at the bottom, where the end of the farm buildings rose high and grey, there was a plum tree which had been crucified to the wall, and which had broken away and leaned forward from bondage. Now under the boughs were hidden great mist-bloomed, crimson treasures, splendid globes" (p. 52). Lettie's previous remark about suffering is completely embodied here in the image of the plum tree crucified to the wall. Leaning forward from bondage, George has become a Christ whose pain is pleasure and whose very crucifixion is a kind of corrupt resurrection, the fruit of his transformation by Lettie. This figure is all part of the *fleur du mal* theme; it shows the interaction between background and character to be an organic one, and it directly relates the meaning of the peacock symbolism to Cyril's point of view.

Embracing the entire man–woman relationship presented in the novel, this symbolism functions in two ways. At first it appears to be merely a conceptual metaphor describing the essentially possessive, sadistic, and destructive nature of women. Lettie and, ultimately, all the female characters come to be explicitly identified with the peacock as destroyers of men. As those destroyed, on the other hand, the male characters give the symbol a quality that expresses their inexplicable longing for death, which it would otherwise not convey. Thus, the peacock may simply designate *woman* or, more comprehensively, may signify and analyze the man–woman relationship, as far as Lawrence attempts such analysis in the work. Later, the symbolism reveals the ways in which all the male characters are dramatic projections of Cyril, as the female characters are of Lettie. The incestuous link to be partially demonstrated between Cyril and Lettie then suggests the cause of Cyril's death wish and the nature of these dramatic projections.

Lettie's gradual transformation first into a swan and then into a peacock is described primarily through imagery of white birds. Both the color's connotation of purity and Cyril's enchantment are evident in the initial comparison of Lettie to a "sail stealing along the water's edge" (p. 9). Though the sail image shares the quality of whiteness with the swan, Lawrence does not render their association more explicit until later in the text: "The swans, as they sailed into shadow, were dim, haunting spectres; the wind found us shivering" (p. 62). Then, long after she has been identified with the swan, Lettie is seen eddying "unevenly down the little stream of courtship" (p. 144). In addition, a change in Cyril's response may be observed, from enchantment in the first passage to harrowing anxiety in the second, to implicit contempt in the third.

As Lettie is further defined through her whiteness, the color takes on, by degrees, the connotation of ugliness and defilement. Immediately before the introduction of the sail image, for example, Lawrence presents the scene in which Cyril expects to find his mother dusting the piano at home, but discovers Lettie instead: " 'That must be mother dusting the drawing room,' I thought. The unaccustomed sound of the old piano startled me. The vocal chords behind the green silk bosom—you only discovered it was not a bronze silk bosom by poking a fold aside,—had become as thin and tuneless as a dried old woman's. Age had yellowed the teeth of my mother's little piano, and shrunken its spindle legs. Poor old thing, it could but screech in answer to Lettie's fingers flying across it in scorn, so the prim, brown lips were always closed save to admit the duster" (p. 6). And immediately after the sail reference, some frightened lapwings are heard "whining, skelping off from a fancy as if they had a snake under their wings" (p. 11). The whining birds and screeching piano bind the natural and domestic scenes together, and the description of Lettie's fingers flying across the piano "in scorn" establishes this salient characteristic as the focal point of her transformation into the white peacock.

The view that the sail image ultimately elicits the swan thus receives auricular reinforcement from the

screeching and whining and evokes an undertone of discord that qualifies the initial impression of Lettie. The
lapwings fly off at her approach, and Cyril, expecting to
find his mother dusting the piano, does not register sur-
prise or even change of expression when he discovers
Lettie instead. Perhaps deliberately he seems to identify
mother and sister. Nor is a sexual element absent in the
identification, since the "green silk bosom" of the piano
is juxtaposed against its tone, "thin and tuneless as a
dried old woman's." Behind appearances there lurks a
sinister reality, associated with Lettie's scorn, and Cyril
is suspended between the allure of this beauty and its
underlying ugliness. The deliberateness of such associations for Lawrence appears even more explicitly when
he describes the effect of one of Lettie's conversations
upon George: "Whatever he said to her, she answered
in the same mad clatter of French, speaking high and
harshly. The sound was strange and uncomfortable.
There was a painful perplexity in his brow, such as I
often perceived afterwards, a sense of something hurting, something he could not understand" (p. 30). The
second sentence, "The sound was strange and uncomfortable," shows how completely realized the entire passage is, and the phrase "mad clatter" reflects the aural
and visual integration of the preceding scene.

Furthermore, the reason for George's "hurting" is
closely related to the significance of the bird imagery:
"Her pose was fine. With her head thrown back, the
roundness of her throat ran finely down to the bosom,
which swelled above the pile of books held by her
straight arms. He looked at her. Their lips smiled curiously. She put back her throat as if she were drinking.
They felt the blood beating madly in their necks. Then,
suddenly breaking into a slight trembling, she turned
round and left the room" (p. 29). The description suggests Lettie's poisonous attraction for George as well as
her swanlike beauty. It is becoming obvious that she is
the victimizer and he the victim; through the bird im-

agery Lawrence is achieving a deliberately ambiguous effect. Lettie is at once sexually attractive and repulsive, pure white and screeching, a goddess and a vampire.

The one place in the novel where Lettie's physical features are specifically mentioned strengthens this view by showing the underlying identity between her purity and mentality (consciousness). Lawrence contrasts her with Emily: "Lettie, as I have said, is tall, approaching six feet; she is lissome, but firmly moulded, by nature graceful; in her pose and harmonious movement are revealed the subtle sympathies of her artist's soul. The other is shorter, much heavier. In her every motion you can see the extravagance of her emotional nature" (p. 97). Lettie's whiteness, "artist's soul," and birdlike lightness suggest the dominance of intellect and will over emotion, represented by Emily. This is why Lettie's very beauty is a source of potential horror for the passive male and why her purity and ugliness are manifestations of psychological dissociation. The first of Lawrence's possessive women, she is incapable of living from an emotional center, but only from a mental one in which intellect reigns and from which the passions are divorced.

Though Lawrence never establishes the sexual basis of Lettie's cruelty beyond asserting in the last section of the novel that all modern women are so, he does associate it with the death of her father: "The death of the man who was our father changed our lives. It was not that we suffered a great grief; the chief trouble was the unanswered crying of failure. But we were changed in our feelings and in our relations; there was a new consciousness, a new carefulness. We had lived between the woods and the water all our lives, Lettie and I, and she had sought the bright notes in everything. . . . Lately, however, she had noticed again the cruel, pitiful crying of a hedgehog caught in a gin, and she had noticed the traps for the fierce little murderers, traps walled in with a small fence of fir, and baited with the guts of a killed rabbit" (p. 43). Not only is the whole of nature made to reflect her state of mind, but the connection between Lettie's ugliness (screeching) and her beauty is more clearly an aspect of her self-division. The new consciousness, the changed feelings, and the fixation upon the crying of the hedgehog all anticipate the sadism implicit in her psychological split. Annable's later description of the white peacock in the cemetery as "all vanity and screech and defilement" (p. 148) clarifies this view of Lettie and enables the reader for the first time to see her from the inside. Her unconscious nature is totally exposed; she is a screaming bird, a "miserable brute" dirtying an "angel" (p. 148). In short, Lettie becomes a female Dorian Gray. Her angelic innocence and purity (the angel) are only a mask for predatory lust and foulness.

For the remainder of the work, only this one side of her nature is manifest, associated as it is with male domination: "Leslie knelt down at her feet. She shook the hood back from her head, and her ornaments sparkled in the moonlight. Her face with its whiteness and its shadows was full of fascination, and in their dark recesses her eyes thrilled George with hidden magic. She smiled at him along her cheeks while her husband crouched before her. Then, as the three walked towards the wood she flung her draperies into loose eloquence and there was a glimpse of her bosom white with the moon. She laughed and chattered, and shook her silken stuffs, sending out a perfume exquisite on the frosted air. . . . As she turned laughing to the two men, she let her cloak slide over her white shoulder and fall with silk splendour of a peacock's gorgeous blue over the arm of the large settee" (p. 251). Lettie's symbolic transformation is now achieved. If she or her group of friends are ironically referred to afterward as goddesses or ministering angels, this description only completes the symbol by extending it to all the female characters in the work. In spite of marrying and bearing children, these women remain sterile, spiritual virgins who never fulfill themselves or provide fulfillment for another.

nceptual significance of the white peacock
sideration of its expressive value in the novel,
.on of the symbol with the male longing for
assumptions behind this discussion, to be
sure, are that Cyril views Lettie as a mother surrogate;
that their relationship is implicitly incestuous; and that
Mrs. Beardsall may be seen as the original white peacock
and the source of Cyril's self-division. One of the defi-
ciencies of *The White Peacock* in this respect is the author's incomplete detachment from his character. The
nature of Cyril's relation to Lawrence, I believe, gives
the peacock image its peculiar intensity, illuminates
Cyril's ambivalent hatred of Lettie and his longing for
her, and suggests the reason for the formal problem of
the novel. The links between male passivity and the
onslaught against women in the second part of the work
never join. Because he identifies with his character too
completely, Lawrence does not always render the Cyril–
Lettie relationship objectively. There is an unstated psychological significance of the relationship that is uniden-
tifiable. Even as the symbols that Lawrence has elaborated
achieve meaning, they are dissipated into the conventional realism of Part Two. From this spending of the
force of the symbols it would seem that Lawrence's failure to objectify Cyril's relation to Lettie properly involves his own emotional turning away from it, a failure
to come to terms with the implications of the theme, and
an attempt to seek refuge in the wooden, plot-centered
realism of Part Two.

With the shift in emphasis, moreover, Lawrence
abandons the original mother–son–sister relationship,
and he offers instead a series of strident generalizations
that place the blame for man's sexual difficulties upon
the peacock conception of womanhood. Since these assertions do not emerge from the experience of Cyril, the
only character in the novel beside Lettie whose background and mental processes can be directly observed,
they are, in effect, rationalizations. They are part of a

rationalizing process that the author superimposes upo
the work, and this process is extended later in the novel
to include an identification between the possessive woman, modern mechanistic society, and Christianity. Formulated as a theory of consciousness in *The Trespasser*,
the process is carried over without modification to subsequent novels. According to the theory, (social) consciousness per se, which is feminine and incorporates
the threefold identification suggested above, is responsible for man's failure to realize himself. It must be
obliterated before the individual can free himself from
the possessive, reductive, and ultimately incestuous domination by women, and before the new consciousness associated with the vital self can evolve. Thus, Lawrence's
indisposition to confront the mother–son relationship in
The White Peacock—his rationalizing it away by a sudden shift in emphasis from personally felt emotion to
formulated concepts of the emotion—is also the source
of much confusion in his later work. The formal problem
of all the novels probably originates here, and there is
some substance to the idea that the later prophet is simply the man who will not accept what the artist tells him.

Internal evidence for the incestuous relationship is
tenuous, but the motif is reflected in the symbolic devices
used to inform the parental ties. As the white peacock,
Lettie is also the mother surrogate who has conditioned
Cyril and for whom he yearns. And if he sometimes
deprecates his father, Cyril also wishes to idealize him
and to create a father in his own image:

> "Fancy being in love and making a row in such a
> twilight," said I as we continued our way. But when we
> came opposite the fallen tree, we saw no lovers there, but
> a man sleeping, and muttering through his sleep. The cap
> had fallen from his grizzled hair, and his head leaned back
> against a profusion of the little wild geraniums that dec-
> orated the dead bough so delicately. The man's clothing
> was good, but slovenly and neglected. His face was pale
> and worn with sickness and dissipation. As he slept, his
> grey beard wagged, and his loose unlovely mouth moved

in indistinct speech. He was acting over again some part of his life, and his features twitched during the unnatural sleep. He would give a little groan, gruesome to hear, and then talk to some woman. His features twitched as if with pain, and he moaned slightly.

The lips opened in a grimace, showing the yellow teeth behind the beard. Then he began again talking in his throat, thickly, so that we could only tell part of what he said. It was very unpleasant. I wondered how we should end it. Suddenly through the gloom of the twilight-haunted woods came the scream of a rabbit caught by a weasel. The man awoke with a sharp "Ah!"—he looked round in consternation, then sinking down again wearily, said, "I was dreaming again." (P. 21)

Mr. Beardsall is not the crude person Cyril later says he is, and the portrayal of the father "alone and palely loitering," asleep against the dead bough from which geraniums are blooming, puts him within the novel's *fleur du mal* theme. The screaming of the rabbit caught by the weasel echoes the same sense of torment and despair that is expressed through similar nature imagery by Lettie, George, and Cyril. Clearly, the same kinds of conflicts exist in him as in the other main characters.

In addition, Mrs. Beardsall has deliberately conditioned both Cyril and Lettie to hate their father: "The marriage had been unhappy. My father was of frivolous, rather vulgar character, but plausible, having a good deal of charm. He was a liar, without notion of honesty, and he had deceived my mother thoroughly. One after another she discovered his mean dishonesties and deceits, and her soul revolted from him, and because the illusion of him had broken into a thousand vulgar fragments, she turned away with the scorn of a woman who finds her romance has been a trumpery tale" (p. 32). Uttered as if rehearsed in his mother's presence, this description does not square with fact or with the prior scene. Cyril's rejection of his father is ambiguous, for Mr. Beardsall is not presented elsewhere as lying, deceitful, dishonest, vulgar, and frivolous. Cyril's inherent regard for his father contradicts the viewpoint superimposed upon him and points to some obscure element in the parental relationship that he will not face. The image of Mrs. Beardsall's soul "broken into a thousand vulgar fragments" is a significant aspect of their relationship, and I shall examine it later in detail.

Nor is the father's death inconsequential in the lives of Cyril and Lettie: "The death of the man who was our father changed our lives. It was not that we suffered a great grief; the chief trouble was the unanswered crying of failure. But we were changed in our feelings and in our relations; there was a new consciousness, a new carefulness" (p. 43). In later assuming the role of mother, even the Magna Mater, Lettie does so with the knowledge of Mrs. Beardsall's victory over her father. In identifying with him, of course, Cyril accepts the father's failure as his own. Again, it is not unwarranted to assume that Mr. Beardsall's marital difficulties are in part sexual, similar to those Annable was subjected to by his first wife (Lady Crystabel) and to those George Saxton has later to endure with Lettie. In fact, the novel includes a hierarchy of male characters in this respect: Cyril, who seems unaffected by women (but is not); Annable, who ostensibly wins his freedom from woman and survives; Mr. Beardsall, who loses; George Saxton, who succumbs without a struggle; and Leslie Tempest, who stupidly and unknowingly gives way and becomes the prototype of Siegmund in *The Trespasser* and of Gerald Crich in *Women in Love*. Mr. Beardsall's failure, however, does not disturb Cyril nearly so much as his victimization. This aspect of his father's life is what he rejects and what leads to his own ambivalent relations with both men and women. On the one hand, Cyril blames all women, and implicitly his mother most heavily of all, for being possessive; on the other, he blames all men for allowing themselves to become victims. Cyril's later contemptuous conceptualization of all women as white peacocks is balanced only by his idealization of all men who reject them. He is man-oriented and homosexually motivated, which is the basis of his relationship with George, his father, and Annable.

The death of the father, then, does not end the presence of the father figure in the work. By a process of idealization and symbolic transference, this role passes to Annable, that refuge for all who fall and seek to rise: " 'Be a good animal, true to your animal instinct,' was his motto. With all this, he was fundamentally very unhappy—and he made me also wretched. It was this power to communicate his unhappiness that made me somewhat dear to him, I think. He treated me as an affectionate father treats a delicate son; I noticed he liked to put his hand on my shoulder or my knee as we talked; yet withal, he asked me questions, and saved his thoughts to tell me, and believed in my knowledge like any acolyte" (p. 146). In this manner the son encounters his spiritual father—the overstressed romantic veneer of Cyril's intellectual superiority concealing his dependence upon Annable, who actually converts Cyril, himself the "acolyte." Beneath the veneer, only two kinds of men exist, those like Annable who win in the struggle with women, and those like George Saxton and Mr. Beardsall who lose. Annable is the symbolic ideal and the means by which Cyril can be reunited with the father as he ought to be. George Saxton is the dramatic extension of the father and possibly Cyril as they actually are. George's failure with Lettie not only parallels Annable's earlier defeat by Lady Crystabel and the father's failure with Mrs. Beardsall, but also anticipates Paul Morel's ambiguous relation with Miriam, the Emily of *Sons and Lovers*.

Moreover, the weakness involved in Lawrence's conception of the male relationship (and implicitly, it must be admitted, with all man–woman relationships based upon the peacock conception of womanhood) receives later confirmation in his characterization of Deerslayer: "But you have there the myth of the essential

white America. All the other stuff, the love, the democracy, the floundering into lust, is a sort of by-play. The
essential American soul is hard, isolate, stoic, and a
killer. It has never yet melted. . . . And this, for America,
is Deerslayer. A man who turns his back on white
society. A man who keeps his moral integrity hard and
intact. An isolate, almost selfless, stoic, enduring man,
who lives by death, by killing, but who is pure white."[2]
Like Deerslayer's, Annable's manhood rests fundamentally upon the act of rejection, a basically negative and
passive reaction that is made to appear active and positive. This peculiar notion of manhood begins to emerge
more forcefully in the last section of *The White Peacock*,
as if Lawrence had already accepted Annable's solution
to the problem of woman as the only one possible. Since
Annable also spurns industrial society and Christianity,
the passage quoted from Lawrence's critical work illustrates how explicitly he continues to repudiate and to
associate these notions with the color white and, by
extension, with modern woman. This suggests rather
clearly that, for the hero of Lawrence's later fiction, the
disavowal of one factor in this unholy trinity will automatically lead to the rejection of the trinity itself.

Annable's point of view, "that all civilization was the
painted fungus of rottenness" (p. 145), is where the
rationalizing process begins. From here it is only a short
step to the notion that our basic innocence, as in Rous-
seau, can be recovered in an incorruptible natural state.
The fault is in civilization, not in man. The perversity of
Annable's whole line of thought, and through it the distortion of the basic experiences presented in the novel,
should also be clear from the man–woman and man–man
relationships already discussed. If he returned to civilization, Annable would be the first to fall victim again
to the predatory woman. His own white purity is only
a manifestation of his reaction against the white peacock

2. D. H. Lawrence, *Studies in Classic American Literature*,
pp. 62–63.

and a measure, really, of her hold upon him. As presented by Lawrence, Annable's profoundly negative escapism leads ultimately to the man–as–master and woman–as–slave doctrine proposed in *The Plumed Serpent*. Cyril's idealization of Annable, then, is fundamental to the process by which the personality of the Lawrentian hero is fabricated.

In these terms, it will be possible to define more precisely the major shortcoming of the work. Cyril's quest for a father, never related to his hatred of women, reveals an unperceived homosexuality that is apparent in his intellectual relationship with Annable and in his emotional attachment to George Saxton. The unstated psychological bond between these two associations is not related by Lawrence to the incestuous tie with Lettie. Cyril's failure to encounter the problem of homosexuality implicit in the incest—a failure that is also Lawrence's —accounts for the formal breakdown in the novel and for the otherwise pointless male longing for death. To perceive the connection between the formal lapse and the character's problem more clearly, it is necessary to examine Cyril's relation with Lettie and the symbolic identification of Lettie with Mrs. Beardsall.

The identification of the two women is based upon a few primary facts, the imagery used, and a series of inferences. One fact is their common first name—clearly intended to identify the relation between the persons as well. Reinforcing this suggestion is the similarity of their mannerisms. The mother's snobbishness in disapproving of Cyril's visits to the Saxtons because they are vulgar, for example, is reflected in Lettie's announcement to George that she is going to marry Leslie Tempest for his money. Both women are also headstrong, domineering, and at the same time self-abnegating in caring for their children. Like her mother, Lettie "determined to abandon the charge of herself to serve her children" (p. 281), and "did not yield her independence" (p. 280) to her husband. This acceptance of Mrs. Beardsall's values implies the two women's psychological identity as well.

In addition, the similarity of their marriages may be assumed, even though it is impossible to determine exactly the nature of Mrs. Beardsall's. Leslie's womanish acceptance of his fate and his wealth are the only differences. With respect to self, husband, and children, Lettie's marriage is an idealization of her mother's. The fact that this observation is outside the framework of the novel and is therefore speculative does not lessen its validity. Enough uncoordinated material is evident in the work to support the identity hypothesis. As Cyril fuses with an idealized father image, so Lettie identifies with the mother. As Cyril's real father dies and is replaced briefly by Annable, so Mrs. Beardsall disappears from the story, and her role is assumed by Lettie.

To establish the incest idea more concretely, however, it is necessary to recall what Cyril has been told of his mother's marriage: "The marriage had been unhappy. . . ." (p. 32). The primary significance of the passage does not turn on the portrayal of the father as a vulgar character full of deceit, but on the ambiguous metaphor of the husband's image that shatters into "a thousand vulgar fragments" within the woman's soul. This is the first time the soul-fragmenting image occurs in the book, and it applies specifically to Mrs. Beardsall. When it recurs in slightly modified form, its basic similarity to the moon-shattering image of Lettie is clear: "Suddenly, as we went by the pond-side, we were startled by great, swishing black shadows that swept just above our heads. The swans were flying up for shelter, now that a cold wind had begun to fret Nethermere. They swung down on to the glassy mill-pond, shaking the moonlight in flecks across the deep shadows; the night rang with the clacking of their wings on the water; the stillness and the calm were broken; the moonlight was furrowed and scattered, and broken. The swans, as they sailed into shadow, were dim, haunting spectres; the wind found us shivering" (p. 62). This description follows a scene in which George and Cyril have been cuffed by Annable in their first encounter with him. Earlier, the symbolic identity of Lettie and the swan has been established. The image-shattering impact of both mother and daughter on the male is now fully evident, the one presented primarily through the narrative, the other through the symbolism.

In the reference to the mother's marriage, a double process of shattering has taken place. Mrs. Beardsall's broken illusion of her husband suggests both the splitting of her own soul and of his. The word *vulgar*, moreover, echoes the ambiguity inherent in the double process and could refer to either the mother or the father, or to both. Mrs. Beardsall is vulgar in the way she gains vengeance over her husband by asserting her failure in marriage as a personal victory. Her turning away "with the scorn of a woman who finds her romance has been a trumpery tale" (p. 32) reflects an element of the peacock pride that Lettie inherits. These details strengthen the notion that mother and daughter are symbolically identical, especially since the swans in the scene near the pond are also engaged in fragmenting the male soul, in this case the mill-pond itself. Though certainly not beyond question at this point, the idea of the pond as the male psyche is not arbitrary, for it occurs elsewhere in Lawrence's fiction. The pond reflecting the moonlight at which Birkin casts stones in *Women in Love* is such a symbol, and so is the pond from which the doctor rescues Mabel in "The Horse Dealer's Daughter." In context here, it is an entirely adequate objective correlative for Cyril's fearful response to the swans, whose identification with woman is implicit: "The swans, as they *sailed* into shadow, were dim, haunting spectres; the wind found us shivering." Surely, as Lettie puts on her mother's personality, so are the sins of the father visited upon the son.

With conditional acceptance of the mill-pond as

Cyril's male soul and the swans as the glittering instrument of its destruction, the nature of the man–woman relationship in the novel becomes a symbolic extension of those among mother, sister, and son. And if "Nethermere," or deep sea, is the reflecting unconscious and "moonlight" the penetrating consciousness, the kernel of Lawrence's future treatment of psychic opposites lies revealed. The polarity of male and female and of light and dark imagery in the later works has its origin in *The White Peacock*. In transfixing and feminizing the male, the female renders him entirely dependent upon the very agent of his destruction—which alone adequately explains Cyril's bittersweet longing for death.

So far, I may have shown only that the influence of Lettie and Mrs. Beardsall upon Cyril is destructive, not that it is incestuous. But, clearly, this influence relates to his otherwise inexplicable wish to die, and this relationship is sufficient to supply a working distinction between the conceptual function of the swan as a symbol of Lettie's character and its effect on Cyril's state of mind. Already cited in part, one passage relating the swan image to Cyril and the incest hypothesis bears more extensive treatment: "After the evening at the farm, Lettie and Leslie drew closer together. They eddied unevenly down the little stream of courtship, jostling and drifting together and apart. He was unsatisfied and strove with every effort to bring her closer to him, submissive. Gradually she yielded, and submitted to him. She folded round her and him the snug curtain of the present, and they sat like children playing a game behind the hangings of an old bed. She shut out all distant outlooks, as an Arab unfolds his tent and conquers the mystery and space of the desert. So she lived gleefully in a little tent of present pleasures and fancies" (p. 144).

Informing the literal sense of the description, Cyril's mocking irony shows his contempt for Lettie and his disapproval of the courtship. Her submission to Leslie is feigned, and the courtship itself merely an elaborate mask for her more palpable designs. On this account Cyril objects to her romanticizing of love, for romantic love is a game that conceals Lettie's actual view of love as conquest. The desert of which she is master suggests at once the sterility of this kind of love, her own inner emptiness, and the nature of the relationship she will have with Leslie. Her later control of him is so complete that it constitutes a reversal of sexual roles, and Cyril's observation of them jostling "unevenly down the little stream of courtship" is a measure of his resentment against Lettie. His anxiety manifests itself in ridicule and proceeds from an implicit identification with Leslie as a male.

It is surprising shortly afterward, then, to notice Cyril's intense anger at the male swan. The reader does not anticipate such a rapid fluctuation of emotion, because Annable has just died and Cyril is sadly walking home alone through the woods after the funeral:

> In a while, I too got up and went down to the mill, which lay red and peaceful, with the blue smoke rising as winsomely and carelessly as ever. On the other side of the valley I could see a pair of horses nod slowly across the fallow. A man's voice called to him [them] now and again with a resonance that filled me with longing to follow my horses over the fallow, in the still, lonely valley, full of sunshine and eternal forgetfulness. The day had already forgotten. The water was blue and white and dark-burnished with shadows; two swans sailed across the reflected trees with perfect blithe grace. The gloom that had passed across was gone. I watched the swan with his ruffled wings swell onwards; I watched his slim consort go peeping into corners and under bushes; I saw him steer clear of the bushes, to keep full in view, turning his head to me imperiously, till I longed to pelt him with the empty husks of last year's flowers, knap-weed and scabius. I was too indolent, and I turned instead to the orchard. (P. 157)

In light of the preceding passage, the two swans are certainly Lettie and Leslie eddying down the little stream of courtship. At the beginning of the description, Cyril has explained how he longs to follow the horses in obedience to the man's voice, which probably reminds him of the dead Annable. He is still the son in search of a father, and the kind of relationship he seeks is an obedient and subservient one. This is significant because he has just scorned Lettie for her own apparent submissiveness to Leslie. When he encounters the swans, however, Cyril becomes enraged at the male swan, "till I longed to pelt him with the husks of last year's flowers." Since one swan is specifically designated "him" and the other "slim consort," the inference is clear that Cyril is jealous of Leslie for absconding with his sister–mother. Along with his mockery of Lettie, his sudden anger at Leslie may be understood within a general framework that suggests incest.

The most direct evidence of incest and its bearing upon his death wish comes in a section of the novel where Lawrence ironically, but very explicitly, associates Cyril, Lettie, and the *fleur du mal* theme with Poe's "Raven." Since, in my view, the raven is an embodiment of the peacock's inner nature, Lettie is both the white peacock and the raven, the Angel of Purity and the Angel of Death. And Cyril's longing for death must be the product of this knowledge: "There was a driving drizzle of rain, like a dirty curtain before the landscape. The nasturtium leaves by the garden walk had gone rotten in a frost, and the gay green discs had given place to the first black flags of winter, hung on flaccid stalks, pinched at the neck. The grass plot was strewn with fallen leaves, wet and brilliant: scarlet splashes of Virginia creeper, golden drift from the limes, ruddy brown shawls under the beeches, and away back in the corner, the black mat of maple leaves, heavy soddened; they ought to have been a vivid lemon colour. Occasionally one of these great black leaves would loose its hold, and zigzag down, staggering in the dance of death" (p. 80).

Again Cyril's state of mind is conveyed through the background, and the *fleur du mal* theme coalesces with the death wish. The juxtaposition of bright colors against the black, heavy rot underlines the impression of life fallen into decay. In addition, "flaccid stalks, pinched at the neck," "fallen leaves, wet and brilliant," and "scarlet splashes of Virginia creeper" give the passage a certain luscious sexual overtone that is not easy to define. This overtone is more clearly emphasized afterward: "She pulled the thick curtain across the window, and nestled down in it, resting her cheek against the edge, protecting herself from the cold window-pane. The wet, grey wind shook the half-naked trees, whose leaves dripped and shone sullenly. Even the trunks were blackened, trickling with the rain which drove persistently" (pp. 81–82). The half-naked trees and blackened trunks clinch the reference as one of phallic deadness and, as the dance of death is evoked by the rain falling black to the earth, link the deadness to the *fleur du mal* theme.

Into this scene steps a crow, which is immediately related by his color to Cyril's death wish. He is obliquely referred to as an "omen" and "a messenger in advance" (p. 81) and is explicitly identified with Poe's raven when Cyril says "He won't even say 'Nevermore' " (p. 82). Bizarre and mocking though it is, this comment provides some extrinsic support for the incest hypothesis, for, of all the poems that could have been introduced here, none is more susceptible than Poe's to this kind of interpretation. Significantly, Lawrence's later analysis of Poe in *Studies in Classic American Literature* deals at some length with this theme. The following passage from the essay may shed some light upon the brother–sister relationship: "The other great story linking up with this group is *The Fall of the House of Usher*. Here the love is between brother and sister. When the self is broken, and the mystery of the recognition of *otherness* fails, then the longing for identification with the beloved becomes a lust. And it is this longing for identification, utter merging, which is at the base of the incest problem. In psychoanalysis almost every trouble in the psyche is traced to an incest-desire."[3]

Though he had not read Freud at the time he wrote *The White Peacock,* in the essay Lawrence seems to be formulating the basic experience he presents in the novel. It is interesting that, in the very next section of this essay about incest, Lawrence goes on to deny the psychological validity of incest desire, raises a brief argument against psychoanalysis that wrenches apart the continuity of his reasoning, and subsumes the idea of incest under the term *mechanical consciousness.* This may suggest, even at the comparatively late date of the Poe study (published in 1923, but begun as early as 1915), that Lawrence was not entirely satisfied with his definition. As his emotional outburst against Freud in the essay would indicate, he was defensive about his view of incest, though he persisted in it. And as Frederick J. Hoffman observes, Lawrence even accused Freud of advocating "the fulfilment of the incest-craving as a means of cure."[4] The introduction of "The Raven" into Cyril's soliloquies and conversations with Lettie clarifies the relevance of the Poe study to the novel.

The crow serves as the device to unite Cyril's sense of self-torment and his death wish: "He [the crow] sat stolidly unconcerned. Then I heard the lapwings in the meadow crying, crying. They seemed to seek the storm, yet to rail at it. They wheeled in the wind, yet never ceased to complain of it. They enjoyed the struggle, and lamented it in wild lament, through which came a sound of exultation. All the lapwings cried, cried the same tale, 'Bitter, bitter the struggle—for nothing, nothing, nothing'—and all the time they swung about on their broad wings, revelling" (p. 84). The reveling of the lapwings

3. Lawrence, *Studies,* p. 76.
4. Frederick J. Hoffman, "Lawrence's Quarrel with Freud," in Frederick J. Hoffman and Harry T. Moore, eds., *The Achievement of D. H. Lawrence,* p. 119.

recalls the dance of the leaves, and the raven looks on as death personified. Not only is the existential despair expressed here rooted in sexual distress, but the distress is inverted and enjoyed. Cyril's "nothing, nothing, nothing" evokes the same futility and sense of personal failure as Lettie's "We can't help ourselves, we're all chess-men" (p. 121). Whereas Cyril's torment is directed inward, however, Lettie's is directed outward. If both characters fail to understand why they feel and act as they do, each reacts predictably to the same stimuli. Lettie's failure to encounter her true self leads to her marriage with Leslie—so that, ironically, she may preserve her spiritual virginity and destroy George.

Cyril's similar failure leads to a symbolic act, beautifully expressed, of narcissistic suicide: "Lettie was twenty-one on the day after Christmas. She woke me in the morning with cries of dismay. There was a great fall of snow, multiplying the cold morning light, startling the slow-footed twilight. The lake was black like the open eyes of a corpse; the woods were black like the beard on the face of a corpse" (p. 103). The symbol fully unites the *fleur du mal* theme with the character's essential state of mind. At the crucial moment Cyril identifies himself completely with his bearded father, whom he had previously encountered asleep under a bough in the woods, suggesting the common cause of their fate. For Cyril, death, like the raven, is everywhere, and it is only fitting that, birdlike, Lettie should hover over him in the cold morning light. Sister and brother have become mother and father, and they symbolically repeat the relationship: "When the self is broken, and the mystery of the recognition of *otherness* fails, then the longing for identification with the beloved becomes a lust. And it is this longing for identification, utter merging, which is at the base of the incest problem."[5] Lawrence suggests the nature of Cyril's relation to Lettie by ob-

5. Lawrence, *Studies*, p. 76.

jectifying it through the symbolic raven, but in the second part of the book, as if deliberately, he turns away from further psychological explorations.

In *The White Peacock* the vital significance of the imagery to the entire psychological process between the characters is undeniable. Nor can the dramatic relationships be understood apart from the symbols used to create them. Though imperfect, Cyril's is the central intelligence that unites all dramatic facets of the novel, and up to a point his state of mind is presented with integrity and precision. But a fundamental deficiency exists that either puts the formulated conceptualizations at variance with the experience or does not make clear how the conceptualizations are derived from the experience. Nowhere is this more obvious than in Lawrence's idealization of Annable and in his treatment of Lettie. Assuming that he perceives Lettie accurately, for example, Cyril still overresponds in his alternating revulsion and attraction. This reaction helps to produce a certain lack of objectivity and objectification in the work, which implies Lawrence's own excessive identification with his character. Perhaps because his feelings lack a cogent motive, the evidence he offers to explain Cyril's responses cannot be accepted as conclusive. Lawrence does not embody within the character the reasons for Cyril's behavior. As it is, one feels that the implications of the incest theme are half-perceived and then left undeveloped. Lawrence's turning away from his theme results in the purely mechanical process that dominates the last part of the novel. His characters make assertions without regard to their dramatic validity, and thesis and plot replace the tightly knit symbolic relationships of the first part of the book. Had the symbolism been maintained throughout the entire novel, the various structural weaknesses could have been overcome. So clear about Poe, Lawrence is partially blinded by his own light, a condition that is destined to prevail in varying degrees in all the works, through *Lady Chatterley's Lover*. Clear comprehension of the symbols and structure of *The White Peacock*, I believe, is basic to an understanding of everything Lawrence wrote subsequently.

///

An Allegory of Self
The Trespasser

The Trespasser is undoubtedly one of Lawrence's worst novels, "a rotten work of genius," as Ford Madox Ford said with some sympathy. Set in a superficial framework and told by a third-person armchair narrator, *The Trespasser* has all the markings of a titillating potboiler. The clumsily handled theme of oppressive fate, the wooden plot, the overblown language, and the weakly drawn attempt to parallel the experiences of Siegmund and Helena with those of Tristan and Isolde do much to justify this view. The style and form of the book leave everything to be desired, and, even more emphatically than in *The White Peacock*, the last section is a mechanical anticlimax. Through it all the one-dimensional characters are scarcely endurable grotesques—Helena a sort of lesbian Lettie, Siegmund an activated Cyril subjected to the oppressiveness of love. From a conventional standpoint, Lawrence shows here no skill at all in the basic mechanics of novel construction.

For this very reason the author's view of his work is illuminating: "I am always ready to believe the worst that is said about my work, and reluctant of the best. Father was like that with us children. I have written the first 135 pages of *The Trespasser*—rewritten them. Shall I send them on? At the bottom of my heart I don't like the work, though I'm sure it has points, and I don't think it retrograde from *The White Peacock*. It surprises me by its steady progressiveness—I hate it for its fluid, luscious quality."[1] To begin with, Lawrence obviously thinks of it in relation to *The White Peacock*, not an unusual thing to do, since *The Trespasser* is only his second book. Yet

1. D. H. Lawrence, *The Collected Letters of D. H. Lawrence*, ed. Harry T. Moore, I, 93.

it is striking to realize that the two novels were written concurrently, the one begun during Lawrence's student days at Nottingham University and finally published in January 1911, the other started much later, "written in feverish haste between Whitsuntide and Midsummer of 1910," and published in May of 1911.[2]

The chronological overlapping is important because it confirms the value of certain internal similarities and permits more certain approach to the work through the themes and imagery it shares with *The White Peacock*. Helena and Lettie, for example, both representative of modern woman, are described by the same white symbolism and, as one critic puts it, "find themselves unable to respond to the physical love of their men."[3] In addition, the concept of Siegmund as a passive, woman-dominated male bears a close resemblance to a combination of qualities noticeable in Cyril Beardsall and George Saxton. Like Cyril, he is an aesthete, withdrawn and highly, overly sensitive. Like George Saxton, he is ultimately destroyed by the predatory woman. From these comparisons, the novels apparently share the same theme, the love relationship between the passive male and the possessive woman, and in many respects *The Trespasser* seems to be a rehash of *The White Peacock*. In each novel the lover is destroyed in a similar manner, through the same agency.

Lawrence goes on to say, however, that *The Trespasser* is not retrograde from *The White Peacock*, and the sense in which it is not, I believe, is well stated in a passing reference by E. W. Tedlock, Jr.: "But Siegmund is troubled by more than the genteel, ideal, and fanciful in Helena. Constantly, in their five days' struggle, he plays the child to her. In most love scenes she rests above or upon him, and he, sometimes oppressed by her weight, looks up. He resents her mother aspect, which would

---

2. E. T., *D. H. Lawrence: A Personal Record*, p. 181.
3. Michael C. Sharpe, "The Genesis of D. H. Lawrence's *The Trespasser*," *Essays in Criticism*, 11, p. 37.

draw him to her, hide him from fate, and save him from searching the unknown. His crying in the night is a crying that woman cannot still."[4] Indeed, woman cannot still his crying because of the kind of love he demands and Helena is all too willing to give. As Tedlock suggests, their relationship is oedipal, though Helena does not hide Siegmund from his fate, but, on the contrary, is the active instrument of it. Thus, the sense in which the novel is not retrograde ought to be clear. Given the author's definition of incest as the destruction of man through the possessive control and assimilation of his passions by woman, the love relationship described in Part One is entirely realized, and it is the novel's *raison d'être*. The author confronts the incest theme more directly here than in *The White Peacock*, and he adopts an explicit viewpoint toward it. Lawrence's dislike of *The Trespasser* is emotional and need not be confined to matters of style alone.

In addition, several other improvements over *The White Peacock* are noticeable: the implicitly ideological nature of the narrator, Cecil Byrne; the experimental symbolic technique used to convey the psychic interaction between the two main characters; and the perception evident in the work that a whole new realm of experience exists below the level of consciousness, ready to be explored, from which a unique conception of self can emerge. The first of these is apparent early in the novel when the narrator refuses to accept aesthetic withdrawal or passive existence as the solution to his problems, a position held by Cyril Beardsall: " 'After all,' said Byrne, when the door was closed, 'if you're alive you've got to live.' . . . 'Wherefore?' she asked indulgently. 'Because there's no such thing as passive existence,' he replied, grinning. She curled her lip in amused indulgence of this very young man. 'I don't see it at all,' she said. 'You can't,' he protested, 'any more than a tree

4. Ernest W. Tedlock, Jr., *D. H. Lawrence, Artist and Rebel*, pp. 51–52.

can help budding in April—it can't help itself, if it's alive; same with you.' "[5] The comparison of Helena to a tree budding in April is ironic in light of future developments. It recalls the *fleur du mal* theme of the earlier novel and suggests the narrator's rejection of it and his refusal to be victimized by the possessive woman Helena so obviously represents. Though he has no positive role to play and does not participate actively in the central experience to be interpreted, Byrne's detachment allows an objective view of the unfolding action and the imagery connected with it. In this respect, he is the prototype of the later Lawrentian hero or thesis-maker, according to whose gradually discovered ideas and sense of self the work evolves.

Later, when Siegmund is introduced, the focus of the novel shifts from the possessive woman so thoroughly exploited in *The White Peacock* to the passive male. Here, too, the narrator's oblique criticism of Siegmund's fatalism helps to expose the root experiences responsible for his downfall and reveals the author's clarification of several key ideas. Reformulating the same basic material that underlies *The White Peacock*, Lawrence ends by repudiating both the victimizing woman and the betrayed male. In so doing, he opens the way for a proposed solution of the incest problem in his later work through a commitment to vitalism and to the pursuit of self in previously unexplored areas of human experience. The rejection of Helena and Siegmund, together with the idea of destructive consciousness that their relationship embodies, is the necessary preliminary to this exploration, which is centered in the pristine (non-Freudian) unconscious.

Since, beginning with *The Trespasser, consciousness* is used in a very restricted sense, the connotations of the word, its precise extension from *social consciousness*, should be fixed immediately. Consciousness, for Lawrence, involves the means the possessive woman

5. D. H. Lawrence, *The Trespasser*, p. 5.

uses (her will to dominate; her ability, sanctified through traditional Christian moral codes, to sublimate her bodily desires; and her attempt to idealize, intellectualize, and distort human relationships) in order to subjugate her man, inhibit him, and ultimately re-create him in her own image. According to this definition, the tale of Helena and Siegmund illustrates what the passive male should not do to retain his masculine identity and survive. This is the meaning behind the ironic treatment of love in the first part of the book and the full sense in which this study uses the terms *consciousness* and *social consciousness*.

And if Lawrence is willing to show what should be avoided, he also has a more positive program. The positive program follows from the essential though negatively expressed point of *The Trespasser*, that Siegmund's inability to win through to the spontaneous wellsprings of his being constitutes a failure of will that ends in his destruction. Invert the negativity of this viewpoint, and the direction of Lawrence's future development stands clear: It will reveal the vital self transcending particular, Freudian aspects of personality, and will show also how that self evolves. This development, of course, is the central theme of *The Rainbow* and, to a lesser extent, of *Sons and Lovers* and *Women in Love*, from which a duality in the art emerges that Lawrence never overcomes. Intellectually, the duality is the product of a series of relatively absolute distinctions Lawrence makes between the two selves culminating in the polar principles of mastery and obedience and male and female. Crucial to his entire concept of human growth, Lawrence's view of mechanical consciousness as contradicting and unrelated to the core of experience that underlies it reveals the psychological dissociation that is inherent in his thought. The progress of this dissociation becomes evident in his intense concentration upon the light imagery, which *The Trespasser* shares with *The White Peacock* and *Sons and Lovers*.

In *The Trespasser*, Lawrence significantly links the familiar nature of light symbolism to the ironic treatment of Adamic material in order to describe the destructive effects of love upon Siegmund. Two examples that point up the difference between Siegmund's view of himself and the narrator's view of him and that obliquely suggest the incest theme through the imagery should adequately demonstrate this treatment. Coming after he has been "reborn" in Helena's image, the climactic moment of irony is Siegmund's belief that he has attained perfect happiness: " 'You know, I felt as if I were the first man to discover things: like Adam when he opened the first eyes in the world.' 'I saw the sunshine in you,' repeated Helena quietly, looking at him with her eyes heavy with meaning. He laughed again, not understanding, but feeling she meant love" (p. 49). Let the reader tentatively accept "sunshine" as one of the metaphors used to signify her all-consuming possessiveness, and seeing the sunshine in Siegmund will immediately suggest Helena's success in molding him to her own desire. The moment of his greatest happiness is also the moment of his reduction, which is related to the incest theme as the "longing for identification, utter merging"[6] with the beloved. Granted this reduction, Siegmund's transformation is the product of incest or, as Lawrence has it, of his total assimilation to Helena's consciousness (her image of him).

His "Helenization," in turn, leads to the fall, the expulsion from Paradise:

> Presently the breeze, and Siegmund, dropped asleep. The sun was pouring with dreadful persistence. It beat and beat on Helena, gradually drawing her from her book in confusion of thought. She closed her eyes wearily, longing for shade. Vaguely she felt a sympathy with Adama in "Adam Cast Forth." Her mind traced again the tumultuous, obscure strugglings of the two, forth from Eden through the primitive wilderness, and she felt sorrowful. Thinking of Adam blackened with struggle, she

6. D. H. Lawrence, *Studies in Classic American Literature*, p. 76.

looked down at Siegmund. The sun was beating him upon the face and upon his glistening brow. His two hands, which lay out on the grass, were full of blood, the veins of his wrists purple and swollen with heat. Yet he slept on, breathing with a slight, panting motion. Helena felt deeply moved. . . . She wanted to kiss him, and shed a few tears. She did neither, but instead, moved her position so that she shaded his head. Cautiously putting her hand on his hair, she found it warm, quite hot, as when you put your hand under a sitting hen, and feel the hot-feathered bosom. (P. 76)

In context, the irony is evoked by juxtaposing the comparison of Siegmund's hair to a hen's bosom against the Adamic fall, his feminization or reduction by Helena. Taking place without his awareness, the entire process also illustrates the technique of psychic interaction around which the fuguelike first section of the novel develops. If he is ultimately what she wants him to be, the fact is not conveyed to the reader by the unperceiving Siegmund, nor by Helena, but through symbol and nuance theoretically supplied by Cecil Byrne, the narrator. Through the symbolism the incest theme is established and an indirect relationship suggested between Siegmund and Cecil Byrne. Cecil supplies the thesis that passive existence ends in catastrophe, and Siegmund illustrates it.

By way of summary, then, Cecil Byrne as narrator and persona represents a new-found determination in Lawrence's work to avoid the disaster described by the action. The action of the first part of the novel is largely interpsychic, and Lawrence experiments with a highly flexible symbolic technique to convey its significance. Though no positive solution to the problem of love is reached, the narrator's ironic detachment from both major characters implies the author's determination to seek the answer beyond consciousness and the kind of relationship it creates. Siegmund's downfall is the inevitable outcome of his complete subjection to Helena and the corresponding decay of his unconscious spontaneity and maleness. The imagery and the accompanying theme of incest, which have still to be fully discussed, together with the ideological nature of the narrator, the experimental technique, and the increasing role of the unconscious in Lawrence's art all suggest the sense in which *The Trespasser* is not retrograde from *The White Peacock*.

To be sure, in the fullness of its recognition and in coming to terms with the incest problem, *The Trespasser* represents a signal advance over the earlier work. What the author evades in *The White Peacock* he now deliberately presents, though with continued distortion. However, because the problem is not encountered through artistic realism, as to some extent it is in *Sons and Lovers*, *The Trespasser* can best be described as an allegorical rather than a symbolic confrontation of self. The characters are one-dimensional, of conceptual significance only, and they lack the complexity of human beings in conflict with themselves and each other. In addition, Lawrence's allegorical method must be held partly responsible for the aesthetic failure of the work, most noticeable in the long-drawn-out denouement. The characters have to be carried some 120 pages through London after their conceptual functions have been exhausted. Yet, the allegory does permit for the first time a detached, if ambiguous, examination of the man–woman relationship in Lawrence's fiction.

The basis of this relationship depends upon two ideas that are closely tied to the incest theme and implicit in the imagery. The first is the specious psychological identity the reader is asked to assume between Helena, womanhood, and Christianity. Lawrence simply carries this notion over without qualification from the last part of *The White Peacock* and posits it as the novel's *donnée*. Since Helena is a static symbol, and since the focal point of the work is not on her, the assumption may easily be granted. Aesthetically, it provides a framework for the action and permits the reader to ascertain the conditions that govern Lawrence's handling of the characters. Initially, the idea is neither debatable nor subject to question; the reader merely suspends disbelief. Within this framework, however, Lawrence is inconsistent at the beginning of the novel in suggesting that the relationship of Helena and her roommate Louisa is lesbian in nature, and then in proceeding to designate Helena as the symbol of all womanhood. From an implicitly deviant character the author creates a norm that falls apart under close scrutiny. Thus, Helena's reduction of Siegmund can be viewed in quite another way than the author intends, and the thesis that, as consciousness, Helena causes Siegmund's fall can be negated. She may actually be what she seems to be, a lesbian who enjoys tormenting men. On the other hand, if she is not what she seems to be, her accepted identity operates within the novel in behalf of more pressing concerns.

The second idea involves the cause-and-effect relationship that the author develops in the book between Helena's dominating will and Siegmund's reduction, which is apparent from the beginning: "Siegmund died out even from his violin. He had infused it with his life, till its fibres had been as the tissue of his own flesh. Grasping his violin, he seemed to have his fingers on the strings of his heart and of the heart of Helena. It was his little beloved that drank his being and turned it into music. And now Siegmund was dead; only an odour of musk remained of him in his violin" (p. 8). Helena not only dominates Siegmund, but she compels him to sublimate his feelings into a kind of abstract ecstasy (music) that finally destroys him by its very oppressiveness. He is intellectualized, and the dichotomy of mind and body that is implicit in their relationship establishes him as the masculine body in the process of being transformed and Helena as the vampire mind that drinks his blood. The peculiarity is not so much in the antagonism of opposed psychic forces as in Lawrence's association of masculinity with the body (and, by extension, with the unconscious or vital self) and femininity with mind (and social consciousness) almost as mutually exclusive principles.

Lawrence is more than half way to the assertion of a male principle that is totally outside and independent of mentality, which is evident in *The Lost Girl* and all the subsequent works. Long before *Psychoanalysis and the Unconscious*, *Fantasia*, and his quarrel with Freud, Lawrence has already imaginatively rejected the Jungian conception of psychic integration as incestuous, a manifestation of "this longing for identification, utter merging, which is at the base of the incest problem."[7] In view of this assertion, the purpose of *The Trespasser* to show how the merging of the masculine and feminine principles ends in Siegmund's destruction should hardly seem surprising. Lawrence's concept of deviant behavior lies in his definitions of *incest, consciousness, masculine,* and *feminine,* not in their application. In my opinion, the critical problem posed by the novel does not reside primarily in a discrepancy between the experience presented and its intellectual formulation, as in *The White Peacock*. Though the discrepancy exists and is especially evident in Helena's tie to Louisa, *The Trespasser* as a whole is the intellectual product of an earlier experience that is not formulated within it. As a work of art it stands alone, independent of its emotional sources. The major difficulty is to accept the deliberately presented cause-and-effect relationship between consciousness and incest, which strains psychological credibility, indicates the dissociation inherent in Lawrence's thought, and suggests the fundamental deficiency of his aesthetic.

Nowhere is the rupture between mind and body, a realized theme in the work, better illustrated than by the wound Siegmund receives while swimming. He catches his thigh "on a sharp, submerged point"; observes "the insidious creeping of blood" over his white

7. Lawrence, *Studies*, p. 76.

skin; comments upon "the sudden cruelty of the sea"; and remarks: " 'That is I, that creeping red, and this whiteness I pride myself on is I, and my black hair, and my blue eyes are I. It is a weird thing to be a person. What makes me myself, among all these?' " (p. 32). As Helena is compared to a vampire drinking his blood, on one level of the story, the same idea is repeated in a different way on another. As the novel progresses, the characters and the natural background alike are more clearly penetrated and transformed by sunlight. One of the elements transformed is the sea, originally a masculine symbol of the vital self, but subsequently a feminine one. In line with this view, the submerged point, the white rock upon which Siegmund cuts himself, is associated by its color with Helena and consciousness. The cut leads him to ask the significant question, "Who am I?" and vaguely to perceive the duality within himself, which is evidenced by the blood running down his thigh, over his white skin. The cut itself is meaningful initially; then, through the effect it creates, it suggests the unconscious in a state of hemorrhage. His long denial of body has opened an incurable psychic wound that makes him feel the undersurface of the sea as cruel and destructive. The sign of this wound, the blood that wells from it, is antithetical to the surrounding whiteness of the sand, morning, sunlight, rock, sea, and skin. And with the congealing of the blood, Siegmund regresses to infantilism, is re-created in Helena's image, and comes to resemble the white marble rock upon which he cuts himself, the symbol at once of his reduction and psychic death.

After Siegmund's fatal self-division, the significance of Helena's effect upon him—the conditions under which consciousness can usurp and alter the essential self—becomes clear through the light imagery:

> "I like sunshine on me, real, and manifest, and tangible. I feel like a seed that has been frozen for ages. I want to be bitten by the sunshine."

She leaned over him and kissed him. The sun came bright-footed over the water, leaving a shining print on Siegmund's face. He lay, with half-closed eyes, sprawled loosely on the sand. Looking at his limbs, she imagined he must be heavy, like the boulders. She sat over him, with her fingers stroking his eyebrows, that were broad and rather arched. He lay perfectly still, in a half-dream.

Presently she laid her head on his breast, and remained so, watching the sea, and listening to his heartbeats. The throb was strong and deep. It seemed to go through the whole island and the whole afternoon, and it fascinated her: so deep, unheard, with its great expulsions of life. Had the world a heart? Was there also deep in the world a great God thudding out waves of life, like a great heart, unconscious? It frightened her. This was the God she knew not, as she knew not this Siegmund. It was so different from the half-shut eyes with black lashes, and the winsome, shapely nose. And the heart of the world, as she heard it, could not be the same as the curling splash of retreat of the little sleepy waves. She listened for Siegmund's soul, but his heart overbeat all other sound, thudding powerfully. (P. 38)

In the last paragraph, the strangeness to Helena of Siegmund's heart and his unconscious God "thudding out waves of life" shows how completely opposed their original conceptual values are. This sign of a hidden, spontaneous existence in him confirms the idea that he is cut off from his inner being, and it is the earliest indication of Lawrence's "dark gods" and his later vitalism.

But the passage as a whole clearly suggests the destructive nature of the man–woman relationship. In the first paragraph, Siegmund's feeling like a frozen seed is actually the direct consequence of being "bitten by the sunshine," a metaphorical restatement of Helena's ghoulish effect upon him as the vampire mind. As she assimilates him, Siegmund's inner life freezes, and his later dream of ice crystals (p. 77) prefigures his death by revealing the continued creeping paralysis of coldness upon his vital self. Thus, his constant desire to thaw out through exposure to sunlight expresses the ironic cause of his freezing and also anticipates the kind of imagery

Lawrence uses in *Women in Love* to describe Gerald Crich's annihilation in the ice and snow of the Tyrol. The self-tormented man's longing for incestuous relationship is at once a manifestation of his death wish and the cause of his death, which he welcomes. In the second paragraph, the sun, coming "bright-footed over the water" and leaving its mark on Siegmund's face, repeats the assimilative idea that underlies the light imagery and extends the meaning of water and sun to include male and female. In addition, Siegmund's ready acceptance of Helena's domination, on the narrative level of the book, parallels his symbolic transformation and explains the narrator's irony. Cecil Byrne's explicit rejection of passive existence and its asserted causes is the real measure of Lawrence's growth in artistry since he wrote *The White Peacock*; it announces the future development of the man–woman relationship in his work as a reversal of that which he documents in *The Trespasser*.

Lawrence's view of the Siegmund–Helena relationship as in fact incestuous, destructive of Siegmund's maleness, and the product of usurping intellect alone now stands forth:

> "The big flowers open with black petals and silvery ones, Siegmund. You are the big flowers, Siegmund; yours is the bridegroom face, Siegmund, like a black and glistening flesh-petalled flower, Siegmund, and it blooms in the Zauberland, Siegmund—this is the magic land." . . . Then she sank down and lay prone on him, spent, clinging to him, lifted up and down by the beautiful strong motion of his breathing. . . .
>
> She looked down at Siegmund. He was drawing in great heavy breaths. He lay still on his back, gazing up at her, and she stood motionless at his side, looking down at him. He felt stunned, half-conscious. Yet as he lay helplessly looking up at her some other consciousness inside him murmured: "Hawwa—Eve—Mother!" She stood compassionate over him. Without touching him she seemed to be yearning over him like a mother. Her compassion, her benignity, seemed so different from his little Helena. This woman, tall and pale, drooping with the strength of

her compassion, seemed stable, immortal, not a fragile human being, but a personification of the great motherhood of women.

"I am her child, too," he dreamed, as a child murmurs unconscious in sleep. He had never felt her eyes so much as now, in the darkness, when he looked only into deep shadow. She had never before so entered and gathered his plaintive masculine soul to the bosom of her nurture. (Pp. 60–61)

The flower imagery that opens this scene repeats the *fleur du mal* theme and is related to the victimization motif of *The White Peacock*. It is intended here to include the wish-fulfilling act of incest with the beloved in which the mother–madonna–victimizer fuses "her soul into his forever" (p. 60), assimilating him to her. The position of Siegmund's body beneath Helena's and the highly erotic tone of the passage declares the reversal of sexual roles that takes place. The incest wish at the heart of the novel, "Hawwa—Eve—Mother," establishes the reason for Siegmund's passivity, his increasing feminization, his infantile reduction, and his longing for death. The author's later association of him with Christ and of Helena with a Christ-crucifying Christianity does little to add to the picture of the Magna Mater that emerges from these pages, except to rationalize further ("philosophically," in this case, not aesthetically) the cause-and-effect relationship between consciousness and incest.

Closely related to Helena's assimilation of him, a corresponding change in the background elements of the novel clarifies still further the nature of Siegmund's reduction and the imagery used to describe it. One such element is the sea, which, as I have said, is gradually altered from a masculine to a feminine symbol:

They went out softly, walked in silence to the bay. There they stood at the head of the white, living moon-path, where the water whispered at the casement of the land seductively.

"It's the finest night I have seen," said Siegmund.

Helena's eyes suddenly filled with tears, at his simplicity
of happiness.

"I like the moon on the water," she said.

"I can hardly tell the one from the other," he replied
simply. "The sea seems to be poured out of the moon,
and rocking in the hands of the coast. They are all one, just
as your eyes and hands and what you say, are all you."

"Yes," she answered, thrilled. This was the Siegmund
of her dream, and she had created him. Yet there was a
quiver of pain. He was beyond her now, and did not need
her. . . .

"Whatever I have or haven't from now [on]," he continued, "the darkness is a sort of mother, and the moon
a sister, and the stars children, and sometimes the sea is
a brother; and there's a family in one house, you see."
(P. 29)

Despite the artificial and overblown rhetoric, the symbolism is readily discernible. Since the imagery that
identifies her with dominating mind has already been
established, the pull of the moon upon the sea easily
corresponds to Helena's psychic control of Siegmund.

Paralleling and readily commenting upon his alteration, the background reflects the transformation process: "The sea seems to be poured out of the moon."
Filtered into the moon, the sea now appears wholly derived from it. The anticipated result of this, Siegmund's
reduction to infantilism, is clear from the rest of the
image, the sea "rocking in the hands of the coast." The
later reference to him as "sea and sunlight mixed" (p.
42) adds to the deliberateness of Lawrence's symbolic
technique. Siegmund's "Hawwa—Eve—Mother," then,
is foreshadowed in the natural scenery. Previously associated with a traditionally masculine symbol, the sun
as the source of power, Helena in her moon aspect now
exercises a romantic, idealistic sway over him. The words
created and *dream* in the fifth paragraph reinforce this
view, for Siegmund becomes Helena's dream: "This was
the Siegmund of her dream, and she had created him."
Like the transformation that takes place in the background, Helena has altered him to an abstraction con-

gruent with her mental image. In *The Rainbow* and *Women in Love*, Lawrence uses light and moon imagery with the same connotations, and *The Trespasser* appears as the major source in his fiction for symbols of this type and the processes they include.

Nor does Helena's will to assimilate end with Siegmund; it extends to the cosmos of natural scenery around her:

> Substance and solidity were shadows that the morning cast round itself to make itself tangible: as she herself was a shadow, cast by that fragment of sunshine, her soul, over its inefficiency.
>
> She remembered to have seen the bats flying low over a burnished pool at sunset, and the web of their wings had burned in scarlet flickers, as they stretched across the light. Winged momentarily on bits of tissued flame, threaded with blood, the bats had flickered a secret to her.
>
> Now the cliffs were like wings uplifted, and the morning was coming dimly through them. She felt the wings of all the world upraised against the morning in a flashing, multitudinous flight. The world itself was flying. Sunlight poured on the large round world till she fancied it a heavy bee humming on its iridescent atmosphere across a vast air of sunshine.
>
> She lay and rode the fine journey. Sunlight liquid in the water made the waves heavy, golden, and rich with a velvety coolness like cowslips. Her feet fluttered in the shadowy underwater. Her breast came out bright as the breast of a white bird. (P. 45)

Maintaining a fine balance between the irony and the romantic appeal of the metamorphosis now occurring, Lawrence shows how material reality is transcendentalized until all is simply an extension of Helena's soul. In cementing the identity between person and metaphor, the use of the background to evoke her as a white bird is similar to the technique and imagery employed in *The White Peacock*. As the embodiment of her soul, such images as "the cliffs were like wings," "the world itself was flying," and "her breast came out bright as the breast of a white bird" all reveal the transforming process. Its reductiveness is of course apparent in the comparison of Helena to a bat "threaded with blood," in whom the world is reflected as "a heavy bee." Like the peacock, the underside of her whiteness is foul, and consciousness is again exposed as a vampire.

Despite the novel's concentration upon Helena's effect on Siegmund, his actual rebirth provides the final link between the theme, the background, and the psychological interaction of the characters:

> Where was Siegmund? she wondered. He also was somewhere among the sea and sunshine, white and playing like a bird, shining like a vivid, restless speck of sunlight. She struck the water, smiling, feeling alone with him. They two were the owners of this morning, as a pair of wild, large birds inhabiting an empty sea.
>
> Siegmund had found a white cave welling with green water, brilliant and full of life as mounting sap. The white rock glimmered through the water, and soon Siegmund shimmered also in the living green of the sea, like pale flowers trembling upward.
>
> "The water," said Siegmund, "is as full of life as I am," and he pressed forward his breast against it. He swam very well that morning; he had more wilful life than the sea, so he mastered it laughingly with his arms, feeling a delight in his triumph over the waves. Venturing recklessly in his new pride, he swam round the corner of the rock, through an archway, lofty and spacious, into a passage where the water ran like a flood of green light over the skin-white bottom. Suddenly he emerged in the brilliant daylight of the next scoop of a bay.
>
> There he arrived like a pioneer, for the bay was inaccessible from the land. He waded out of the green, cold water on to sand that was pure as the shoulders of Helena, out of the shadow of the archway into the sunlight, on to the glistening petal of this blossom of a sea-bay.
>
> He did not know till he felt the sunlight how the sea had drunk with its cold lips deeply of his warmth. Throwing himself down on the sand that was soft and warm as white fur, he lay glistening wet, panting, swelling with glad pride at having conquered also this small, inaccessible sea-cave, creeping into it like a white bee into a white virgin blossom that had waited, how long, for its bee. (P. 46)

The reductive process in the entire scene establishes beyond doubt the nature of Siegmund's rebirth as a reflecting image of Helena. The place in which he is now swimming, for example, is later referred to as a "virgin bay" (p. 48), and from internal evidence his entrance into the bay will appear as a symbolic reversion to the womb, from which he emerges at the end of the passage as a newborn baby. The central idea behind the description is a kind of profane Immaculate Conception in which the Madonna, Helena, gives birth to the Christ-like Siegmund.

Though his insight is out of character and compromises Lawrence's detachment, which has been completely controlled up to this point, Siegmund's later identification with Christ reinforces this image: "The carved Christ upon His cross hung against a silvery-grey sky. Helena looked up wearily, bowing to the tragedy. Siegmund also looked, and bowed his head. 'Thirty years of earnest love; three years' life like a passionate ecstasy —and it was finished. He was very great and very wonderful. I am very insignificant, and shall go out ignobly. But we are the same; love, the brief ecstasy, and the end. But mine is one rose, and His all the white beauty in the world'" (p. 65). In a basic sense, Siegmund must be considered the complete product of a woman-dominated and repressive Christianity that has been conveyed to him through the mother surrogate, Helena. For Lawrence, the possessive woman, Christianity, and the psychic assimilation of the passive male are now integrally related.

The first paragraph of the preceding scene establishes Siegmund's identity as an adjunct of Helena, for he is described as childlike, "white and playing like a bird," and "a restless speck of sunlight." The sterility of the relationship is suggested in their comparison to a pair of birds "inhabiting an empty sea." The irony is almost blatantly obvious, since, far from recognizing his reduction, Siegmund views himself as a second Adam, a pioneer discovering new lands. His statement that the water is as full of life as he is receives special ironic emphasis because the sea has already been described as empty. No life exists; sunlight has sterilized all.

The last four paragraphs show his rebirth in biological detail. Finding "a white cave welling with green water," in the second paragraph, represents his entry into the womb. With a single imaginative stroke Lawrence then reverses the direction of the movement by describing Siegmund swimming "in the living green of the sea, like pale flowers trembling upward," and he now represents him on his journey forth. The author reinforces the upward movement by the reference to mounting sap in the preceding sentence. The flower image is also significant because it relates Siegmund's rebirth to the *fleur de mal* theme carried over from *The White Peacock*, and because his hands have already been described as "two scarlet flowers" (p. 27) groping for Helena.

In the third paragraph, Siegmund swims "round the corner of the rock, through an archway, lofty and spacious, into a passage where the water ran like a flood of green light over the skin-white bottom." If Lawrence is being clinically exact here, he is describing the stage of birth at which the fetus passes from the womb through the cervix into the vagina. The "skin-white bottom" at once conceptualizes the reductive nature of the image, calls attention by "skin" to the biological process, and implies by the color white the sterility of the ensuing "birth." His emerging "in the brilliant daylight of the next scoop of a bay" at the end of the third paragraph; wading "out of the green, cold water on to sand" in the fourth paragraph; and lying "glistening wet, panting, swelling with glad pride" in the fifth paragraph visualize the process of birth. References to the sand as "white fur" and to Siegmund creeping "like a white bee into a white virgin blossom" complete the physiological process by evoking the image of a baby (white bee) crawling from the mother's pubes (white fur) to her breasts (white virgin blossom). By recalling Helena's reduction of the world to a "heavy bee" (p. 29), the deliberateness of this entire process in the comparison of Siegmund to a white bee becomes apparent. With Helena towering above him, he has indeed become a Lilliputian in the Land of Brobdingnag, and the short step to "Hawwa—Eve—Mother" is inevitable.

Anticipating *Sons and Lovers*, both *The White Peacock* and *The Trespasser* with increasing clarity deal with several interrelated themes conveyed through a common imagery. Reflecting the formal problem at their core, each novel splits into two unintegrated halves. Part One of each includes a symbolic description and partial analysis of a state of mind; Part Two shifts in scene (to London in *The Trespasser*) and falls to seed in a realism that is mechanically written, plot-centered, and only conceptually coordinated with the governing symbolism. Whatever realism exists in Lawrence's first two novels is in the nature of an afterthought, a weak attempt to provide a credible external framework for an intensely subjective and symbolically formulated experience. His solution to the aesthetic problem is evident in *Sons and Lovers*, where he endeavors to subordinate the symbolism to realism.

IV

Self-Encounter and the Unknown Self
Sons and Lovers

Criticism of *Sons and Lovers* has demonstrated that any interpretation of the book depends finally upon the reader's view of the conclusion: Paul Morel's repudiation of "the drift towards death" in favor of life and his departure "towards the faintly humming, glowing town." Granted the importance of the ending, however, critics have been more successful in dividing themselves into two factions explicating the reasons for their respective opposing points of view than in interpreting the work. It is not necessary to defend or to reject the conclusion merely because the affirmation does or does not follow from the real nature of the evidence presented about Paul Morel. The affirmation is one of degree, and the book ends, understandably, with an emotional pronouncement out of all proportion to the author's conceptual tentativeness. The peculiar sense of despair that attends Paul's assertion of hope suggests a double conclusion, which takes full advantage of the author's uncertainty over the outcome. Lawrence is split between the emotional and conceptual import of Paul's decision; he perhaps leaves the conclusion deliberately ambiguous in order to conceal the formal problem, the lack of coherence between the realistic and symbolic levels of the work, between the psychoanalytic and life matrices.

Whatever hope Paul has is intrinsically related to the mercy killing of his mother: this deliberate act is the only means by which he can overcome her possessiveness and his fear of being assimilated by her, can assert his inner freedom, and can arrive ultimately at wholeness of being. To achieve a sense of human completeness, he must begin by rooting out his own consciousness, which is formed entirely in Mrs. Morel's image, and take the risk that his action (the mercy killing) may be a form of psychic suicide. The critical issue raised by the ending, then, is whether Paul can survive this form of death. Events make clear that the mercy killing and the psychic rooting out are, in effect, synonymous; that Mrs. Morel's control of Paul is so complete that the two feel united as a single mental construct; that Lawrence's definition of incest as a commingling and merging of conscious minds holds true of *Sons and Lovers* as it did of *The White Peacock* and *The Trespasser*; and that, given his definition, Lawrence does not deny the oedipal tie between mother and son. In fact, the mercy killing is the consequence of the nature of their relationship, and the formal incongruity in the novel can be traced to the weakness inherent in Lawrence's view of the intellect and its relation to the vital self.

As in the earlier work, an understanding of the light imagery is the best means for putting the formal difficulty clearly into perspective. This imagery not only binds Paul and his mother into a single identity, but it also describes the similar qualities of Mrs. Morel and Miriam. Miriam is apprehended, then, as being deliberately presented as a mother surrogate, and the cause for Paul's rejecting her and killing his mother is the same. Both women theoretically prevent him from attaining wholeness of being, and he eliminates them to ensure his future growth. But the inconsistencies between the different levels of the work—Lawrence's insistence on the realistic plane, for example, of the contrast between the vital Mrs. Morel and the predatory Miriam, when all the evidence on the symbolic level denies this view—raises the question of means and ends. Nowhere does the author's notion of psychic processes become more suspect and the formal problem associated with it more obvious than in Paul's assertion of a vital self independent of his mother's influence: "Paul would have died rather than his mother should get to know of this affair [with Clara]. He suffered tortures of humiliation and self-consciousness. There was now a good deal of his life of which necessarily he could not speak to his mother. He had a life apart from her—his sexual life."[1] If Paul's sexual life is not independent of his mother's influence, nor his own, the idea of the vital self cannot stand, and the discrepancy between means and ends will be clear.

Furthermore, Lawrence seems to overlook an important distinction that ought to have been enforced between the concept of the vital self and adolescent sexuality: "This was the end of the first phase of Paul's love affair. He was now about twenty-three years old, and, though still virgin, the sex instinct that Miriam had over-refined for so long now grew particularly strong. Often, as he talked to Clara Dawes, came that thickening and quickening of his blood, that peculiar concentration in the breast, as if something were alive there, a new self or a new centre of consciousness, warning him that sooner or later he would have to ask one woman or another" (p. 252). The vital self is not so inseparable from adolescence that it need be confused with the sexuality accompanying it. In blurring the distinction between the new self and sexual development, Lawrence tends to enlist evidence in support of one as proof of the other and in effect smooths over the radical duality between his theory of consciousness and the newly created doctrine of vitalism. To be sure, final judgment of the doctrine must await direct textual examination of the Paul–Clara relationship, where the vital self is supposed fully to emerge.

Nevertheless, the impossibility of reconciling these ideas is evident from their mutual exclusiveness, from the psychological dissociation upon which Lawrence constructs his view of psychic processes. Though the consequences are not entirely apparent until after *Women in Love*, the developing direction in the body of the

1. D. H. Lawrence, *Sons and Lovers*, p. 345.

novels is quite clear. Since consciousness and the vital self are mutually exclusive principles as in the later works *male* and *female* are, the only solution for Lawrence will be to cut the Gordian knot and to maintain one principle over the other, the vital unconscious over mechanical mind. Only when the ego is thoroughly uprooted can the vital self emerge and the kind of psychic integration occur that Lawrence associates with a totally new kind of consciousness evolving in connection with the vital self. His very attempt to trace this evolution with fidelity is in large measure responsible for the aesthetic imbalance in the novels and raises the whole question of the psychological credibility of his viewpoint. In this context, then, the reference above to "a new self or a new centre of consciousness" suggests *Sons and Lovers* as the initial statement of this issue. If the psychological opposites at work in the novel are irreconcilable, Lawrence must be asserting the gradual eclipse of one self by the other. Certainly, the "new self" and "that peculiar concentration in the breast" do anticipate the doctrine of unconscious centers of being that he enunciates later in *Fantasia of the Unconscious*. The thesis of this work—that all superimposed forms of behavior distort the vital self and must be rejected on behalf of a new kind of awareness directly reflecting the unconscious centers and subject to their laws—surely implies Lawrence's repudiation of the mental life as an obstacle to self-fulfillment.

In *Sons and Lovers* the author works toward his goal by showing the evolution of the vital self until an approximate balance is struck between the opposed psychic forces. He then uses the upsetting of this balance through the mercy killing to suggest the removal of the last impediment to a further development of the vital self. Since this growth ostensibly takes place in *The Rainbow* and *Women in Love*, *Sons and Lovers* may be considered a study preparatory to the later work. In summing up Lawrence's earlier novels and in anticipating the later, *Sons and Lovers* is of central importance to the whole Lawrence canon because it contains the psychological basis of much of the later doctrine. If the author does not show the vital self emerging coherently upon the destruction of consciousness in this work, the underlying assumptions governing the later novels are questionable. *The Rainbow*, in particular, is the product of the vital assertion first formulated in *Sons and Lovers*.

Granted these premises, existing criticism has failed by its very one-sidedness to take Lawrence's purpose fully into account and has left little room for a dispassionate, independent viewpoint. American critical opinion begins with Schorer's "Technique as Discovery" and bifurcates loosely thereafter into the vitalist–ethical approach of Mark Spilka, Julian Moynahan, Maurice Beebe, Dorothy Van Ghent, and John Edward Hardy, and into the Freudian perspective of Daniel Weiss, Seymour Betsky, Louis Fraiberg, and, implicitly, of Schorer himself. Freudian critics reject the conclusion of *Sons and Lovers* and often succeed remarkably well in discerning the cleavage between intention and performance. But in focusing upon Paul's subconscious and unrealized incestuous desires, they tend to reduce the novel to a case study of neurosis that illuminates Lawrence more than Paul Morel. The vitalists, on the other hand, raise ingenious arguments in defense of the work. Nevertheless, they are unable to evaluate it, I believe, without appearing vague and somewhat inconsistent. They tend to substitute poetic generalities and idealism for textual evidence.

In noting the discrepancy between intention and performance, Schorer paves the way to and half-enters the Freudian door:

> The novel has two themes: the crippling effects of a mother's love on the emotional development of her sons; and the "split" between kinds of love, physical and spiritual, which the son develops, the kinds represented by two young women, Clara and Miriam. The two themes should, of course, work together, the second being, actu-

ally, the result of the first: this "split" is the "crippling." So one would expect to see the novel developed, and so Lawrence, in his famous letter to Edward Garnett, where he says that Paul is left at the end with the "drift towards death," apparently thought he had developed it. Yet in the last few sentences of the novel, Paul rejects his desire for extinction and turns towards "the faintly humming, glowing town," to life—as nothing in his previous history persuades us that he could unfalteringly do.

The discrepancy suggests that the book may reveal certain confusions between intention and performance.[2]

The only possible answers to the criticism are that the letter does not adequately reveal Lawrence's intention and that evidence exists in the novel to anticipate, if not entirely justify, Paul's decision. Schorer also suggests that the Mrs. Morel–Paul and the Paul–Miriam–Clara themes do not cohere because the novel fails to end in Paul's "drift towards death." From this, one may conclude, Paul's ties with Mrs. Morel and Miriam, at least, are interchangeable aspects of his mother fixation. Since Lawrence does not discover the exact nature of his own relation to Paul, the exploratory technique he uses does not result in achieved content, a clear, wholly formed point of view that objectively interprets the experience presented. In identifying with his characters, Lawrence the artist succumbs to Lawrence the man, a fissure opens between intention and performance, and "the sickness was not healed, the emotion not mastered, the novel not perfected."[3] Behind the work and unconsciously distorted within it is an unrecognized neurosis that is directly responsible for the formal lapse. Without attempting to discover whether Lawrence's intention in fact differed from that announced in the letter, Schorer presents a view of *Sons and Lovers* obliquely directed toward biographical criticism and Freudian analysis.

Daniel Weiss does not stop short of full Freudian commitment, and his *Oedipus in Nottingham* is a frank

2. Mark Schorer, "Technique as Discovery," *Hudson Review*, 1 (1948), 76.
3. Schorer, "Technique as Discovery," p. 78.

attempt to analyze the novel according to the Freudian materials it conceals. Like Schorer, Weiss also assumes a psychological connection for Paul between Miriam and Mrs. Morel, but he extends Schorer's argument to include Clara Dawes within the role of mother surrogate and views Paul's relation to his mother as explicitly incestuous: "With Paul's last embrace of a living woman all three women are finally joined and identified as one, the mother. When she dies, the regressive, incestuous phantasies her life had fed sicken and die with her. The pleasantly deathly consummation with Miriam and the Nirvana-like 'impersonality of passion' with Clara resolve themselves in Paul's horror at the coldness of his mother's lips, a horror he inverts and feels in Clara when he lies with her. Gertrude's death releases both Clara and Miriam from their functions as mother surrogates. They do not die for Paul; it is he, finally, who samples death, first pantomiming it in Clara's arms and, at the last, feeling it on his mother's mouth. Clara's horror of him is based on this: that Paul is trying to 'die' on her."[4] As a result of his Freudian commitment, however, Weiss attributes almost every difference between his own assessment and the novel itself to Lawrence's ignorance of his unconscious nature. Though such an assumption is perhaps true in some quite general sense, it ultimately reduces the merit of the criticism as an objective study by opposing the author's intention diametrically to his achievement. The critic pays too little attention to the formal significance of the material, and the work as art is in danger of disappearing into the case study presented.

Nevertheless, except for his failure to perceive the extent of Lawrence's deliberateness, Weiss's view of the Paul–Miriam relationship is not difficult to accept: "Paul's entire relationship with Miriam is the unconscious purgation of his own attitude towards her, accomplished by attributing to her that same attitude, which accurately

4. Daniel A. Weiss, *Oedipus in Nottingham: D. H. Lawrence*, p. 65.

describes his infantile need for love. Needing her love, yet unable to accept it, he accuses her of the same thing Gertrude Morel accused her of, of 'sucking' the soul out of him."[5] Granted this argument, Lawrence's assertion that Paul rejects Miriam because of her possessiveness rather than his own inadequacy is untrue. Paul projects his own shortcomings onto her, and Weiss shows us that a legitimate Freudian entrance into the novel is possible. But to accomplish this without sacrificing the formal demands of Sons and Lovers by failing to discuss them and without submerging the representational aspects of the work in the Freudian hypothesis, the author's intention should be clearly grasped. Since "intention" is not a matter of content divorced from form, the entire structural organization of the book and, most importantly, the symbolism are relevant to this question.

Louis Fraiberg's "The Unattainable Self: D. H. Lawrence's Sons and Lovers" and Seymour Betsky's "Rhythm and Theme: D. H. Lawrence's Sons and Lovers" conclude the Freudian survey. Betsky confirms the view of the Paul–Miriam relationship as aesthetically unsatisfying and psychologically false, refers to it as "the novel's great weakness," which can be "clarified only by biography, if even there," and notes the cleavage in Paul's attitude toward Miriam between "conscious reason" and "unconscious rejection."[6] In attacking the novel at its weakest point and in suggesting Lawrence's failure to realize the Paul–Miriam relationship within the scope of the work, Betsky repeats several of the propositions commonly held by Freudian critics. Other shared viewpoints, which owe much to Schorer, are the failure of Lawrence the man to separate himself from Lawrence the artist; the cleavage between intention and achievement; Paul's ignorance of his actual motives; Lawrence's

5. Weiss, *Oedipus in Nottingham*, p. 52.
6. Seymour Betsky, "Rhythm and Theme: D. H. Lawrence's *Sons and Lovers*," in Frederick J. Hoffman and Harry T. Moore, eds., *The Achievement of D. H. Lawrence*, pp. 138–39.

inability to integrate the formal realistic method and the chronological organization of the novel with the psychological significance of the material; and the ultimately incestuous identity for Paul of Mrs. Morel, Miriam, and, according to some critics, Clara Dawes.

In essential agreement with him about the inadequacy of the conclusion and Lawrence's incomplete detachment, Fraiberg generally extends Schorer's main arguments as they apply to Paul Morel alone. He considers the author's failure to balance his own view of Paul with the facts presented about him to be responsible for the formal lapse, and he notes "a partial gap between his accurate reporting (or invention) of his characters' behavior and its artistic significance."[7] More importantly, Fraiberg relates the aesthetic fault of the work both to its chronological structure and to Lawrence's inability to develop his character sufficiently: "The chronological plan of the novel—the essential part of which is Paul's life between childhood and the end of adolescence—does not work because the events do not bring associated changes in character. Paul's responses are fixed. He cannot develop; he can only repeat his suffering."[8] The notion of a psychological development in Paul, incapable of objectification through the plot movement, would be a useful alternative to this view. Pursuing this direction, it would be possible to maintain that a chronological framework is not a suitable means of showing the character's growth. But before the question of Paul's development can really be argued one way or another, the imagery of the novel must be recognized and must be considered relevant to this problem. The symbolic residue carried over from *The White Peacock* and *The Trespasser* conditions *Sons and Lovers* in spite of Lawrence's serious attempt through realism to save the book from too one-

7. Louis Fraiberg, "The Unattainable Self: D. H. Lawrence's *Sons and Lovers*," in Charles Shapiro, ed., *Twelve Original Essays on Great American Novels*, p. 182.

8. Fraiberg, "The Unattainable Self," p. 182.

sided a dependence upon the light imagery. This residue and the hypothesis of a possible psychic development in Paul suggest symbolism—not the realism with which it clashes—as the more appropriate way of illustrating the hero's growth.

Finally, like the other Freudians, Fraiberg considers the discrepancy between intention and achievement entirely the outcome of an abnormality in Paul that Lawrence does not perceive: "Accordingly, in the attempts of Paul to love Miriam and Clara there is a reading of love as a sinking—not a rising into oneness with nature. But though at moments Paul attains this apparent spiritual success, it leads him not to peace, but to frustration, and ultimately he is forced to recognize its equation with death, thus defeating Lawrence's attempt to establish passion as the road to selfhood. The search for life and its meaning perversely becomes for Paul the inadvertent but welcome union with death, the obliteration of self. This is both a logical and fictional contradiction, and it prevents the book from achieving full aesthetic integration."[9] However, in no other Freudian view of the conclusion is even the possibility of Paul's reaching momentary spiritual success admitted, and it is worth while to observe the effects on the Freudian thesis when this phenomenon occurs. As soon as even partial winning through to wholeness of being is suggested (since this is the only way in which success can be understood in this context), the only Freudian alternative is to depict Paul's success as an aspect of his total failure. While this is perhaps again true in some general sense, Fraiberg and the other Freudians never demonstrate how their judgment can be convincingly maintained without reducing the novel to a case study. Those who wish to remain within the confines of the work are not persuaded by this argument.

Unless *Sons and Lovers* itself can explain why Paul's success must end in catastrophe, the ordinary Freudian

9. Fraiberg, "The Unattainable Self," pp. 186–87.

view of the ending will appear merely doctrinaire and speculative. It applies more to the author than to the work and disregards the formal nature of art. True, the evidence presented in the novel does not justify the conclusion—Paul's departure for the town—but the surrounding context qualifies Lawrence's dogmatic pronouncement about life, and renders it more tentative and less harsh than it appears on the surface. Even as stated, moreover, the conclusion is at least poetically preferable to the only other alternative possible—Paul's lying down beside his mother and dying. One might assert that the Paul–Miriam relationship is a projection of Lawrence's own oedipal plight, that Paul does not realize his difficulties because Lawrence does not and that his fixed responses are also Lawrence's. Yet, if Paul in some sense appears to attain momentary spiritual success, his psychological growth must to some extent be admitted. It is then unnecessary to drag the author into the novel and hold him personally responsible for the conclusion. At the beginning, Paul is completely bound to his mother; by the end, even though he asserts his freedom on behalf of the vital self, he yet must tear himself away from her. With this surrounding context, then, the conclusion is not so dogmatically stated that it can be debated on such tenuous grounds as those set forth by Schorer and Fraiberg. In following their assumptions, the only course left open is to identify Paul Morel fully with D. H. Lawrence and use biographical information where possible to supply the missing links in the argument. The question is not whether this can be done, but whether it is necessary to do so, at least to the degree the Freudians imply. Though there is a very deep sense of personal involvement between the author and his hero, which is detrimental to the work as a whole, *Sons and Lovers* is not that bad a novel.

Operating through the light imagery and integrally related to his definition of incest, the author's theory of consciousness is sufficient to mediate between formal demands and Freudian observations. A study of this imagery will reveal that Lawrence is discussing incest throughout the book and that the nature of the vital self is in fact predicated upon its asserted value as an alternative to mentality. If the formal problem merely involved Lawrence's awareness of incest, there would be no difficulty at all in satisfying psychological considerations without sacrificing the representational qualities of art. In this respect, *Sons and Lovers* is perfectly realized, and the vitalist critics are right in insisting upon the integrity of the work.

But the weakness inherent in his view of incest—Lawrence's claim that neurosis affects consciousness alone and that the vital self remains pristine—limits the novel too severely. He does not perceive entire areas of experience beyond the scope of the light imagery, which, nevertheless, condition his response to experience. The disproportion between the characters' response to stimuli and the stated causes of their response; Lawrence's insistence that the vital self and the mechanical mind are wholly separable and antagonistic principles; his ultimate identification of the predatory woman, consciousness, industrial society, and Christianity—all are manifestations of this one-sided view of reality. The impulse of Freudian critics to explore the man behind the work, their insistence upon the discrepancy between intention and achievement, simply reflects the belief that *somehow Sons and Lovers* tails off into autobiography and abnormal psychology. This is a view with which I can sympathize and can understand.

Lawrence's fear of a psychic encounter of opposites certainly conceals an attempt to repress a constant, subliminally felt incestuous drive. And exactly because the drive is felt, it, too, emerges to expression in the work and influences the structural design. Furthermore, in the process of repression, what originally may have been a healthy and counteracting segment of the unconscious becomes so entangled with neurosis that the two become

hopelessly enmeshed, never quite destroying one another, but always on the verge of mutual chaotic collapse.
Lawrence's assertion of the vital self as autonomous is
thus negated by the existence of Freudian components
within it. In *Sons and Lovers* the effects of this inter-
meshing are not fully apparent; only in the beginning
stages is it still possible to consider momentary abate-
ment of self-conflict as evidence of progress in an uphill,
finally hopeless struggle.

Maurice Beebe's "Lawrence's Sacred Fount: The
Artist Theme in *Sons and Lovers*" counters Schorer's
thesis of the split between intention and achievement.
Beebe views *Sons and Lovers* as a portrait-of-the-artist
novel in which the "concept of the artist as an exile from
life" is juxtaposed against the theme of the sacred fount,
the notion that "the artist must experience life in order
to depict it in art."[10] The tensions between the opposing
themes are then resolved through the emergence of a
third theme, "the liberating force of artistic creativity.
Unless there is some such resolving theme, we should
have to agree with Schorer that the novel is split not
only between intention and performance, but also between idea and form, and we should have to agree with
critics who feel that the entire last part of the novel is a
failure."[11] Beebe's contention that if Schorer is right there
is no resolving theme in the work puts the argument
between Freudian and vitalist critics squarely into focus.

The weakness of the essay is in Beebe's either-or
interpretation of the novel, for he disregards the significance of Freudian claims after apparently taking them
into account: "Paul begins to free himself from the op-
pression of his mother when he assumes the role of the
father. Thus when he makes love to Clara he reverts
unconsciously to the speech of Walter Morel. But the

10. Maurice Beebe, "Lawrence's Sacred Fount: The Artist
Theme of *Sons and Lovers*," *Texas Studies in Literature and Language*, 4 (1962), 540.

11. Beebe, "Lawrence's Sacred Fount," p. 542.

return to the father is best represented in terms of Paul's relationship with Baxter Dawes, Clara's estranged husband. As Daniel Weiss has pointed out, Baxter is physically similar to Walter Morel in appearance and, like him, works with his hands and is the rejected husband of an educated woman."[12] Weiss's actual concerns are with Paul's homosexual orientation toward Dawes as father surrogate, which is simply another manifestation of his oedipal plight. The quite opposed view of Beebe is that Clara is a bridge for Paul and not a goal and that he, for that reason, seeks to reconcile Clara and Dawes. The case for artistic creativity appears superficial and evasive when it encounters direct Freudian criticism drawn from the text. In addition, Beebe's assertions can usually be turned against him, as his view of the mercy killing suggests. Mrs. Morel's death is supposed to free Paul from "his dead self" so that he will ultimately attain wholeness of being.[13] The counter-Freudian view argues the mercy killing to be a manifestation of the very incestuous drives Paul ostensibly overcomes; his assertion of freedom is merely the mask of his bondage. Again exclusive positions confront each other, and the problem of accepting one view without entirely rejecting the other is clear.

Dorothy Van Ghent focuses upon the sociological aspect of the novel and assumes that Lawrence's purpose is to show the "organic disturbance" of normal "sexual polarities . . . as a disease of modern life . . . in all its personal, social, political, and industrial manifestations."[14] Undeniably, modern industrialism can severely exacerbate existing sexual disturbances, and Lawrence does construct much of his later fiction around the thesis that modern life is diseased. But even if this were the author's

12. Beebe, "Lawrence's Sacred Fount," p. 549.
13. Beebe, "Lawrence's Sacred Fount," p. 550.
14. Dorothy Van Ghent, "On *Sons and Lovers*," in Mark Spilka, ed., *D. H. Lawrence: A Collection of Critical Essays*, pp. 16–17.

purpose here, evidence is lacking to establish a cause-and-effect relationship between modern life and sexual disturbance. In her unquestioning acceptance of this aspect of his thought, Van Ghent blurs the issue. Is sexual disturbance caused by modern life, or is it only exacerbated by it and caused by something else, such as heredity? Lawrence's conception of sexual polarities is not normative, as both Van Ghent and Spilka claim, but reductive, and the identity he wishes to establish between sexual polarity and vitalism is questionable. The author's whole notion of vitalism must be rejected if his theory of sexual polarity is a manifestation of sexual disorientation rather than of sexual health. In addition, Van Ghent uses the phrase "unsuccessful struggle to establish natural manhood" to describe Paul, but does not actually apply it to him.[15] His refusal to let Miriam possess him is taken as a sign of his "coming through." By not commenting upon the connection between Paul's refusal to be possessed, his search for manhood, and the nature of his relationship with Mrs. Morel and Miriam, Van Ghent evades the oedipal problem that is inherent in the novel. It is demonstrable that both Van Ghent and Beebe skirt this issue while giving lip service to the Freudian point of view.

His easy acceptance of Lawrence's doctrine also leaves Mark Spilka's analysis in *The Love Ethic of D. H. Lawrence* open to question. It may be true that "a man is born at the end of *Sons and Lovers*," but it is something of a breech delivery, not a natural birth.[16] Spilka is able to defend Paul's vital growth only by minimizing the oedipal tie with his mother, by denying any basically Freudian similarity in his relation to Mrs. Morel, Miriam, and Clara, and by blaming the three women for his inadequacies. From Spilka's viewpoint, Paul's development consists more in his evaluating others according to the doctrine of vitalism, which Lawrence assumes a priori,

15. Van Ghent, "On *Sons and Lovers*," p. 16.
16. Mark Spilka, *The Love Ethic of D. H. Lawrence*, p. 31.

than in gradually discovering the existence, source, and nature of the vitalism in himself:

> the conflict in all future novels centers upon a single man and woman, a specific couple whose relationship is judged or resolved in terms of its own vitality. We have already seen such conflicts, incidentally, in the floral scenes in *Sons and Lovers*, where vitality, or the full glow of the life-flame, is the chief criterion in Paul's specific relations with his mother, and with Miriam and Clara—where each affair is judged, in other words, in terms of its effect upon the life-flow, or the "livingness," of the man and woman involved. And as a matter of fact, each of Paul's three loves is actually significant in itself, since each contributes something vital to his development, yet finally proves destructive and inadequate. So all three loves—spiritual, oedipal, and possessive—resemble the counterfeit loves of later stories, and this in spite of the obvious Freudian twist which Lawrence seems to give them in his final draft.[17]

Spilka minimizes the "Freudian twist" by regarding Paul's tie with each of the women as existing by itself in an isolated and separate matrix. Granted that all three relationships are destructive, each evokes a fundamentally different response from Paul. Clearly, though, a Freudian critic could explode the whole notion of separate matrices by demonstrating how similar Paul's responses are in each instance. He could then introduce the incest and mother-fixation themes as an alternative view. This shift in perspective would inevitably lead to a reassessment of the actual value of Spilka's argument, especially his sentimental view of Mrs. Morel in relation to Paul.[18]

John Hardy's "*Sons and Lovers*: The Artist as Savior" clears much of the fog from a too-easy commitment to Lawrence's vitalism. Hardy's purpose is to show how the struggle of the artist-hero to emerge "from the still present and undifferentiated mass, stone, of the life experience" results in a final self-confrontation through

17. Spilka, *Love Ethic*, pp. 61–62.
18. Spilka, *Love Ethic*, p. 74.

which Paul overcomes the passive, Christ-like role of the artist-as-savior (victim) and asserts his manhood.[19] Like Beebe, Spilka, and Van Ghent, Hardy underestimates the oedipal problem and considers Miriam and Clara to be mere instruments in Paul's freeing himself "from the involvement with his mother to the task of the final self-confrontation."[20] But he is aware of Paul's compulsiveness and of the importance of the mercy killing: "An extreme and desperate measure; and one, as we have observed, that nearly defeats its purpose. But what the purpose is, is quite plain. Paul must kill his mother, before it is too late—that is, before the radical dependence of his will upon her, which he realizes, is irrevocably fixed by her death. Only, now, in the literal sense of the word, in preventing the natural death, in murdering her, can he assert his will; avail himself of the last chance to deny that his love for her has been self-destructive; and so preserve the idea of her goodness."[21] In this way, Lawrence forces the novel to a conclusion, and Hardy perceives the significance of Paul's act as the author's rejection of the Christ role and of "women who required him to take that role."[22]

However, his notion that Lawrence compels the character to reject victimization is not thorough enough. The view of Paul's act as an extreme and desperate measure is well taken and good, but the assertion that Paul arrives at a direct self-confrontation through murder needs further discussion. In regarding the mercy killing as a prerequisite to self-realization, Hardy assumes the underlying validity of Lawrence's doctrine and its successful embodiment in the character a priori. Of course the idea of Paul as a transformed vital hero follows, and by considering Mrs. Morel, Clara, and

19. John Edward Hardy, "*Sons and Lovers*: The Artist as Savior," in *Man in the Modern Novel*, p. 52.
20. Hardy, "*Sons and Lovers*," p. 54.
21. Hardy, "*Sons and Lovers*," p. 63.
22. Hardy, "*Sons and Lovers*," p. 65.

Miriam to be simple pawns in the process of Paul's victory over himself, Hardy removes the remaining obstacle to his argument. Again, if Paul does not react differently in different circumstances and thus does not free himself, the question of a successful self-encounter is not only left in doubt; it requires an altogether opposed set of motivations to account for his action. Lawrence's thesis in the book may be that Paul frees himself, and evidence exists in support of it, as Hardy and the other vitalist critics demonstrate. Yet, side by side with their view is evidence that either disqualifies or considerably modifies it.

In his assessment of *Sons and Lovers* and of Lawrence generally, Julian Moynahan follows the pattern of vitalist criticism. But unlike Spilka and to a lesser extent Hardy, he gives much greater attention to the psychological significance of character relationships and to the apparent discrepancies in the formal organization of the work:

> Actually, *Sons and Lovers* has three formal orders or matrices, which inhabit the same serial order of narrated words. To a degree, they blend with each other, and enrich one another. The first matrix is autobiographical narrative; the second a scheme taken over from the psychoanalytic theory; the third is difficult to name because Lawrence was the first novelist to use it as a context, as opposed to a quality, of human experience, but it might be called the matrix of "life." . . .
>
> Now that the form of *Sons and Lovers* has been defined, it becomes possible to deal with the charge of formal confusion. Confusion arises owing to a final inescapable conflict between the psychoanalytic and the vital contexts. Each approaches experience from a somewhat different angle, interprets it differently, and posits a different sort of hero.[23]

Moynahan's adaptation of the matrix theory is valuable, since it crystallizes and offers a completely fair test of

---

23. Julian Moynahan, *The Deed of Life: The Novels and Tales of D. H. Lawrence*, pp. 14–17.

the Freudian and non-Freudian points of view relating to the novel. Indeed, the concessions to the psychoanalytic viewpoint show how willing he is to take the Freudian charges seriously and to deal justly with them.

Yet, the form of his concessions, "a final inescapable conflict between the psychoanalytic and vital contexts," implies Moynahan's willingness to sacrifice the form of the work in order to maintain his argument: "Paul Morel at the end is of necessity and by virtue of his own free act released from the material bondage which, if long continued, would have destroyed him."[24] The question is whether, having noted the opposition between the two contexts, the critic can still legitimately assert Paul's vital nature. He treats the novel's defect of form as something quite mechanical and unrelated to the hero's conflict. On the contrary, it may be claimed, the opposition between the contexts is the result of Lawrence's view of incest and his refusal to recognize its Freudian implications, which are present in the work in spite of him. Final self-confrontation is evaded, and the failure of form is inseparable from the hero's failure to encounter himself.

The critical issue ought to be clear: Paul's freedom and future growth depend upon how directly he confronts himself. Since, in my estimation, he does not face himself honestly, he is not free and will never attain wholeness of being. Lawrence's failure in *Sons and Lovers* is in effect a failure of nerve. Intellectually, the flaw is largely the outcome of his theory of consciousness and the psychological dissociation inherent in it. To assure the autonomy and incorruptibility of the vital self, Lawrence posits incest as an exclusively mental process and the psyche as a construct of opposed and separable principles. As a result, the very psychological problems he is evading slip in unperceived, and both the Freudian and the vital unconscious become irreparably blurred and confused with each other in the work. Therefore,

24. Moynahan, *Deed of Life*, p. 31.

Lawrence's theory is primarily a rationalization of the Freudian view of incest, and the mercy killing must be interpreted in two contrary ways, a circumstance that exposes the lapse in form. Paul's act represents a deliberate rooting out of consciousness in order to overcome neurosis; it is also a manifestation of neurosis, by which Lawrence evades the real nature of his character's plight. Unless the mercy killing is viewed in both ways, the author's achievement will appear diametrically opposed to his intention, which it is not, and content will seem to be more completely divorced from form than is actually the case.

Because it reflects each way of viewing Paul's action, the extremely ambiguous conclusion is crucial. In the context of Lawrence's rejection of the Freudian notion of incest and the close identification between author and character, *Sons and Lovers* becomes an exercise in deliberate ambiguity. If at the last possible moment Paul resists the temptation of dying at his mother's side and instead, departs, "towards the faintly humming, glowing town," his decision does not have the ring of absolute conviction in the total context. It is, rather, somewhat tentative, if more than an alternative possibility. Nor is the ambiguity unrelated to Lawrence's constant shifting back and forth between the vital and the psychoanalytic matrices. He was more aware than is usually admitted of the Freudian implications in the novel, and the note of ambiguity could have insinuated itself at least as a partial effort to conceal the radical thesis and the problem of form. Since this is exactly what happens in *Lady Chatterley's Lover*, the hypothesis is not without possibilities. Carrying through to the conclusion, the ambiguity may well be a manifestation of the author's wish to evade unpleasant realities. Thus, either concluding alternative alone would lack conviction as the book stands. The cleavage between intention and achievement does not emerge solely because the ending does not follow from the evidence but because Lawrence does not integrate the psychoanalytic and life matrices. A larger and prior problem that is glaringly reflected only in the conclusion, this defect is responsible for the structural weakness that ambiguity glosses over.

The novel's rationale is for the most part conveyed by two sorts of imagery that occasionally intrude upon the realistic manner of the composition. The light imagery, as I have suggested, is carried over from *The White Peacock* and *The Trespasser* and is identified with Mrs. Morel and Paul in the opening chapter, "The Early Married Life of the Morels," where its use is undisguised and direct. Later, when Lawrence blunts this imagery to maintain the realistic façade of the writing, it becomes more complex and contributes to the confusing ambivalence that the continual shifting of narrative perspective between the matrices causes. Illustrating the psychoanalytic matrix, the light imagery statically predominates in Mrs. Morel and Miriam, but as he develops, Paul's "whiteness" is gradually replaced by the dark imagery of the life matrix. This second kind of imagery is synonymous with unconscious growth and implicitly includes a vision of life that exceeds any individual's grasp, though it is presented through a single person's increasing awareness of his own inner nature. In addition, since all the characters participate to some extent in both kinds of being, they may be placed on a hierarchic scale and evaluated as "good" or "bad" according to their degree of light (bad) or darkness (good). And because all the characters remain static except Paul, it becomes possible to measure his growth through his changing relationship with the other characters: Mrs. Morel, Miriam, and Clara Dawes follow the scale suggested and convincingly mark each step of his progress.

The thesis Lawrence advances through the imagery and the symbolic arrangement of characters is the familiar one that Paul's relation to women is incestuous in inverse ratio to his vital growth; that the oedipal tie does not affect his male unconscious; and that his movement toward selfhood is the consequence of rejecting consciousness in the guise of the three women. The ultimate identity of the self as unconscious, vital, and male is diametrically opposed to the mental life as mechanical, dead, and feminine. Therefore, Lawrence's purpose must be to show how Paul confronts and defeats one part of himself in order to win the freedom he so desperately needs. The stages of the novel, from his original tie with Mrs. Morel to his theoretically successful efforts to break away from her through Miriam and Clara, are well-defined movements toward this end.

Before the imagery in Chapter One provides the basis of the mother–son relationship, the marital struggle of the Morels is established on the narrative level as a simple clash of wills. When Mrs. Morel discovers the duplicity of Morel's mother in charging them an exorbitant house rent, "Something in her proud, honourable soul . . . crystallised out hard as rock" at Morel's weakness (p. 13). The first step in her transformation, the destruction of her illusions about her husband, is completed long before Paul is born and recalls the situation of Cyril's mother in *The White Peacock*. On the level of realism, the marriage is a contest of opposites in which the "soft, non-intellectual, warm, a kind of gambolling" Morel contrasts with the "puritan, like her father, high-minded, and really stern" Mrs. Morel (pp. 9–10). And from this conflict the light and dark imagery emerges to comment upon the alteration of both parents and upon the consequences for Paul. As the following passage illustrates, Paul is the product of his mother's transformation, but his tie to her is ambiguous from the beginning. He remains on her side throughout the book, in opposition to his father and to anyone else who comes between them, but the prevailing dark imagery originally associated with Mr. Morel replaces Paul's "whiteness" as he matures, and suggests his ultimate identification with his father as a male. However, since Morel is weak and his spontaneity crushed early in marriage through his own fault, he is not treated sympathetically, and Paul never comprehends his need for him.

Having established the marriage bond as "a fearful, bloody battle that ended only with the death of one" (p. 14), Lawrence shows through the imagery the irony of Mrs. Morel's victory. Triumphing, she changes from a life- to a death-centered person and injures the child in her womb, who in becoming her victim takes on her identity as well. For Paul the act of birth is an ironic ascent into death, and his later description of Mrs. Morel on her deathbed as a maiden who had never lived, mutely echoes the bitterness Lawrence feels over the transformation now taking place:

> The moon was high and magnificent in the August night. Mrs. Morel, seared with passion, shivered to find herself out there in a great white light, that fell cold on her, and gave a shock to her inflamed soul. . . . She walked down the garden path, trembling in every limb, while the child boiled within her. For a while she could not control her consciousness; mechanically she went over the last scene, then over it again, certain phrases, certain moments coming each time like a brand red-hot down on her soul; and each time she enacted again the past hour, each time the brand came down at the same points, till the mark was burnt in, and the pain burnt out, and at last she came to herself. . . .
>
> She hurried out of the side garden to the front, where she could stand as if in an immense gulf of white light, the moon streaming high in face of her, the moonlight standing up from the hills in front, and filling the valley where the Bottoms crouched, almost blindingly. . . .
>
> She became aware of something about her. With an effort she roused herself to see what it was that penetrated her consciousness. The tall white lilies were reeling in the moonlight, and the air was charged with their perfume, as with a presence. Mrs. Morel gasped slightly in fear. She touched the big, pallid flowers on their petals, then shivered. They seemed to be stretching in the moonlight. . . . It almost made her dizzy.
>
> Mrs. Morel leaned on the garden gate, looking out, and she lost herself awhile. She did not know what she thought. Except for a slight feeling of sickness, and her

consciousness in the child, herself melted out like scent into the shiny, pale air. After a time the child, too, melted with her in the mixing-pot of moonlight, and she rested with the hills and lilies and houses, all swum together in a kind of swoon. (Pp. 23–24)

The first paragraph notes the change in Mrs. Morel from a self-divided person, in whom natural vitality and passion are gradually uprooted by the sense of injustices suffered, to a totally conscious woman dominated by pride and deathlike self-sufficiency. The white light falling cold on her and the remembrance of her husband's wrongs as a brand coming down on her soul illustrate the transforming process. These effects are reinforced in the second paragraph by the blaze of moonlight "as if in an immense gulf of white light," and in the third paragraph by the phallic frame of reference, the lilies reeling and stretching in the moonlight, which is an ironic commentary upon the change in her. The whiteness of the lilies and the moonlight, the phrase "drank a deep draught of the scent," and the statement "she roused herself to see what it was that penetrated her consciousness" strengthen the sense of psychic displacement and passional loss. As she is transformed, moreover, her perceptions change, and though the vital reality that transcends the individual remains, she no longer experiences it except as something lost or vaguely menacing. She feels "forlorn . . . in the mysterious out-of-doors," and "the white ruffles of the roses" remind her of "the morning-time and sunshine" (p. 24). She is not unaware of her passional nature and does not reject it; it is simply taken from her. Paul's later insistence that his own vitality is inherited from his mother, an apparent contradiction of her symbolic value, derives from this nocturnal event.

The final paragraph illuminates the direct effect of the mother's experience upon the unborn child by describing them as fused together "in the mixing-pot of moonlight." As the culminating step in the entire process of her alteration, this image evokes the central theme of the book: "this longing for identification, utter merging, which is at the base of the incest problem."[25] The "true centrality of the self"[26] has been broken prenatally in Paul by his mother's "light" operating subliminally upon him, and his victimization is almost complete before he is born. By the end of Chapter One, then, the essential question, whether Paul can ever gain independence from his mother and assert his own identity, has been implicitly posed. In view of the later mercy killing, he can answer affirmatively only by assuming that uprooting part of his mind will not end in the destruction of his entire personality, that parts of the psyche are separable, and that incest is the product of the mental nature alone. Thus, the completely satisfying resolution of the mother–son relationship exists on theoretical grounds quite independent of the Freudian reasons for the satisfaction. The conclusion takes full advantage of the ambiguity created to blur over the formal problem and to win the reader's emotional assent to propositions that are not psychologically credible.

After establishing the mother's prenatal effect upon the child, Lawrence proceeds to bind Paul even more completely to his mother in the first part of the novel. When Morel throws a table drawer and cuts his wife over the brow, the blood-tie in consciousness is irrevocably cemented: "He was turning drearily away, when he saw a drop of blood fall from the averted wound into the baby's fragile, glistening hair. Fascinated, he watched the heavy drop hang in the glistening cloud, and pull down the gossamer. Another drop fell. It would soak through to the baby's scalp. He watched, fascinated, feeling it soak in; then, finally, his manhood broke" (p. 40). United to her in suffering and baptized in the blood soaking through to his scalp, Paul's assimilation

25. D. H. Lawrence, *Studies in Classic American Literature*, p. 76.
26. Lawrence, *Studies*, p. 77.

to his mother is complete. Deprived of a male frame of reference by Morel's broken manhood, his future development will be entirely in her image. The symbolic guidelines to his character are clearly and objectively presented, and up to this point in the book all the evidence suggests the impossibility of Paul's ever breaking away from Mrs. Morel, let alone asserting his manhood, assuming an identity, or encountering himself.

But in applying the light imagery with a conflicting purpose to the Paul–Miriam relationship, Lawrence violates the objectivity and sets the different layers of the work at cross purposes. Though it is denied on the narrative level, for example, the view of Miriam as mother surrogate appears incontrovertible from the light imagery used to describe her:

> Then she saw her bush.
> "Ah!" she cried, hastening forward.
> It was very still. The tree was tall and straggling. It had thrown its briers over a hawthorn-bush, and its long streamers trailed thick, right down to the grass, splashing the darkness everywhere with great spilt stars, pure white. In bosses of ivory and in large splashed stars the roses gleamed on the darkness of foliage and stems and grass. Paul and Miriam stood close together, silent, and watched. Point after point the steady roses shone out to them, seeming to kindle something in their souls. The dusk came like smoke around, and still did not put out the roses. . . .
> She looked at her roses. They were white, some incurved and holy, others expanded in an ecstasy. The tree was dark as a shadow. She lifted her hand impulsively to the flowers; she went forward and touched them in worship.
> "Let us go," he said.
> There was a cool scent of ivory roses—a white, virgin scent. Something made him feel anxious and imprisoned. The two walked in silence. (Pp. 159–160)

Taking place near the Leivers' farm, this scene once more illustrates the author's by-now familiar technique of using background to comment upon character. As the rose bush ensnarling the hawthorn with briers, Miriam tries to possess Paul, and as in the prior scene that showed Mrs. Morel's transformation, the phallic frame of reference is at once ironic and perverse. Miriam's touching and looking at the white, glistening roses recalls the similar flower imagery and evokes the same kind of conceptualized and sublimated response to the mysterious out-of-doors that Mrs. Morel sensed in an earlier scene. The ironic reference to her as a rose and the comparison of roses to the sun reveal her feminine and predatory qualities, which explain Paul's feeling anxious and imprisoned in the white, virgin scent and his resistance to her back-to-the-womb allure. His resistance, in turn, presupposes the earlier maternal conditioning that, together with the light imagery, establishes Miriam's identity as mother surrogate. Since they share the same qualities, both women pose the same threat.

As Lawrence proceeds from the symbolic description of Miriam to a consideration of Paul's adolescent sexuality, however, the dislocation between the life and psychoanalytic matrices becomes increasingly apparent. Not only is the identity of the two women rejected literally, but Paul is compelled to deny it with a vengeance when he agrees with his mother that Miriam had in a "subtle way undermined his joy" of life (p. 258). Since Mrs. Morel has still not cut the umbilical cord binding him to her, Paul's praise of her passionate nature in contrast with Miriam's is evidence of the opposition between matrices. When the reader notices that Mrs. Morel has been described through the imagery as even more possessive, dominating, and abstractly "religious" than Miriam, the point becomes evident. The only way the discrepancy between the matrices can be accounted for, I believe, is to assume the author's gradual and, in some respects, unconscious identification with his character. The argument that Paul is projecting the oedipal tie with his mother onto his relation with Miriam is

certainly true, though as a point of departure for and
not the end of analysis.

The effect of Lawrence's intrusiveness is to distort
further the actual identity that Miriam and Mrs. Morel
have for Paul by suggesting different motivations for
his later rejection of them. Theoretically Paul defeats
Miriam and is released by his mother, but the cause of
his rejection of them is essentially the same: both stand
in the way of his freedom and must be eliminated. Lawrence's denial of their similarity of effect and symbolic
function on the realistic plane of the work leads him to
pursue differences where none exist, which suggests that
the light imagery has an area of application he does not
perceive. Paul's self-encounter will fail, then, because
the author does not permit him to confront the real problem, an indication that there is not much real psychological growth between *The White Peacock* and *Sons
and Lovers*. Similarly, Lawrence's refusal to discern the
Freudian implications of Paul's relations to Miriam and
to his mother clearly compromises the assertion that Paul
is following the trail of wholeness of being. The argument for the vital self becomes primarily an escape from
a dilemma; it is so hopelessly enmeshed with Freudian
elements in Paul's character that he never really acts
upon the basis he affirms. Lawrence does not embody
the concept successfully in his hero as a clear and psychologically convincing motivating force.

To illustrate this point, there is the similarity of
Paul's response to his mother and Miriam. Long before
the mercy killing proves their connection, the oedipal
tie, the longing for death, and the desire for incest are
implicit in his relation to Miriam: "She put her hands
over him, on his hair, on his shoulders, to feel if the
raindrops fell on him. She loved him dearly. He, as he
lay with his face on the dead pine-leaves, felt extraor-
dinarily quiet. He did not mind if the raindrops came on
him: he would have lain and got wet through: he felt as
if nothing mattered, as if his living were smeared away

into the beyond, near and quite lovable. This strange, gentle reaching-out to death was new to him. . . . To him now, life seemed a shadow, day a white shadow; night, and death, and stillness, and inaction, this seemed like *being*. To be alive, to be urgent and insistent—that was *not-to-be*. The highest of all was to melt out into the darkness and sway there, identified with the great Being" (p. 287). As in *The Trespasser* and in the previous scene with Miriam, the assimilation of the male is accompanied by an ironic juxtaposition of imagery suggesting fulfillment against the reductive process. The rain contrasts with Paul's childlike passivity, and Miriam's continuing attempt to possess him through touch recalls Helena's effect upon Siegmund.

Consequently, life now becomes "a shadow, day a white shadow," and *not-to-be* seems like *being*. Paul's assent to reduction leads inevitably to his longing for death, and the implicitly incestuous wish to fuse with the darkness is reinforced by the similar description of Mrs. Morel's transformation and its prenatal effect upon him in the opening chapter. The complete association of death, incest, Miriam, and the oedipal tie emerges immediately afterward when Paul remarks that Miriam gives him "a feeling of home almost like his mother" (p. 289). In addition, a cherry-picking scene just before the previous passage establishes his association of beauty, death, and sexual desire. From the tree, Paul notices some cherry stones on the ground "hanging bleached, like skeletons, picked clear of flesh," and then quickly glances at some cherry clusters (virginity) hanging over Miriam's ears, "so small, so tender, so soft" (p. 285). Around the stones are four dead birds, would-be despoilers of virginity, with whom he identifies.

Lawrence's only partial recognition of the psychological limits of the light imagery is also evident in Paul's silent reply to Miriam's accusation that he is a child: "He did not answer, but said in his heart: 'All right; if I'm a child of four, what do you want me for? I don't want another mother.' But he said nothing to her, and there was silence" (p. 296). His response implies a rejection of his mother and Miriam that in its bitterness goes far beyond Lawrence's purpose by linking the women emotionally in Paul, almost putting the work on a Freudian basis. The reader may infer an identification between Miriam and Mrs. Morel far below the level of awareness suggested by the light imagery.

The use of the imagery even to describe Mrs. Morel upon her deathbed helps to confirm this view by showing how ambiguous and mixed Paul's actual feelings for her are: " 'My love—my love—oh, my love!' he whispered again and again. 'My love—oh, my love!' . . . She lay raised on the bed, the sweep of the sheet from the raised feet was like a clean curve of snow, so silent. She lay like a maiden asleep. With his candle in his hand, he bent over her. She lay like a girl asleep and dreaming of her love. The mouth was a little open as if wondering from the suffering, but her face was young, her brow clear and white as if life had never touched it. . . . He bent and kissed her passionately. But there was coldness against his mouth. He bit his lips with horror" (pp. 398–399). The perception of his mother's brow, "clear and white as if life had never touched it," fixes her symbolic value with terrible clarity, conveys an attitude of slight contempt toward her for not having lived, which is expressed in spite of the genuinely felt remorse and tinges his sorrow with an element of maudlin and overemphatic rhetoric. The sheet raised "like a clear curve of snow," for example, is an objective detail that has no significance at all outside the imagery and is unrelated to the sorrow expressed elsewhere in the passage. Together with the underlying tone of coldness, it suggests a detachment from the scene not born of remorse and opposed to the tenderness of "My love—my love—oh, my love!"

The author's letter to Edward Garnett in the spring of 1913 in which he disclosed the double nature of his own involvement is external evidence for this assessment: "I only just realised the amazing brutality of sons and lovers. How that brutality remains, in spite of Christianity, of the two thousand years; it's better like that, than the civilized form it takes! It's only the top plaster [Lawrence: the civilization], and I'm sure brutality ought to develop into something finer, out of *itself*, not to be suppressed, denied! Paul [Morel] says to his mother, when she is dying, 'if I'd got to die, I would be quick about it, I would *will* to die.' Doesn't it seem awful! Yes, one *does* feel like that, but not only that, after all."[27] In addition, scenes in *The Rainbow*, *Women in Love*, and in the stories generally show preoccupation with a mother's death to be a recurring theme in Lawrence's fiction. Paul's ambiguous response to his mother before and after the mercy killing, then, suggests the same positive desire for incest and extinction, coupled with the last-minute revulsion in horror, that mark his relationship with Miriam. Lawrence's failure to connect and to explain this similarity; his insistence upon a basic difference between Miriam and Mrs. Morel in spite of their identical symbolic functions; the contradiction in this respect between the realistic and symbolic levels of the novel; and the disparity in many situations between Paul's response to his mother and Miriam and the apparent causes of his response—all imply a notion of the Oedipus complex beyond the limits of the imagery used to interpret it.

But if the formal problems of *Sons and Lovers* were related only to unperceived incestuous ties, any analysis would be grossly oversimplified. The existence of unrecognized Freudian elements must be linked to the conception of the vital self presented before the significance of the formal lapse can be rightly determined. Schorer's observations about the conclusion and various Freudian interpretations are useful points of departure,

27. D. H. Lawrence, *The Collected Letters of D. H. Lawrence*, Harry T. Moore, ed., I, 208.

but in no sense finished and final judgments. Lawrence wishes not only to assert the validity of the vital self through Paul's successful development but to show its relation to the author's quite explicit views of consciousness and incest. The conclusion, Paul's winning through to life and to "the faintly humming, glowing town," is merely the final dramatic manifestation of the purpose. Before the merit of Schorer's evaluation can be demonstrated, that there is nothing in his previous history to persuade the reader that Paul could successfully turn to life, it must be tested against the psychic conflict embedded in his character, through which the final assertion emerges.[28]

The author's view of the conflict and his claims for the vital self permeate the entire Paul–Miriam relationship and give it a firm theoretical basis. From this garden scene, for example, two distinct but crucially related ideas emerge: " 'See,' said Paul to Miriam, 'what a quiet garden!' She saw the dark yews and the golden crocuses, then she looked gratefully. He had not seemed to belong to her among all these others; he was different then—not her Paul, who understood the slightest quiver of her innermost soul, but something else, speaking another language than hers. How it hurt her, and deadened her very perceptions. Only when he came right back to her, leaving his other, his lesser self, as she thought, would she feel alive again. And now he asked her to look at this garden, wanting the contact with her again" (p. 165). Though not synonymous with it, Paul's adolescent sexuality is a manifestation of the vital self, "his other, his lesser self, as she thought." In this manner, adolescence and vitalism are yoked together, and Lawrence tends to view evidence for one as substantial proof of the other. In addition, Paul feels threatened by Miriam's very presence; to maintain contact with her, he must repress his essential maleness. The basis of their relation is established as an extension of the conflict within Paul, to be

28. Schorer, "Technique as Discovery," p. 76.

resolved only by the victory of one over the other, the vital over the mental self. Chapter Nine, "Defeat of Miriam," presents the apparent outcome of this struggle.

Lawrence's continual shifting back and forth from Miriam's to Paul's point of view in an apparent effort to fix responsibility for the conflict objectively does not conceal his partiality. The a priori commitment to the vital self and the symbolic value assigned to Miriam only assure the author's judgment against her: "With Miriam he was always on the high plane of abstraction, when his natural fire of love was transmitted into the fine stream of thought. She would have it so. . . . And in this passion for understanding her soul lay close to his; she had him all to herself. But he must be made abstract first. Then, if she put her arm in his, it caused him almost torture. His consciousness seemed to split" (p. 173). Holding Miriam responsible for Paul's shortcomings is really the easy way out of a dilemma, for Lawrence seems to deny the whole point of the opening chapter, that Paul is prenatally split as a result of the conflict between his parents. The apparent cause of the split, Miriam, is now regarded as the essential cause: she reduces him to the abstract.

Only the author's view of sexuality and the vital self as existing independently of the rest of the psyche will illuminate his inconsistency. The nature of Paul's tie to his mother (and to Miriam) makes this fact clear: "Paul would have died rather than his mother should get to know of this affair [with Clara Dawes]. He suffered tortures of humiliation and self-consciousness. There was now a good deal of his life of which necessarily he could not speak to his mother. He had a life apart from her— his sexual life. The rest she still kept" (p. 345). Implying Lawrence's whole argument for the vital self, Paul's life apart from his mother and Miriam, "his sexual life," this passage cannot be otherwise understood without misrepresenting the thesis. Paul's sexual life is a manifestation of the vital self; it is separate and dissociated from consciousness; and it is free from Mrs. Morel's and Miriam's possessive control. According to Lawrence, the vital self can be disturbed but not uprooted or perverted by the predatory woman.

Moreover, as he becomes aware of his vital nature, Paul fights "against his mother almost as he fought against Miriam" (p. 223). Since the very violence of his response to both women would ordinarily suggest their subconscious identity for him, it is clear that the vital self should have been perverted as a result. Yet, once again, Paul's acceptance of his mother's assertion that Miriam is "sucking the soul out of him" illustrates Lawrence's viewpoint. Not only is the vital self an automatic guarantee of Paul's sexual health, but he is sound in spite of previous passional failure: " 'I know,' he cried, 'you never will! You'll never believe that I can't—can't physically, any more than I can fly up like a skylark——.' 'What?' she [Miriam] murmured. Now she dreaded. 'Love you.' . . . And he came back to her [Mrs. Morel]. And in his soul was a feeling of the satisfaction of self-sacrifice because he was faithful to her. She loved him first; he loved her first. And yet it was not enough. His new young life, so strong and imperious, was urged towards something else. It made him mad with restlessness. She saw this, and wished bitterly that Miriam had been a woman who could take this new life of his, and leave her the roots" (pp. 221–223).

Showing defeat asserted as victory, the scene demonstrates the limits of the author's detachment from his character. Whereas Paul observes the possessiveness of Miriam alone, Lawrence notices Mrs. Morel's desire to retain Paul's roots as well. The irony of his return home with a feeling of self-sacrifice is seen by Lawrence but not by Paul. Yet neither author nor character discerns any connection between Paul's love for his mother and his passional failure with Miriam. Instead, Lawrence blames Miriam completely and reasserts Paul's vital self. And both agree with Mrs. Morel that Miriam might have taken Paul's new life and have left her the roots, though this division would preclude any fulfilling sexual role with Miriam. In short, Lawrence uses both women in different ways to excuse Paul's shortcomings, thus placing the responsibility for it beyond him. The rationalization inherent in this, the assertion of Paul's new life in spite of his "can't physically," is the only way to explain why the claim for the vital self and the admission of impotence do not immediately negate each other. It underlies, to repeat, Lawrence's use of the light imagery and is the reason for the aesthetic imbalance in the work, the separation of the psychoanalytic and life matrices, and the discrepancy between the narrative and symbolic levels.

Consequently, the introduction of the Paul–Clara relationship to illustrate the emergence of the vital self conceals the imperfection that is carried over from the previous section of the novel. Lawrence's purpose in introducing the new relation after the defeat of Miriam is almost blatantly clear: "This was the end of the first phase of Paul's love affair. He was now about twenty-three years old, and, though still virgin, the sex instinct that Miriam had over-refined for so long now grew particularly strong. Often, as he talked to Clara Dawes, came that thickening and quickening of his blood, that peculiar concentration in the breast, as if something were alive there, a new self or a new centre of consciousness, warning him that sooner or later he would have to ask one woman or another" (p. 252). Fully evident in his later sexual encounters with Clara, the "new self or a new centre of consciousness" is the answer to Miriam's and his mother's possessiveness, the means of initiating Paul into manhood. The nearly forced bravado of "that thickening and quickening of his blood, that peculiar concentration in the breast" clarifies Lawrence's viewpoint and anticipates his later doctrine of unconscious centers of being, as announced in *Fantasia of the Unconscious*. Paul's sexual initiation with Clara, then, is the author's proof for the validity of the vital self.

However, since he is not yet entirely liberated from his earlier condition, not every encounter is presented as successful, and the reader must discriminate between valid and invalid expressions of sexuality. In a number of scenes the sexual relation is obviously false, a carry-over, as it were, from Paul's sublimated tie to Miriam. The following scenes—both invalid—recall the destructive effects of Lettie upon George Saxton in *The White Peacock* and of Helena upon Siegmund in *The Trespasser*. The first occurs in the Theatre Royal in Nottingham, where Paul takes Clara to see Sarah Bernhardt in *La Dame Aux Camélias*: "The drama continued. He saw it all in the distance, going on somewhere; he did not know where, but it seemed far away inside him. He was Clara's white heavy arms, her throat, her moving bosom. That seemed to be himself. Then away somewhere the play went on, and he was identified with that also. There was no himself. The grey and black eyes of Clara, her bosom coming down on him, her arm that he held gripped between his hands, were all that existed. Then he felt himself small and helpless, her towering in her force above him" (p. 331). Though the author in this scene realizes the projective fantasy of Paul's wish to merge, Paul himself attributes the same power to Clara that Miriam exercised over him previously. Why Lawrence should admit the nature of the character's desire in one instance and not in the other is of course clear from his view of Clara as relatively opposed to Miriam through her dark, sensual mystique. Yet Paul, like Cyril, George Saxton, and Siegmund before him, betrays the same longing for reduction. His seeing Clara "towering in her force above him" while he holds her arm "gripped between his hands" clearly indicates this desire.

Unless the reader is aware of Lawrence's theory of consciousness, the theater scene would appear not merely perverse and of doubtful dramatic value, but also suggestive of a glaring weakness in the Paul–Clara relationship. Paul is supposed to gain a clearer awareness of the

vital self by being with her, but a perverse scene is admitted of no more apparent purpose than to point out
that his victimization continues into the present and will
probably persist into the future as well. The evaluation
of the implications of the theater scene raises questions:
Is it significant because it reveals perversity within Lawrence or because it marks a step in Paul's evolution
toward wholeness of being? If the first alternative should
be true, the relation with Clara would be unconsciously
perverse, and intention and achievement would be diametrically opposed. If the second, how is it justified?
Only the theory of consciousness, I suggest, explains why
Lawrence himself does not consider the scene a manifestation of inherent abnormality.

The second scene to illustrate the function of perverse love takes place in Clara's bedroom after their
return from the theater: "His eyes were dark, very deep,
and very quiet. It was as if her beauty and his taking it
hurt him, made him sorrowful. He looked at her with a
little pain, and was afraid. He was so humble before her.
She kissed him fervently on the eyes, first one, then the
other, and she folded herself to him. . . . She stood letting
him adore her and tremble with joy of her. It healed her
hurt pride. It healed her; it made her glad. . . . It was her
restoration and her recognition" (pp. 338–339). Both in
his fantasy at the theater and in the actual love-making
at home, Paul's bodily position is beneath or lower than
Clara's. In both instances he is in a sexually passive,
highly self-conscious state, reveling in, almost identifying with the female form. Yet the function of the present
scene is quite clearly a part of the dramatic structure.
Because Paul worships her, Clara's pride, hurt in her
marriage to Baxter Dawes, is healed. One implication is
that Paul's action, perverse in itself, makes Clara whole
so that she can now enjoy the vital connection with
him that has been in theoretical preparation all along.
Another is that Paul responds to her in the way she
wishes him to, and the process of assuring her wholeness

will ultimately lead to his own. Nevertheless, assuming this healing to be the function of the scene, the psychological premises upon which it rests are specious. A healthy sexual relationship will emerge from a perverse one, Lawrence suggests, if the people involved simply act out the perversion and change their attitudes toward one another concurrently.

Although this alteration in attitude actually encompasses the entire psychic transformation of the individual, as *The Rainbow* in particular illustrates, the change in Paul is merely assumed. The unsuccessful encounters are only juxtaposed against the single success in which Paul assertedly experiences the vital self fully for the first time. Without showing how it is accomplished, Lawrence asks the reader to accept the change allowing for the successful engagement as a preliminary to the encounter itself. The actual value of this meeting must therefore be determined:

> She caught him passionately to her, pressed his head down on her breast with her hand. She could not bear the suffering in his voice. She was afraid in her soul. He might have anything of her—anything; but she did not want to *know*. She felt she could not bear it. She wanted him to be soothed upon her—soothed. She stood clasping him and caressing him, and he was something unknown to her—something almost uncanny. She wanted to soothe him into forgetfulness.
>
> And soon the struggle went down in his soul, and he forgot. But then Clara was not there for him, only a woman, warm, something he loved and almost worshipped, there in the dark. But it was not Clara, and she submitted to him. The naked hunger and inevitability of his loving her, something strong and blind and ruthless in its primitiveness, made the hour almost terrible to her. . . .
>
> All the while the peewits were screaming in the field. When he came to, he wondered what was near his eyes, curving and strong with life in the dark, and what voice it was speaking. Then he realised it was the grass, and the peewit was calling. The warmth was Clara's breathing heaving. He lifted his head, and looked into her eyes. They were dark and shining and strange, life wild at the

source staring into his life, stranger to him, yet meeting him; and he put his face down on her throat, afraid. . . . They had met, and included in their meeting the thrust of the manifold grass stems, the cry of the peewit, the wheel of the stars.

When they stood up they saw other lovers stealing down the opposite hedge. It seemed natural they were there; the night contained them.

And after such an evening they both were very still, having known the immensity of passion. They felt small, half-afraid, childish and wondering, like Adam and Eve when they lost their innocence and realised the magnificence of the power which drove them out of Paradise and across the great night and the great day of humanity. It was for each of them an initiation and a satisfaction. To know their own nothingness, to know the tremendous living flood which carried them always, gave them rest within themselves. . . .

But Clara was not satisfied. Something great was there, she knew; something great enveloped her. But it did not keep her. In the morning it was not the same. They had *known*, but she could not keep the moment. She wanted it again; she wanted something permanent. She had not realised fully. She thought it was he whom she wanted. He was not safe to her. . . . She had not got him; she was not satisfied. She had been there, but she had not gripped the—the something—she knew not what—which she was mad to have.

In the morning he had considerable peace, and was happy in himself. It seemed almost as if he had known the baptism of fire in passion, and it left him at rest. But it was not Clara. It was something that happened because of her, but it was not her. They were scarcely any nearer each other. It was as if they had been blind agents of a great force. (Pp. 353–354)

Far transcending its immediate sexual expression, the vital frame of reference is evident throughout the passage, is successfully embodied in the characters to the extent that they are beyond conscious "knowing," and offers conclusive evidence that Lawrence intends the encounter as a valid one. The first paragraph presents Paul in his characteristically passive state, caressed rather than caressing, highly self-conscious, with his head on

Clara's breast. The second paragraph illustrates the first step in his transformation: he no longer knows, but has forgotten, and "the struggle went down in his soul." But his alteration is not complete, for he still worships Clara and wonders that she submits to him. The fact of her submission, or of love as an act of submission on her part, is perhaps too emphatic and suggests a faint will in Paul to dominate her. Yet, his discovery that it is not Clara as conscious self who accepts him but a "woman . . . there in the dark," the anima, indicates that the love relationship is not a matter of his will, but of the change in his perception of her. The next sentence, beginning with "The naked hunger," almost ruins the effectiveness of the paragraph with its tone of forced male bravado, and there is no indication of how and in what sense the encounter is primitive. The climactic orgasm then unites the lovers and ends in Paul's momentary completeness, as the first line of the following paragraph makes clear.

This paragraph manifests Paul's new relation to the cosmos as a result of successful consummation. The peewits "screaming in the field," the grass "curving and strong with life," Clara's eyes, "life wild at the source staring into his life"— all suggest the personal transformation that follows the encounter. His altered relation to the universe emerges in the ascending line of development from earth to stars in the last sentence: "They had met, and included in their meeting the thrust of the manifold grass stems, the cry of the peewit, the wheel of the stars." Paul is now the active partner and no longer appears passive, caressed in Clara's arms.

The last four paragraphs present the aftermath of the experience and a reflective view of it. The images, such as "the night contained them" and "the tremendous living flood which carried them always," are ambiguous. They imply the transcendental release of the inner nature and womblike enclosure in safety as well. Whereas the passage as a whole illustrates the success of the initiation, the imagery that expresses the achievement is susceptible to Freudian interpretation. Together with the imagery of enclosure, the idea of knowing their own nothingness suggests that incest of another sort than that illustrated by conscious merging has been unwittingly included within the scene. Thus, while part of the passage crucial to the concept of the vital self may be an expressively valid embodiment of it, part is not.

Additional evidence in the last two paragraphs supports this viewpoint. Clara is not satisfied with her experience: "In the morning it was not the same. They had *known*, but she could not keep the moment." Clara, who began the scene as the one not wanting to know, is now dissatisfied because she does not know Paul or because she has not succeeded in possessing him. The observation, "she had not got him; she was not satisfied," is too self-assured to ring quite true. Paul himself has introduced the idea of Clara's possessing him, and the only other time possession has been a factor in their relationship was during Paul's fantasy at the theater. Though intended to suggest the inaccessibility of the vital self beyond her reach, Clara's response to him here is contrived. Unless sexual engagement is successful for both persons, it is not usually fulfilling for one. The statement that Clara is dissatisfied implies Paul's projection onto her of his own feelings, an indication that the sexual encounter has not been so happily consummated after all. The difficulty in assessing the value of Lawrence's achievement once more involves the seemingly hopeless entanglement of the vital self with an unrecognized self that is to be fully understood only within a Freudian context.

Lawrence's claims for the vital self and his inability to make it convincing independently of Freudian psychology are serious flaws in the novel, explain the sense in which the author's vision exceeds his grasp, and bring the cleavage between intention and performance into clear perspective. Had he not insisted that Paul's sexuality was independent of his mother's influence and that Clara,

Miriam, and Mrs. Morel affected Paul's mental state alone, Lawrence might more adequately have confronted the problem inherent in the novel. As it is, he does belatedly and obliquely relate the dissolution of the Paul–Clara relationship to Paul's discovery of his mother's fatal illness. The ambiguity that derives from the implicitly causal connection between the two events conceals an insight the author deliberately and half-successfully withholds from himself.

The passage that describes the alteration in the union after Paul discovers his mother's illness suggests at once the nature of the ambiguity and provides the necessary link between the dissolving relationship, Mrs. Morel's illness, and the mercy killing: "Occasionally she would [take him]. But she was afraid. When he had her then, there was something in it that made her shrink away from him—something unnatural. She grew to dread him. He was so quiet, yet so strange. She was afraid of the man who was not there with her, whom she could feel behind this make-believe lover; somebody sinister, that filled her with horror" (p. 387). The difficulty is not in the language that conveys the sense of the "unnatural" sexual act, but in the use Lawrence makes of the psychological problem inherent in the encounter. On the one hand, the scene illustrates the change in the relationship brought about at least in part by Mrs. Morel's illness. Therefore the mother, and not Paul, can be held responsible for any implied perversity, and Lawrence can still maintain that Paul's aberration does not extend beyond consciousness. On the other hand, the scene describes a terrible wrenching apart of the inner man. If Mrs. Morel is responsible for Paul's deviance, then she does control his sexual nature and his vital self. By the very way in which the artist arranges his dramatic material, Paul is brought to the brink of an unwilling recognition that the nature of his tie with his mother, Clara, and Miriam precludes a meaningful assertion of the vital self.

Lawrence's response to this dilemma by devising the mercy killing is an attempt not to solve but to conceal the problem and to cut the Gordian knot by maintaining both propositions at once: that Paul has a vital self for the integrity of which he kills his mother and that his mother is responsible for his passional failure. His action is again an effort to turn defeat into victory through defiant assertion, and Schorer is correct in the assessment that Paul's departure for the town and his affirmation of life do not follow from the evidence presented in the work. And yet the extreme nature of the mercy killing and its symbolic import do suggest Lawrence's awareness, at least subconsciously, of its Freudian implications.

The double conclusion to the novel may substantiate this hypothesis by clarifying Lawrence's dissociated emotional and intellectual response to his own vital assertion. For if the book does end with Paul's unjustifiable departure "towards the faintly humming, glowing town," to "life" as Schorer says, side by side with this claim is the only other alternative Lawrence feels to be possible: " 'Mother!' he whispered—'mother!' She was the only thing that held him up, himself, amid all this. And she was gone, intermingled herself. He wanted her to touch him, have him alongside with her" (p. 420). The possibility of death alongside the mother, as well as the desperate act of the mercy killing itself, qualifies the vital assertion and makes it more tentative. This uncertainty must give pause to Freudian critics who state that Lawrence is unaware of the psychological implications of *Sons and Lovers*. For, even as he intellectually denies the Freudian viewpoint and fails to perceive that his doctrine of the vital self is a manifestation of the very duality he seeks to overcome, the author is compelled by his own dramatic arrangement of scenes and events to move toward an unwilling emotional recognition. If the artist selects the life alternative at the end, he does not make his choice at the total expense of the other possibility. The hope against hope that is evident in Paul's turning toward the town and life is at least poetically justified, though contrary to the basic insights Lawrence is on the verge of receiving. Interpreted in this way, Paul's departure is a last desperate effort by the author to maintain the validity of a vital self that is everywhere threatened by repressed awareness ready to explode into consciousness. In anticipating this last contingency by making Paul's action against his mother the symbolic equivalent of rooting out his own mind, Lawrence reveals a powerful, if perverse, emotional understanding of the Freudian mechanisms embodied in the work.

V

Symbolic Transformation
and the Impersonal "I"

The Rainbow

In *The Rainbow*, the central image binds two related but far from identical themes together: the emergence of the vital self to its own separate identity and its
apocalyptic opposition to the modern industrial order
and abstraction. My viewpoint is that the novel is not
completely successful, though more so than *Sons and
Lovers*, because the themes are not fully integrated and
ultimately operate against each other. These basic faults
result in a complete shift in emphasis as the work
evolves. The reader expects Ursula, for example, to transform herself and also seeks to learn how she accomplishes her transformation. But such expectations are
defeated; Lawrence turns attention away from the vital
self and the obstacles attending its development over
three generations of Brangwens to an attack upon the
social order. The struggle of the vital self to realize its
potentialities is partly abandoned, and the positive accomplishment of the work as a whole is thereby blurred.
Thus, the conclusion, the promise of the rainbow fulfilled, "the old, brittle corruption of houses and factories
swept away, the world built up in a living fabric of
Truth, fitting to the over-arching heaven,"[1] appears
forced and merely defiant.

The reason for the shift in emphasis in Part Two,
the Ursula section, and for the disunity that attends it
is most apparent when the basis for the synonymous
treatment of the industrial order and the psychic processes of modern man emerges in the light imagery.
For the first time in his work, Lawrence universalizes

1. D. H. Lawrence, *The Rainbow*, p. 495.

the idea of consciousness as an impediment to self-fulfillment by extending it to society as a whole and proposes the vital self as a new norm, antithetical to the old conventions. Since he considers the social order integrative and therefore incestuous and feminine, the conclusion to be reached is clear. To arrive at the vital self and the new society it envisions (the rainbow), Lawrence explicitly repudiates psychic integration, a counter-theme in the work, as a means to self-fulfillment, and the results, I believe, are damaging to the art. In no other way could the disparate themes have been made to cohere and the resulting aesthetic imbalance in the novel been overcome. In my judgment, the vitalist critics are quite mistaken in their view of *The Rainbow* as aesthetically and also psychologically integrated.

As in *Sons and Lovers*, Lawrence claims ultimate defeat as final victory. In the struggle between psychic opposites, depraved consciousness is theoretically overcome, and the vital self strides forth victorious from battle, pristine and incorruptible. The ensuing formal problem, the cleavage between intention and performance, is inseparable from the concept of selfhood pursued, and it is enlarged by the assertion in the work that society alone is responsible for the failure of the vital self to win through. The shift in emphasis, the symbolic straining to incorporate the social order within the framework of psychic drama, and the continuing breach between symbolism and realism are manifestations of the aesthetic imbalance. Lawrence's solution to the predicament of the "sick" individual, his projection of consciousness upon the social mechanism, is also the *donnée* of *Women in Love* and an underlying cause of the psychological catastrophe evident in the "leadership" novels, *Aaron's Rod*, *Kangaroo*, and *The Plumed Serpent*.

The sources of the formal problem posed by *The Rainbow*, then, are to be found in the nature of the vital self asserted, in the manner in which psychic renewal is pursued, and in the relationship of the vital self to the industrial system. In Part One, up to the birth of Ursula, Lawrence succeeds almost completely in maintaining the forward thrust of the novel toward vital fulfillment. At the same time, the assumption that is implicit from the beginning—that the extent of each character's involvement in the social order destroys the very fulfillment he seeks—is sustained. The potential conflict between the themes is avoided only by concealing one within the other, by emphasizing the development of the vital self through succeeding generations of Brangwens. Yet, the technique used to give the illusion of a single theme actually amounts to a dialectic of thesis-antithesis-synthesis.

Briefly put, the thesis is that the Industrial Revolution has destroyed the Brangwen men's original connection to the earth and has made them the victims of their wives' social aspirations. The antithesis involves a search for identity on a more individuated plane than the old, undifferentiated relationship allowed—an attempt, Lawrence believes, to overcome the split inflicted upon the male by his discovery of his vital self. According to this scheme, woman is a substitute for the original harmony with the earth and a means of transcending duality to the unified life beyond. The dialectic of rhythmic opposition between these two processes, between mechanical mind and the vital self—one disintegrating, the other renewing and evolving—creates the tension that binds them tenuously together. Unity is achieved at times only through the momentary transcendence of self, when the synthetic product of the dialectic, the vital self, overcomes the dialectic, and wholeness of being is reached. Thus, each generation represents one stage in the total process toward self-perfection and progressively clarifies the problem of self in relation to disintegrating elements within and outside it.

The basic nature of the vital self can be perceived initially in the "Ur" generation, before the Industrial

Revolution. Even here a sense of contrast is evident between the Brangwen men and women: "She faced outward to where men moved dominant and creative, having turned their back on the pulsing heat of creation, and with this behind them, were set out to discover what was beyond, to enlarge their own scope and range and freedom; whereas the Brangwen men faced inwards to the teeming life of creation, which poured unresolved into their veins" (p. 3). The description of the men suggests their unconscious, virile qualities, but the word *unresolved* in the last line relates the undifferentiated nature of the men to a strain or condition in their lives that is susceptible to change. The women, on the other hand, suggest aspiring mentality that is not creative because it is not organically related to life or to creation. Lawrence's ungrammatical use of the pronoun *their* in the first part of the passage to refer to the subject *she* momentarily obscures the impact of the contrast he presents. The men are creative because they are vital and not mental; the women are not creative, and therefore not vital, because they are mental. As the Brangwen woman looks outwards, she loses her sense of the pulsing heat of creation, her organic relatedness to life and, in pursuit of scope and range and freedom, destroys her naturally subordinate relation to the dominant and creative male. Implicitly carried over from *Sons and Lovers* and the earlier novels, the contrast between men and women is established in *The Rainbow* as a working hypothesis regarding the nature of Man and Woman.

While uprooting the unindividuated wholeness of the men, the Industrial Revolution announces their fall into duality and, with their fall, the rise of full domination by the women over them. The severing effect of the new colliery pits and of the canal constructed about 1840, which shut off the Brangwen farm from the rest of the community, confirms the notion of a split in the male psyche: "At first the Brangwens were astonished by all this commotion around them. . . . Then the shrill whistle of the trains re-echoed through the heart, with fearsome pleasure, announcing the far-off come near and imminent. As they drove home from town, the farmers of the land met the blackened colliers trooping from the pit-mouth. As they gathered the harvest, the west wind brought a faint, sulphurous smell of pit-refuse burning. As they pulled the turnips in November, the sharp clink-clink-clink-clink-clink of empty trucks shunting on the line, vibrated in their hearts with the fact of other activity going on beyond them" (p. 7). The organic relationship of the men with the earth, apparent even in the rhythm of "the cows yielded milk and pulse against the hands of the men, the pulse of the blood of the teats of the cows beat into the pulse of the hands of the men" (p. 2), has been replaced by a metallic clink-clink-clink-clink-clink. With the sexual displacement implicit in the sound and the "fearsome pleasure" inherent in machine civilization, the novel proper begins. Tom Brangwen appears as the first victim of the Industrial Revolution and of the mentality associated with it.

Tom's dissociation from creativity as a result of his mother's influence is clear from the beginning: "But when he had a nice girl, he found that he was incapable of pushing the desired development. The very presence of the girl beside him made it impossible. . . . Again, if he had a loose girl, and things began to develop, she offended him so deeply all the time, that he never knew whether he was going to get away from her as quickly as possible, or whether he were going to take her out of inflamed necessity. . . . But he despised the net result in him of the experience—he despised it deeply and bitterly. Then, when he was twenty-three, his mother died, and he was left at home with Effie. His mother's death was another blow out of the dark. . . . He had loved his mother" (p. 15). If the baldly analytic style is not in itself reminiscent of *Sons and Lovers*, Tom's reactions to the "nice girl" and to the "loose girl" are similar to

Paul Morel's conditioned responses to Miriam and Clara. In each case, initial sexual attraction is followed by revulsion, guilt, and possible contempt indirectly associated with the mother. This process is obliquely suggested when the death of Tom's mother is mentioned immediately after his sexual problem is described. In the absence of a logical relationship between them, the statements are in effect juxtaposed and a psychological explanation invited, if not explicitly called for. In addition, Paul's and Tom's identical ages, twenty-three, seem to reveal their related significance for Lawrence. The portrait of Tom begins where that of Paul ends, and Tom's relation to women includes the author's view of the abnormalities associated with Paul. Since Paul's solution to his problems is more apparent than real, acceptance of Lawrence's point of view in *The Rainbow* may be too easy. Superficially, Tom does achieve an apparently balanced and healthy marriage with Lydia, who is foreign and dark, unlike the Brangwen women generally. But in this novel Lawrence rejects the basis upon which the success of the marriage is accomplished.

In appearing to reverse his usual application of the light (female) and dark (male) imagery respecting Lydia, Lawrence is probably suggesting that the gateway to the vital self lies through the sexual connection. White Tom becomes dark Tom as he is released from matriarchal domination and encounters his deeper self. Certainly the first rainbow symbol shows the psychic opposites successfully fused and illustrates the success, and the limits, of the Tom–Lydia relationship: "Anna's soul was put at peace between them. She looked from one to the other, and she saw them established to her safety, and she was free. She played between the pillar of fire and the pillar of cloud in confidence, having the assurance on her right hand and the assurance on her left. She was no longer called upon to uphold with her childish might the broken end of the arch. Her father and her mother now met to the span of the heavens, and she, the child, was free to play in the space beneath, between" (p. 92).

The image of the two pillars connected by the arch seems clearly integrative, and the spatial qualities of the imagery—the child playing between the parents who meet "to the span of the heavens"—do give a transcendental dimension to the equilibrium that has apparently been achieved. The pillar of fire is literally associated with the father and, by extension, with passion (fire), the male principle (pillar), and the unconscious; the pillar of cloud with the mother, the female principle, and consciousness (cloud, air, ether); and the connecting arch with the tension binding the opposites together. Nevertheless, the imagery is ambiguous because at this point in the novel it is unclear whether the dualities are actually reconciled or merely held in balance. The biblical source of the rainbow symbol, to be introduced shortly, will help resolve the ambiguity by implying that Tom's death by drowning is actually the result of reconciliation, the form of merging that Lawrence continues to regard as incestuous.

Had the novel ended here, however, the vitalist and particularly Spilka's view of the over-all significance of the symbol would have been difficult to contest: "The rising tower, then, and the horizontal farmland, are the two 'elements' which will be criticized in the novel: for the one represents an outworn form of spirituality, and the other, an inadequate, mindless immersion in the teeming life of the farm. But at the same time, both elements—vertical and horizontal, spiritual and sensual —will contribute to the symbol that *relates* them both: the rainbow, the symbol of a new kind of oneness with the Infinite (or more accurately with the 'twofold' Infinite), and of a new kind of 'holy knowledge.' "[2] But the rainbow as integrative applies to the Tom–Lydia re-

2. Mark Spilka, *The Love Ethic of D. H. Lawrence*, p. 95.

lationship alone, and not really to it. The significance
of the symbol unfolds only as the remaining character
relationships develop and as Lawrence's conception of
the vital self becomes increasingly clear.

Though it may be read as a simple realistic description of a man drowning, the following scene relates the
nature of Tom's marriage, which is implicit in the first
vision of the rainbow, to his epochal death by water:
"Fear took hold of him. Gripping tightly to the lamp,
he reeled, and looked around. The water was carrying
his feet away, he was dizzy. He did not know which way
to turn. The water was whirling, whirling, the whole
black night was swooping in rings. He swayed uncertain-
ly at the centre of all the attack, reeling in dismay. In
his soul, he knew he would fall" (p. 243).

To illuminate this passage convincingly, to show the
connection between Tom's death and the rainbow, is
to understand the significance of water throughout Lawrence's fiction. As a recurrent image, water may sym-
bolize potential renewal or possible destruction, may be
associated with the apocalyptic release of unconscious
energies, or may accompany a character's efforts to cast
off the bondage of mechanical mind. In "The Horse
Dealer's Daughter," for example, the young doctor who
saves Mabel from drowning simultaneously experiences
the vital reality that the pond represents. In *The Virgin
and the Gypsy*, the flood that inundates the vicar's house,
the symbol of Western middle-class civilization, destroys
it along with all the inhabitants of the house except
Yvette and the gypsy; in freeing her from the deadness
of the past, the flood releases her vital self. In *Women
in Love*, Birkin tries to destroy mental consciousness by
throwing stones at the image of the moon in the pond.
As he does so, waves spread in circles from the fixed
center formed by the moon's reflection, outward to the
shores. Since the center does not break, Birkin remains
the victim of his cerebral nature. And in *The White*

Peacock, Lawrence had already used water imagery: the image of the moon in the pond is crucial, and its use here anticipates the pond scene in *Women in Love.*

The story of the source of the rainbow as related in Genesis 9:12–15, when God speaks to Noah after the flood, more nearly relates image and idea:

> And God said, this is the token of the covenant which
> I make between me and you and every living creature that
> is with you, for perpetual generations.

> I do set my bow in the cloud, and it shall be for a token of
> a covenant between me and the earth.

> And it shall come to pass, when I bring a cloud over the
> earth, that the bow shall be seen in the cloud.

> And I will remember my covenant, which is between me
> and you, and every living creature of all flesh;
> and the waters shall no more become
> a flood to destroy all flesh.

Because the covenant has not been granted, because Tom has failed to create himself and to risk living from his own center, he dies engulfed by water.

Certainly the significance of his death, suffocation within the imprisoning unconscious, is suggested by the water "whirling, whirling, the whole black night was swooping in rings" around him. Trapped within the narrowing circle of his bondage to Lydia, he disintegrates, merges with her foreign darkness, and loses his own identity. Tom's failure to separate himself—the first step in the process of self-transformation and the step illustrated by the Will–Anna relationship—ends with his regression to the womb. For those who fear and fail to encounter it directly, the unconscious is indeed a womb, a reductive agency that holds the passive male in subjection to the possessive woman. Previously, in the "Anna Victrix" chapter, Lawrence has used the same cluster of imagery to describe Will who, at the beginning of his marriage, feels "so secure, as though this house were the Ark in the flood, and all the rest was drowned"

(p. 143). Though Will's hope of finding security through Anna is illusory—as in time he discovers—Lawrence is obviously aware of the biblical source of the water imagery, deliberately applies it to the man–woman relationship, and by repeating the word *drowned* suggests the same possible consequence for Will unless he encounters himself.

A final reference to drowning in "Anna Victrix" and one that confirms the tie Tom and Will have as characters with similar sexual problems, suggests the actual thematic design that underlies Lawrence's presentation of the rainbow as it is gradually defined through succeeding generations of Brangwens: "For how can a man stand, unless he have something sure under his feet? Can a man tread the unstable water all his life, and call that standing? Better give in and drown at once. . . . What was he afraid of? Why did life, without Anna, seem to him just a horrible welter, everything jostling in a meaningless, dark, fathomless flood?" (p. 184). Clearly, as the man–woman relationship throughout the novel implies, unless the self-divided male becomes independent, he is destroyed in the way he most fears and compulsively desires. The primary function of the rainbow, then, is to sum up the progress each generation makes and to set the direction for the next. Each marriage is an extended analysis of the same problem with the solution of the author superimposed upon the whole.

As Tedlock points out: "The solution is that the relationship be made to transcend the personal and find its place in a metaphysic. The woman must yield precedence to larger relationships and purposes, granting the man the higher activity of cultural and religious pioneer."[3] Had anything approaching this phenomenon happened to Tom, according to Lawrence, he would have survived instead of being reduced by Lydia to "the subtle sense of the Great Absolute wherein she had her

3. Ernest W. Tedlock, Jr., *D. H. Lawrence, Artist and Rebel*, p. 67.

being" (p. 99). His death underscores the necessity for pursuing the vital self through the process leading to "star equilibrium" (transcendental separateness in oneness) in the direction suggested by Tedlock, and any integrative view of the rainbow may be questioned. If the first rainbow image initially appears to reconcile psychic opposites, as Spilka for one suggests, Lawrence would consider the very concept of psychological integration to be incestuous. And though the definition of star equilibrium may be used to infer a kind of balance between opposed psychic forces (if one argues that balance is integration), the actual working out of the definition in *Women in Love* and in the leadership novels is by no means integrative.

Furthermore, in *The Rainbow* Lawrence views Christianity as the ethical extension of the integrative concept, and his repudiation of one is inextricably linked to his rejection of the other. When Tom says at Anna's wedding feast, for example, that "an Angel is the soul of man and woman united in one: they rise united at the Judgment Day" (p. 135), religion and psychology are on the verge of being equated. Tom's traditional notions of marriage, the man–woman relationship, and Christianity are all based upon the reconciliation of psychic opposites that ends in catastrophe, not in finding and creating the self, but in losing it. The effect is to make all three ideas synonymous by identifying them with the usurping, feminine intellect. This identification is why Tom's proposal of an ideal relation between man and woman is a false start, and why it must give way to a radically new departure founded upon male separateness, the primacy of the unconscious, and the destruction of the mental self. Reflecting the first stage in this endeavor, the Will–Anna relationship culminates in the star equilibrium of Birkin and Ursula in *Women in Love*.

Will's achievement in freeing himself from Anna is crucial to an understanding of the work, for Lawrence asks its acceptance as an implicitly normative stage in the total process of self-renewal he presents. Unlike the marriage of Tom and Lydia, in which the husband is reduced to a state of sexual servitude, the relation of Will and Anna revolves around the husband's declaration of independence: "He could sleep with her, and let her be. . . . He had come into his own existence. He was born for a second time, born at last unto himself, out of the vast body of humanity. . . . Before he had only existed in so far as he had relations with another being. Now he had an absolute self—as well as a relative self. But it was a very dumb, weak, helpless self, a crawling nursling. . . . He had an unalterable self at last, free, separate, independent" (p. 187). Since his "separate identity" (p. 187) grows out of his very alienation from Anna, alienation is a necessary step in the psychic quest. In addition, the metaphor of being born "out of the vast body of humanity" as "a crawling nursling" shows the central significance of the womb imagery to the entire process of self-transformation. Before Will can stand alone, he must struggle out of the blood and mire into which Tom had sunk.

Viewed in this way, the brief harmony in their marriage is a point of departure, not an end, and Will's early fall from bliss is fortunate. His marriage serves a different purpose from Tom's, and the initial unity with Anna is only a momentary fusing with her, an experience that Will falsely idealizes and identifies with transcendental reality: "As they lay close together, complete and beyond the touch of time or change, it was as if they were at the very centre of all the slow wheeling of space and the rapid agitation of life, deep, deep inside them all, at the centre where there is utter radiance, and eternal being, and the silence absorbed in praise: the steady core of all movements, the unawakened sleep of all wakefulness. They found themselves there, and they lay still, in each other's arms; for their moment they were at the heart of eternity, whilst time roared far off, for ever far off, towards the rim" (p. 141). Will cannot sustain this level of relatedness because he has yet to be initiated into the mysteries of self-transformation. He first must encounter himself and then discover that his failure to create himself further—beyond the separateness he has achieved—is not his fault, but Anna's —Anna, who will not accept his primacy. In the context of the work, then, Will's accomplishment theoretically guarantees the male's ultimate release from the womb that makes the later relationship between Birkin and Ursula possible. As a corollary to my viewpoint, the development from *Sons and Lovers* to *The Rainbow* may be observed in the altered direction of the psychic quest. In the earlier novel, Lawrence seems to consider the vital self more immanent, more wholly attainable, and more closely identical with the individual unconscious. In *The Rainbow* the vital self lies beyond the personal unconscious and seems scarcely attainable.

The limits of Will's development are evident in his failure to complete the wood carving of Adam and Eve, which links the extent of his growth to the thesis of the work:

> Will Brangwen worked at his wood-carving. It was a passion, a passion for him to have the chisel under his grip. Verily the passion of his heart lifted the fine bite of steel. He was carving, as he had always wanted, the Creation of Eve. It was a panel in low relief, for a church. Adam lay asleep as if suffering, and God, a dim, large figure, stooped towards him, stretching forward His unveiled hand; and Eve, a small vivid, naked female shape, was issuing like a flame towards the hand of God, from the torn side of Adam.
>
> Now, Will Brangwen was working at the Eve. She was thin, a keen, unripe thing. With trembling passion, fine as a breath of air, he sent the chisel over her belly, her hard, unripe, small belly. She was a stiff little figure, with sharp lines in the throes and torture and ecstasy of her creation. But he trembled as he touched her. He had not finished any of his figures. There was a bird on a bough overhead, lifting its wings for flight, and a serpent wreathing up to it. It was not finished yet. He trembled with

passion, at last able to create the new, sharp body of his Eve. (Pp. 115–116)

Will cannot evolve beyond separateness because he cannot create Woman in his own image, out of himself, like God creating Eve "from the torn side of Adam." In this manner the pattern of the novel emerges, the various Brangwen generations representing stages in the quest for psychic renewal. Tom Brangwen fails to separate himself and is destroyed, but he does gain a vital relationship with Lydia and, through her, an awareness of himself. Will does not create himself, but he does win through to personal independence and is not destroyed in the process. He has his own dark being, uncorrupted by Anna and opposed to her. Thus, the measure of Will's growth beyond Tom's involves his standing alone, alienated from his wife, trying to re-create her in his own image—an endeavor, incidentally, almost the reverse of that in *The Trespasser*. The abortive nature of the attempt is mirrored in the unfinished wood carving, which marks the extent of his development. As Ursula's later relationships with Skrebensky and Birkin reveal, the struggle for male superiority is an essential aspect of the quest, and victory in the struggle is the final step that leads to the rainbow. The figures in the carving help to confirm this estimate by anticipating the entire evolution of the maleness theme through *The Plumed Serpent*. Adam (being), the bird (love or spirit), and the serpent (sensual power), the psychic components of the quest, bear an identical relation to Don Ramón, Kate, and Cipriano.

Further reference to the carving, the use of light and dark imagery to describe the characters, and Lawrence's view of Will's relation to the Church demonstrate more exactly the importance of male primacy to the novel's rationale. Anna's mockery of Will's inability to finish the carving clarifies the theoretical basis of their conflict and gives the reason for the deficiency at the core of the work: " 'Why don't you go on with your wood-carving?' she said. 'Why don't you finish your Adam and Eve?' But she did not care for the Adam and Eve, and he never put another stroke to it. She jeered at the Eve, saying, 'She is like a little marionette. Why is she so small? You've made Adam as big as God, and Eve like a doll.' 'It is impudence to say that Woman was made out of Man's body,' she continued, 'when every man is born of woman. What impudence men have, what arrogance!' " (p. 171). This tug of war embodies the whole question of male primacy and Lawrence's advocacy of it. What partially conceals the narrator's viewpoint is the irony of putting the thesis into the mouth of the woman most antagonized by it and the basic truth of her remarks on the most immediate psychological level of the story.

Anna's jeering, of course, marks her sexual dissatisfaction with Will, suggests her will to power over him, and reflects his own inadequacy. Identifying herself with Eve and Will with a would-be Adam, she expresses an absolute scorn for his aspiring pretensions. Because he is not a man—in her terms—he cannot create a woman, only a doll. In content and title Lawrence's short novel, *The Captain's Doll*, is a variation of this theme. Implicit in Will's character, then, is a sexual difficulty that, together with Anna's peacock pride, torments and renders him incomplete. And side by side with the personal problem is Lawrence's (and Will's) full commitment to the idea that man must create woman in his own image in order to fulfill himself. For even though Anna exposes Will's shortcomings, the whole point of the novel is diametrically opposed to her assertion, "Every man is born of woman." Lawrence perceives the sexual difficulty, but he does not relate it to the thesis of male primacy, and the formal weakness is in part a result of this deficient recognition. The attempt to describe objectively Will and the nature of his marriage conflicts with the author's claim of illustrating the thesis through the sexual experiences he presents. The imbalance between means and ends is evident in this section of the work and becomes increasingly clear as the connection between Lawrence's conception of the vital self and his rejection of mental consciousness and psychic integration unfolds.

Not unexpectedly, the light imagery that establishes Anna as a scaled-down Magna Mater continues to reflect the attitude toward mind that is inherent in the author's thought. Though it is not always possible to determine who is responsible for the impasse between Will and Anna, the mental life is to blame: "Crimson clouds fumed about the west, and as night came on, all the sky was fuming and steaming, and the moon, far above the swiftness of vapours, was white, bleared, the night was uneasy. Suddenly the moon would appear at a clear window in the sky, looking down from far above, like a captive. And Anna did not sleep. There was a strange, dark tension about her husband" (p. 177). While the identification of Anna with the moon is not so clear as the similar description of Ursula later on, the technique illuminates the continual psychological pull in opposing directions that operates in many of Lawrence's characters. Anna will feel like a captive to whichever side of her divided self is uppermost at the moment. The predominance of light or dark in a character implies her state of mind, and in this scene, even though she is pregnant, Anna is the chaste, frigid moon goddess who produces the dark tension about her husband. Her reflected light beats into him, exacerbating the frustration he feels. Clearly, the cause of the lacerating cruelty in the marriage is consciousness, which is symbolically attributed to Anna.

Moreover, Lawrence's use of the light imagery to account for Will's inadequacy is apparent almost from the beginning of his relationship with Anna, as the ritualistic sheaves scene makes clear:

> She set her sheaves against the shock. He saw her hands glisten among the spray of grain. And he dropped

his sheaves and he trembled as he took her in his arms. He had overtaken her, and it was his privilege to kiss her. She was sweet and fresh with the night air, and sweet with the scent of grain. And the whole rhythm of him beat into his kisses, and still she was not quite overcome. He wondered over the moonlight on her nose! All the moonlight upon her, all the darkness within her! All the night in his arms, darkness and shine, he possessed of it all! All the night for him now, to unfold, to venture within, all the mystery to be entered, all the discovery to be made.

Trembling with keen triumph, his heart was white as a star as he drove his kisses nearer.

"My love!" she called, in a low voice, from afar. The low sound seemed to call him from far off, under the moon, to him who was unaware. He stopped, quivered and listened. . . .

He was afraid. His heart quivered and broke. He was stopped. (Pp. 119–120)

The failure to engage Anna sexually is evoked by nothing more than the moonlight on her nose, which suggests Will's inability to overcome his own or her mental resistance. Though responsibility for the impasse is not assigned and does not seem important on the realistic level of the work, for the author consciousness is symbolically feminine and is usually associated with a female agent. Perhaps deliberately, Lawrence blurs the question of responsibility to maintain the façade of objectivity, for the opposition of Will and Anna is essentially a dramatic extension of the psychic conflict waged throughout the novel. Only when the actual drama, the psychic drama occurs, does the objectivity evaporate, and only here does Anna's symbolic value in evoking Will's state of mind emerge—her significance as a psychic agent.

Though the scene focuses upon Will, its meaning depends upon Anna's strangling the vital self in him and upon the expression of this process through the dark imagery: "All the night in his arms . . . to venture within, all the mystery to be entered, all the discovery to be made." The passion that Will cannot finally arouse is

identified by "night" and the cluster of images surrounding it with Anna's womb where the vital self lies imprisoned. That is to say, consciousness assimilates him
to itself, and though Will expresses a desire for sexual
engagement, he is unwittingly betrayed. This betrayal is
the reason why his heart "quivered and broke" and why
it is "white as a star," the product of a prior split that
he is unable to overcome through Anna. In addition, the
presence of womb imagery in *The Rainbow* strengthens
the assertion in the last chapter of *Sons and Lovers*, when
Clara and Paul were "contained by the night," that night
and darkness generally have sexual significance in Lawrence. There is further evidence for this assertion in
Women in Love, where the entire structure of the work
is organized around Birkin's release from the womb and
Gerald's gradual burial within it. Night as a metaphor
for womb, then, need not be considered pseudo-Freudian
potpourri.

An interesting aspect of Lawrence's use of dark
imagery—one that is only hinted at in *Sons and Lovers*,
though corrected and controlled in *Women in Love*—is
his tendency to apply the imagery somewhat indiscrim-
inately to the vital self or to enclosure in the womb.
The quite opposite processes implicit in the symbolism
are occasionally blurred, and one process does not definitely exclude the other. When, for example, vital darkness of being is momentarily ascribed to him, Will manifests the same will to power and desire for keen triumph
evident in the previous scene with Anna. On behalf of
the vital self or as a necessary stage in its development,
he tries to seduce and bully a street-girl in Nottingham
(p. 224), and after this confrontation he gains a more
satisfying sexual relationship with Anna based upon his
own separateness. Much in the same manner and for
the same theoretical purpose, Ursula later "destroys"
(p. 320) Skrebensky. Since, up to the creation of *Aaron's
Rod* Lawrence generally identifies the will to power with
consciousness alone, a possible interpretation is that its

transfer from one area of Will's (or Ursula's) psyche to another suggests an unintentional confusion on the author's part.

As in *Sons and Lovers*, a homosexual orientation that originated in a prior oedipal split is unknowingly repressed, is then asserted as the product of the mental nature alone, and becomes hopelessly enmeshed with the vital self. The outcome in *The Rainbow* is that Lawrence comes close to rejecting his own vital doctrine. Viewing the unconscious as a womb of darkness associated with woman, he compels the male to penetrate beyond it to the infinite, or to life, in order to arrive at independent selfhood. His subsequent doctrines of star equilibrium and of the polarity within the vital self between the love and power modes are in all probability the consequence of the prior oedipal split that he describes so well in the Tom–Lydia and the Will–Anna sections of *The Rainbow* and in *Sons and Lovers*. When he ascribes a polarity to life itself through a basic rhythm of attraction and repulsion operating in all matter, Lawrence evades the difficulty altogether. Creating a metaphysic out of the problem without ascertaining its recognizable psychological causes, he pronounces his theory of consciousness as normative. Thus, the basic criticism of *The Rainbow* follows from the very nature of the vital self proposed in the work.

Directly related as one of the stages preliminary to the vital self, Will's rejection of the Church and its traditional moral code is implicit in the second vision of the rainbow. Though his attraction to it is born of an apparent need to reconcile the duality within himself, he gradually arrives at Lawrence's view that the Church is to be repudiated for the reason that it stands for psychic integration. The concept is a symbolic expression of the incestuous merging of psychological opposites and can only make Will more dependent and regressive than he is. Like Tom, he feels the compelling tug of Tradition and, failing to create himself with Anna, he looks momentarily to the Church for assistance:

> He looked up to the lovely unfolding of the stone. He was to pass within to the perfect womb.
>
> Then he pushed open the door, and the great, pillared gloom was before him, in which his soul shuddered and rose from her nest. His soul leapt, soared up into the great church. His body stood still, absorbed by the height. His soul leapt into the gloom, into possession, it reeled, it swooned with a great escape, it quivered in the womb, in the hush and the gloom of fecundity, like seed of procreation in ecstasy.
>
> She [Anna] too was overcome with wonder and awe. She followed him in his progress. Here, the twilight was the very essence of life, the coloured darkness was the embryo of all light, and the day. Here, the very first dawn was breaking, the very last sunset sinking, and the immemorial darkness, whereof life's day would blossom and fall away again, re-echoed peace and profound immemorial silence.
>
> Away from time, always outside of time! Between east and west, between dawn and sunset, the church lay like a seed in silence, dark before germination, silenced after death. Containing birth and death, potential with all the noise and transition of life, the cathedral remained hushed, a great, involved seed, whereof the flower would be radiant life inconceivable, but whose beginning and whose end were the circle of silence. Spanned round with the rainbow, the jewelled gloom folded music upon silence, light upon darkness, fecundity upon death, as a seed folds leaf upon leaf and silence upon the root and the flower, hushing up the secret of all between its parts, the death out of which it fell, the life into which it has dropped, the immortality it involves, and the death it will embrace again.
>
> Here in the church "before" and "after" were folded together, all was contained in oneness. Brangwen came to his consummation. Out of the doors of the womb he had come, putting aside the wings of the womb, and proceeding into the light. Through daylight and day-after-day he had come, knowledge after knowledge, and experience after experience, remembering the darkness of the womb, having prescience of the darkness after death. Then

between-while he had pushed open the doors of the cathedral, and entered the twilight of both darkness, the hush of the two-fold silence where dawn was sunset, and the beginning and the end were one.

Here the stone leapt up from the plain of the earth, leapt up in a manifold, clustered desire each time, up, away from the horizontal earth, through twilight and dusk and the whole range of desire, through the swerving, the declination, ah, to the ecstasy, the touch, to the meeting and the consummation, the meeting, the clasp, the close embrace, the neutrality, the perfect, swooning consummation, the timeless ecstasy. There his soul remained, at the apex of the arch, clinched in the timeless ecstasy, consummated. (Pp. 198–199)

In this most beautifully written description, perhaps the most lyrically controlled and ironically deceptive in all of Lawrence, the very juxtaposition of the words points to the meaning. The tone of the passage reveals a two-directional movement toward a superficial and momentary acceptance of the rainbow by the character and the author's rejection of the character's point of view. In viewing the rainbow as a symbolic device that reconciles horizontal and vertical, time and eternity, life and death—in short as an integrative symbol—the passage appears as Will's eyes apprehend it. In appearing to reconcile opposites, the apparent functions of the first and second visions of the rainbow are the same. The major difference lies in the characters' appreciation of the symbol, for Will, unlike Tom, comes to realize its illusory nature. The clue to Lawrence's viewpoint and to Will's own later rejection of the Church and the concept of psychic integration it includes is clear: "He looked up to the lovely unfolding of the stone. He was to pass within to the perfect womb." According to the thesis and the entire structural organization of the novel, Will's act is regressive and self-defeating. The association of church and womb suggests its female rather than male character, its reductive rather than developing agency. The very fact that the Church is the apparent means of reconciling the opposites, and that the opposites are to be reconciled, makes the image of the rainbow suspect and its hope a mirage. Given its association with consciousness, the Church can be depended upon to assimilate Will, and through the pointed rhetoric Lawrence makes it possible to distinguish between the narrator's rejecting point of view and Will's mood of passing acceptance.

In the second and third paragraphs, Lawrence carries this ironic counterpointing of perspective further. Will is enraptured upon entering the church, but when his soul leaps up and his body remains behind, what is actually taking place is the separation of body and soul and the assimilation of the soul into the womb. The identification of church and womb and the reference to the gloom of fecundity suggests the deathlike nature of this process. The twilight in the church signifying the very first dawn and the last sunset sinking is only an apparent integrative image, as is the fusion of darkness and light. Indicating both a beginning and an end, twilight in fact anticipates the revolutionary notion to be introduced shortly afterward. This idea proposes that the Church will be surpassed as the transmitter of moral and religious values and as the agency through which psychic reintegration is achieved. Because the reconciliation of opposites is no longer possible nor advocated, the rainbow in its ultimate significance can scarcely be considered integrative, but as only the vague utopian end of a long process that begins with the apocalyptic release of dammed-up psychic energies. For the release to be meaningful, the Church as part of the thickened outer crust of things will have to be removed. If it is not, the circular route of Will's thought and experience, noted in the fifth paragraph in his flight from "out of the doors of the womb" to "darkness after death," "remembering the darkness of the womb," will continue. The oneness of the beginning and the end shows the dilemma at the heart of the novel to be still unresolved.

In the fourth paragraph, then, the rainbow expresses a way of interpreting experience that is no longer relevant for Will. The abstractness of before and after folded together into one unit of changeless time out of time is misleading in its offer of Buddhistic escape from reality. The image evoked is one of enclosure, which suggests that the oedipal problem cannot be evaded but will hauntingly follow Will in a chain of endless anxieties, all resolving themselves into the original experience: "Through daylight and day-after-day he had come, knowledge after knowledge, and experience after experience, remembering the darkness of the womb, having prescience of the darkness after death." The manner in which Anna shortly afterward brings his attention to the leering gargoyles along the sides of the cathedral is a cruel but necessary way of crushing his illusions of the Church as a categorical absolute. In the last paragraph, Lawrence subtly conveys his own rejection of the Church, the nature of the rainbow associated with it, and the direction of the character's present quest. The flight of Will's soul to the apex of the church suggests a view of Christianity and the crucifixion bordering upon mockery. For "the meeting, the clasp, the close embrace, the neutrality, the perfect, swooning consummation, the timeless ecstasy" at the apex is of course the cross. Will's momentary identification with Christ, the crucified victim, whose role Paul Morel had rejected at the end of *Sons and Lovers* is ironic. Otherwise it would be an affirmation of the same vicious circle of experience he is endeavoring to overcome.

Several references to Christianity before and after this scene confirm this assessment and relate the passage more clearly to the novel's thematic design. In an earlier church scene, for example, Anna's contempt for Will's perverse religious piety illuminates Lawrence's rejection of the Christ role: "What was he doing? What connection was there between him and the lamb in the glass? Suddenly it gleamed to her dominant, this lamb with the flag. Suddenly she had a powerful mystic experience, the power of tradition seized on her, she was transported to another world. And she hated it, resisted it. Instantly, it was only a silly lamb in the glass again. And dark, violent hatred of her husband swept up in her. What was he doing, sitting there gleaming, carried away, soulful?" (p. 156). Will merges with the lamb, is made abstract (p. 155) by it, and so victimizes himself. When this passage is related to Ursula's later pronouncement that Christianity is a religion based upon love and crucifixion or "submission in identification" (p. 341), Anna's hatred of Will becomes fully understandable. Above and beyond her function as a sadistic and possessive character, Lawrence uses Anna as a persona, just as he later employs Ursula, to convey the doctrinal message. By raising the message to consciousness and therefore feminizing and perverting it, the author makes his point that Christianity betrays the vital self.

Will's belated rejection of the Christ role demonstrates the essential thematic connection between his intellectual dismissal of the Church, his refusal to be victimized by the predatory woman, and the nature of the psychology associated with Christ's suffering, the torment of the passive male. The causes of the suffering —the Church and the predatory woman—become in effect synonymous. They are the forces outside of Will that are responsible for his failure to transcend himself, as abstract intellect is the inner mechanism that represses the vital self. Later, with Ursula, the burden shifts to society, and the industrial order appears among the synonymously treated concepts, the material extensions of one aspect of the psychic drama. In this manner, the divisions of the novel, the three major character groupings, define and develop the theme. The man–woman relationship and the problem of man's relationships to man, society, and the cosmos are all manifestations of the conflict between the divorced parts of the self.

Consequently, the significance of Will's rejection of

the Church cannot be underestimated, for it implies a psychological and a social revolution at once and a change in the characters' conception of the rainbow. In the Will–Anna section of the novel, Lawrence has clearly shown that the rejection of Christianity includes the repudiation of psychic integration and that the redirection of the quest through Ursula is conditioned by the conceptual implications of Will's action. But though he sets the stage for Ursula to surpass him, for the transformation of the known self into the impersonal or transcendental "I," Will himself continues in the old form without believing in it: "But now, somehow, sadly and disillusioned, he realised that the doorway was no doorway. It was too narrow, it was false. Outside the cathedral were many flying spirits that could never be sifted through the jewelled gloom. He had lost his absolute. . . . Still he loved the Church. As a symbol, he loved it. He tended it for what it tried to represent, rather than for that which it did represent. . . . He had failed to become really articulate, failed to find real expression. He had to continue in the old form" (p. 203). His failure to forge his being anew ends in his sad alteration to a Ruskinized teacher of arts and crafts and, together with Anna's descent to the status of middle-class housewife, signals the end of the road for this generation of Brangwens.

However, Lawrence's redirection of the quest through Ursula is not without blemish. In spite of the connection between personal and social renewal anticipated previously, the sudden shift in emphasis from pursuit of the rainbow to social criticism thwarts the reader's expectations. The author encourages hope that Ursula will more nearly approach her goals than any of the other characters and that discovery of the means by which she accomplishes her ends will ensue. One reason for the disappointment is that the misplaced emphasis obscures the process and progress of Ursula's search. The search is blurred, I believe, because the assumptions underlying the shift in emphasis are not integrally embodied within the questing character. Though the value of the rainbow alters with Ursula's developing point of view, her character does not develop psychologically.

Since this is the case, the assumptions that govern both character and social criticism bear repeating. The person who lives in a world that crushes his spontaneity is in danger of becoming a mere reflection of events, symbolically interchangeable with the world. In order to save the individual from this social reduction, his vital self—the guarantee of his individuality and singleness—must be assured. Because the social order and the vital self are diametrically opposed, any self-transformation must involve social revaluation as well. According to Lawrence, the personal and social changes effected in this novel will be normative because Ursula is a Brangwen, the Brangwens represent humanity, and their problems are universal in scope. Yet no dramatic proof is ever presented to show that the Brangwens' problems are actually rooted in common humanity, nor to establish a basic similarity in fact between the abstractness of the Church and a dehumanizing social machine.

In short, the novel is too loaded. Intellectual concepts are not adequately objectified in dramatic terms, and the attack upon traditional values and modern society follows more from the peculiar nature of the Brangwens than from a common humanity. A plausible explanation for the revolutionary slant of the attack is its origin in the psychological split of Tom, Will, and Ursula. Obviously, Lawrence's rejection of Tradition involves a transfer of consciousness from the projecting self to woman and then to society at large. While there is room for doubt, it is difficult to disagree with Vivas' conclusion (though not with his methods and suppositions) respecting *The Rainbow* as well as *Women in Love* and *Lady Chatterley's Lover*: "I believe I have shown that if we read *The Rainbow*, *Women in Love*, and *Lady Chatterley* with care, we find in them, too, a profound emotional disorder, an obdurate major disharmony, informed with genius as the substance of their drama. To go to these books for the wisdom that our civilization needs, without rigorous discrimination, is folly."[4] Vivas suggests that sexual abnormalities condition Lawrence's point of view, and I believe they influence the form of the novels and are indirectly responsible for their aesthetic imbalance.

Yet, there are several more immediate reasons for the reduction in creative force in the last part of the work. One is Lawrence's preoccupation with the transition to *Women in Love*; the other involves his method of formulating the doctrine. Since Ursula's quest for the vital self ends only in star equilibrium with Birkin, her search forms part of that novel's thesis. Considered in this way, the Ursula section of *The Rainbow* is supposed to prepare for *Women in Love* by clarifying the nature of the rainbow and of the vital self through the Ursula–Birkin relationship. *The Rainbow* is aesthetically incomplete, then, and the emphasis on the social implications of Ursula's quest, rather than on the psychic process of it is in part self-defeating. Before fully defining the vital self, Lawrence asks acceptance of the connection he proposes between it and revolutionary social goals as essential. Whether or not deliberately, he turns away from the primary consideration.

In addition, the experiences presented and gradually formulated in Part One are now dogmatically asserted. This strong attitude is reflected in the tone and language of the Ursula section, which is conceptual, by and large, rather than poetic. And while the shift from poetic-symbolic to conceptual-abstract language is in part a product of Ursula's developing intellectual capacity, the basic purpose of the language is nevertheless to convey the doctrinal message. Ursula is merely Lawrence's persona, and nowhere is this relationship more

4. Eliseo Vivas, *D. H. Lawrence: The Failure and the Triumph of Art*, p. 270.

evident than in the passages dealing with the author's non-Christian ethical viewpoint and with his divergence from the futurism of Marinetti. The author, not Ursula, announces the newly discovered beliefs, and his use of her as a mask is transparent: "In religion there were the two great motives of fear and love. The motive of fear was as great as the motive of love. Christianity accepted crucifixion to escape from fear; 'Do your worst to me, that I may have no more fear of the worst.' . . . Fear shall become reverence, and reverence is submission in identification; love shall become triumph, and triumph is delight in identification. . . . Her God was not mild and gentle, neither Lamb nor Dove. He was the lion and the eagle . . . they were not passive subjects of some shepherd, or pets of some loving woman, or sacrifices of some priest" (pp. 340–341). The view of Christianity as a religion of fusion and victimization that marks the limits of Will's development now becomes an articulation of Ursula's point of view as it was almost from the beginning of the novel. No longer content to live in the old form without believing in it, she presents in its incipient stages the power doctrine upon which the later Lawrentian hero rests his claim for psychic and social renewal.

But in preferring to be a lion rather than a dove, not even Ursula, as a woman, would consider Christians to be "pets of some loving woman." Lawrence directly intrudes here, the independence of Ursula as a character breaks down, and the resulting pronouncements are not assimilated into the dramatic texture of the dialectic. Perhaps nowhere else in the novel does the identification of Christianity, victimization, and the predatory woman tie the author so closely to his character and illuminate so clearly the relationship between them. If it is possible to show an oedipal split different from Lawrence's conception of it (the theory of consciousness) operating within the context of the novel, the impossibility of separating the author from his work will have been demonstrated; it will be impossible to evaluate *The Rainbow* as a work of art in itself, independent of the artist "paring his fingernails" behind it.

Lawrence also uses Ursula's attendance at a biology lecture to present Marinetti's futuristic viewpoint, to show his own divergence from it, and to clarify somewhat the nature of the vital self through the differences observed. Dr. Frankstone's scientific explanation of life as "a complexity of physical and chemical activities, of the same order as the activities we already know in science" (p. 440), closely resembles the futurists' physiology of matter, the reduction of psychic processes to physical laws. The author's letter to Edward Garnett explaining his rejection of futurism by contrasting that doctrine with the conception of character that governs *The Rainbow* shows the relation of Dr. Frankstone's (Marinetti's) remarks to his own thought:

> That is where the futurists are stupid. Instead of looking for the new human phenomenon, they will only look for the phenomenon of the science of physics to be found in human beings. They are crassly stupid. But if anyone would give them eyes, they would pull the right apples off the tree, for their stomachs are true in appetite. You mustn't look in my work for the old stable *ego*—of the character. There is another *ego*, according to whose action the individual is unrecognisable, and passes through, as it were, allotropic states which it needs in a deeper sense than any we've been used to exercise, to discover are states of the same single radically unchanged element. (Like as diamond and coal are the same pure single element of carbon. The ordinary novel would trace the history of the diamond—but I say, "Diamond, what! This is carbon.") . . . Again I say, don't look for the development of the novel to follow the lines of certain characters: the characters fall into the form of some other rhythmic form, as when one draws a fiddle-bow across a fine tray delicately sanded, the sand takes lines unknown.[5]

Like the futurists, Lawrence would reduce human proc-

5. D. H. Lawrence, *The Collected Letters of D. H. Lawrence*, Harry T. Moore, ed., I, 282.

esses to certain chemical (allotropic) or, in his case, psychic rhythms, and he would also consider the individual a mechanism less interesting in what he is (conscious ego) than in what he reveals about the general psychic laws underlying and governing the ego. Unlike them, he worships life, the carbon (unconscious) from which the diamond (intellect) is created, and he considers life a mystery greater than the sum of its parts.

Ursula's answer to the futurists, the identity she formulates between the vital self and life, parallels Lawrence's argument in the letter and again illustrates his intrusiveness. The degree of conceptualization in her response is disproportionate to her character, and the author is present when Ursula speaks of "physical and chemical activities nodalised," "mechanical energy," and "Self" as "a oneness with the infinite . . . a triumph of infinity" (p. 441). Her sudden illumination and her momentary projection beyond reality into a mystical oneness with life are contrived. The epiphany leads directly to the star equilibrium, or transcendental balance in polarity, of *Women in Love* where the simultaneous identification of the character with life and with Self might be more permanently achieved.

In *The Rainbow*, the definition of the vital self as "a oneness with the infinite" helps to establish the ultimate apocalyptic value of the rainbow symbol and the direction of Ursula's search for it. Since the quest leads to infinity, it may well include an effort to evade and to reject consciousness and the unconscious alike, in which case the rainbow obviously lies beyond human comprehension. The chaotically insurgent inner life, the means of breaking down the existing social and individual framework of encrusted consciousness, is in fact merely a preparatory tool directed toward a nihilistic and self-destructive end:

> That which she was, positively, was dark and unrevealed, it could not come forth. It was like a seed buried in dry ash. This world in which she lived was like a circle

lighted by a lamp. This lighted area, lit up by man's com-
pletest consciousness, she thought was all the world: that
here all was disclosed for ever. Yet all the time, within
the darkness she had been aware of points of light, like
the eyes of wild beasts, gleaming, penetrating, vanishing.
And her soul acknowledged in a great heave of terror only
the outer darkness. . . .

But she could see the glimmer of dark movement just
out of range, she saw the eyes of the wild beast gleaming
from the darkness, watching the vanity of the camp fire
and the sleepers; she felt the strange, foolish vanity of the
camp, which said "Beyond our light and our order there
is nothing," turning their faces always inward towards the
sinking fire of illuminating consciousness, which comprised
sun and stars, and the Creator, and the System of Right-
eousness, ignoring always the vast darkness that wheeled
round about, with half-revealed shapes lurking on the
edge. (Pp. 437–438)

Reflecting the violent and compulsive cast of Lawrence's psychology, this passage centers around the
nearly complete estrangement and opposition between
psychic processes. According to the author, Ursula's
vision of inner terror, of wild beasts within the darkness,
exists independently of the rest of the psyche, for the
conflicting parts of it are not considered dynamically
interrelated but almost mechanistically separate. The
beasts are not produced by repressive consciousness,
merely exacerbated by it, and the imprisonment of the
vital self is not Ursula's fault. Designating both the
psychic source of her anxiety and the social order, consciousness is responsible, and it is projected from the
mind to society, that "circle of light in which she lived
and moved, wherein the trains rushed and the factories
ground out their machine-produce" (p. 437). In blurring
the distinction between the two, Lawrence in effect identifies them. He also suggests that, sadistically restrained
as they are, the forces of the unconscious are destructive
by nature. His intention is to demonstrate that, insofar
as they share the same qualities, Ursula and the social
order must be destroyed to be renewed. Unchaining the

beasts, then, is a precondition of arriving at wholeness of being, no longer identified with the vital unconscious, but with the rainbow beyond.

The achievement, however, is dubious. Lawrence not only asks acceptance of his view of the conscious–unconscious duality a priori, without explanation, but he rejects the very idea of any interplay between them. The psychological dissociation inherent in his theory of consciousness and in the sadistic nature of the imagery conveying the theory is regarded as a virtue! This passage illustrates, I believe, that Lawrence's concept of the pristine unconscious is determined, after all, by his view of consciousness, but in a way he neither observes nor would admit. One part of the mind pressing down upon the other prevents the normal release of psychic energies, and he asks the reader to accept the distorted and perverse result as normative. Granted the author's assumptions, a new notion of personality identified with the infinite and beyond the reach of predatory consciousness and the apocalyptic unconscious alike will of course follow. What is psychologically suicidal will be seen as transcending the lesser self and arriving at the rainbow. To understand the basis of this incredible theory, it is necessary to examine the sexual experiences that are imperfectly assimilated into the final vision of the rainbow unfolding.

The fuguelike scene late in the novel—of horses attacking Ursula in a wood, anticipating her psychic destruction—crystallizes the problem. The scene occurs after her rejection of the lesbian Winifred Inger and the "mechanical" man Anton Skrebensky. It is intended to illustrate the final stage in the progress toward the rainbow. Yet Skrebensky's apparent failure with Ursula actually conceals her failure with him, and Lawrence's assertion of defeat as victory again compromises his final achievement by undermining the value of the rainbow vision. In the first place, Ursula's experiences with Skrebensky are not related to her lesbian affair with Miss

Inger, even though the two exist side by side. While Lawrence would not endorse any assumption that would explain the nature of Ursula's tie with Skrebensky through her liaison with Winifred Inger, he makes no provision against such a claim. Skrebensky, after all, is held entirely responsible by author and character alike for the failure of the relationship. In light of Ursula's connection with Miss Inger, then, some explanation or qualification of this assertion is due, yet none is forthcoming. Instead, the thesis that society is decadent is simply reiterated in the marriage of Miss Inger and the homosexually inclined Tom Brangwen, manager of the colliery (Western Civilization). Ursula's final rejection of Skrebensky, Miss Inger, and Tom Brangwen theoretically shows that her psychic quest is sane and normative, in contrast to the corrupt world they represent. The real difficulty is evaded, thereby rendering the means and ends of the quest suspect.

The dramatic necessity for Ursula's destruction preliminary to her renewal is of course never in doubt. Though she distinguishes herself from the rest of the decadent cast assembled through her willingness to undergo such a painful initiation, she is a product of the same social milieu. Winifred Inger, Tom Brangwen, Anton Skrebensky, and the colliery all form the social order with which she is in part identified. Like Gudrun and Gerald Crich of *Women in Love*, Winifred and Tom function symbolically as the deviant, socially conditioned part of the self that Ursula must overcome before she can sight the rainbow. Dramatically, they are a warning to her of what marriage with Skrebensky would be like and where it would lead, thereby justifying her complete rejection of the three. But in making modern society the cause of her sexual difficulty, Lawrence equivocates. By way of projection, Ursula's problem becomes, in effect, the issue of predatory intellect transferred to the social order.

Thus, when the horses attack her, the processes of

the destructive unconscious can be viewed according to the perverse effects of Lawrence's theory of consciousness or as a final preliminary to her release and psychic transformation: "She was aware of the great flash of hoofs, a bluish, iridescent flash surrounding a hollow of darkness. Large, large seemed the bluish, incandescent flash of the hoof-iron, large as a halo of lightning round the knotted darkness of the flanks. Like circles of lightning came the flash of hoofs from out of the powerful flanks. . . . Her heart was gone, her limbs were dissolved, she was dissolved like water. . . . As she sat there, spent, time and the flux of change passed away from her, she lay as if unconscious upon the bed of the stream, like a stone, unconscious, unchanging, unchangeable, whilst everything rolled by in transcience, leaving her there, a stone at rest on the bed of the stream, inalterable and passive, sunk to the bottom of all change" (pp. 487–489). A conclusive reading of this passage is perhaps unlikely. In itself, it can be accepted in an almost Jungian sense as an integrative experience that involves a collision and the ensuing reconciliation of psychic opposites. As archetypes of unchained power (masculine) dissolving the superficially imposed restraints of consciousness (feminine), the symbolism of the horses would have an undeniable function in any integrative process that was taking place. Ursula's anxiety at the confrontation, as if her doom were impending, may be considered normal and controlled in view of the circumstances. The last sentence, in which "time and the flux of change passed away from her," may also be used to suggest the end in view, self-transformation and the realization of the rainbow. Consequently, vitalist criticism may be correct, and the final vision of the rainbow, "the old, brittle corruption of houses and factories swept away, the world built up in a living fabric of Truth, fitting to the over-arching heaven" (p. 495), may follow from an integrative experience after all.

Still, an alternative reading is equally possible and

actually preferable. It is based essentially upon two factors, the nature of the psychic quest discussed previously and the sexual experiences of Ursula and the other Brangwens informing the quest. Since various attempts to find self-identity throughout the novel form basically one sole quest, the relationship between the nature of the quest and the sexual problems encountered by the Brangwens is an intrinsic one. Tom's troubles are met and partially overcome by Will, who is surpassed by Ursula. But the apparent reconciliation of opposites in the Tom–Lydia marriage is not finally the solution to their problems. Psychic integration works neither for Tom whose death is the consequence of it; nor for Will who belatedly rejects it; nor for Ursula who offers alternatives to it. Given the continuity of the characters' experience and the developing pattern of the quest (and the rainbow), an interpretation of the scene other than the vitalist or Jungian becomes imperative.

After Will's repudiation of the Church and all it implies, the direction of the quest drastically alters and clarifies. The pursuit of self now becomes an exclusive exploration of the unconscious, which involves the apocalyptic release of energies aimed at destroying consciousness. Since these forces are ultimately to be identified with life, the reader must assume that the self envisaged by the rainbow lies beyond the structure of the human mind as we know it. The wild beasts of Ursula's first vision and her dream of the attacking horses formulate attempts to penetrate the psychic polarities to the transcendent unity beyond them. But to get to the beyond, the conflicting parts of the psyche must be destroyed. Thus, the nature of Lawrence's psychology differs remarkably from Jung's (it is very similar, I believe, to Blake's), and Ursula's vision of the horses can scarcely be integrative in the Jungian sense. This observation is not to render aesthetic judgment against Lawrence for failing to be Jungian, incidentally, but simply to suggest that the vitalist critics are wrong about him in this respect. Lawrence does not wish to reconcile opposites, but to destroy mental or social consciousness, release the dammed-up energies of the unconscious, pass through it, and arrive at a state of being beyond the realm of the psychologically verifiable.

To interpret Ursula's dream, then, requires the whole directional surrounding context of the work. The attacking horses can then be easily seen as the life force emerging from the unconscious but distinguishable from it, obliterating Ursula's socially conditioned mental nature, and projecting her to the timeless world beyond. Since it is difficult not to consider this entire process a radical evasion of self, the interpretive problem involves the basis upon which the novel can be evaluated. Within the work itself, the only verifiable element that informs the quest is the sexual experience of the Brangwens. This experience, I suggest, calls the validity of the search into question, for it is conditioned and accompanied by an oedipal split that becomes ultimately apparent in Ursula's lesbianism. Lawrence's awareness of the split is beyond doubt, because each of the characters encounters the sexual problem as part of the over-all attempt to reach the rainbow. Consequently, no critical argument can be directed at Lawrence's ignorance of the split per se, since it is part of the theme. The characters seek to transform themselves, and for a very good reason. My point is simply that they will not succeed, that Lawrence compels them to take the wrong road, and that the compulsion is evident from the imperfect assimilation of sexual materials into the thematic design. His doctrine of the vital self, it follows, is a manifestation of the very psychological dissociation that his characters seek to overcome, and any psychological theory that would permit the artist to unify his work more closely would be more aesthetically fruitful than the one Lawrence in fact employs for this purpose. Assuming the complete separation of psychic and sexual polarities, the quest is neurotically conditioned.

The reasons for the split are to be found in the "Ur" generation at the beginning of the book. The Brangwen woman is "the restraining hand of God," the "conscience-keeper," "the symbol for that further life which comprised religion and love and morality" (p. 13). The Brangwen men who "depended on her for their stability" (p. 13) have in fact renounced their manhood, and Tom, "his mother's favourite" (p. 9), is raised in her image. Like Paul Morel, he begins as a character victimized by the past and is later unable to enjoy the "nice girl" or the "loose girl" (p. 15) or the prostitute in the tavern. It may be speculative, of course, but hardly improbable that Tom's difficulty with the prostitute and then with Lydia is the direct consequence of his absorption within the matriarchal value system, the source of his sexual dilemma. More significantly, the ironic epithets used to describe the Brangwen women not only place Tom within the matriarchal scheme of things, but they fit into the patterned thematic design that culminates in Will's unfinished wood carving and his alienation from Anna. Because he is alienated, Will rejects religion and love and morality, all associated with women's predominance in consciousness over man. Later, when he remains within the old form without believing in it, Ursula carries out the implications of her father's rejection by attempting to live outside traditional norms and by discovering the basis for new ones.

The effect of Tom's past, his victimization by the matriarchy, is most evident early in his marriage:

> "My dear!" she said. He knew she spoke a foreign language. The fear was like bliss in his heart. He looked down. Her face was shining, her eyes were full of light, she was awful. He suffered from the compulsion to her. She was the awful unknown. He bent down to her, suffering, unable to let go, unable to let himself go, yet drawn, driven. She was now the transfigured, she was wonderful, beyond him. He wanted to go. But he could not as yet kiss her. He was himself apart. Easiest he could kiss her feet. But he was too ashamed for the actual deed, which were

like an affront. She waited for him to meet her, not to bow down before her and serve her. She wanted his active participation, not his submission. She put her fingers on him. And it was torture to him, that he must give himself to her actively, participate in her, that he must meet and embrace and know her, who was other than himself. There was that in him which shrank from yielding to her, resisted the relaxing towards her, opposed the mingling with her, even while he most desired it. He was afraid, he wanted to save himself. (P. 90)

The neurotic complexion of Tom's attraction is established through the words *compulsion, mingling, submission, fear, ashamed, suffering, shrank, torture,* and the phrase *unable to let himself go.* Conditioned by these feelings, his view of Lydia as "transfigured," "with her eyes full of light," is on the order of a projection, for she is then described more matter-of-factly as not wanting him "to bow before her and serve her." Lydia's value is thus ambiguously heightened through the light imagery to which he bows in submission as before God, or his mother, and the connection is evident between the Brangwen women who mold Tom's life through religion and love and morality and the light that shines in Lydia's eyes. Later on, Will explicitly identifies these values with women and consciousness, rejects them, and moves a step closer toward wholeness of being.

Considering the transition it provides to the Birkin–Ursula relationship, the last section of the novel confirms the movement away from matriarchy to male superiority. Or, if one wishes to argue for an organic tie between the Ursula section and the rest of *The Rainbow,* Ursula's very inability to establish a satisfactory sexual connection with men may be interpreted, as indeed it is, as a social criticism of the times. What she desires, but cannot find, is a man to whom she will be subordinate. The bargeman of the Annable and the Ciccio-like (*The Lost Girl*) Italian servant whom Ursula and Skrebensky meet at a London hotel anticipate this development. Either view of the conclusion, then, involves a sexual problem, debatable in terms of thematic design, that can be very easily and clearly related to the original dilemma of Tom Brangwen. In like manner, Tom's link with Paul Morel binds *The Rainbow* thematically to *Sons and Lovers*. Though the movement of *The Rainbow* is of course forward rather than backward, the neurosis common to both characters illuminates the psychic quest.

Furthermore, since the Will–Anna relationship is a direct continuation of the marriage between Tom and Lydia, the nature of the sexual experiences within the work confirms the oedipal hypothesis. Will's encounter with the street-girl in Nottingham, for example, recalls Tom's contempt for the "loose girl" (p. 15) as a young man. Will's sadistic compulsion to the deviant is clearly related to the less obvious torment suffered by Tom: "What matter! It was one man who touched Anna, another who now touched this girl. He liked best his new self. He was given over altogether to the sensuous knowledge of this woman, and every moment he seemed to be touching absolute beauty, something beyond knowledge. . . . But he was patiently working for her relaxation, patiently, his whole being fixed in the smile of latent gratification, his whole body electric with a subtle, powerful, reducing force upon her. . . . She was sinking, sinking, his smile of latent gratification was becoming more tense, he was sure of her. He let the whole force of his will sink upon her to sweep her away. . . . With a sudden horrible movement she ruptured the state that contained them both. 'Don't!—Don't!' " (p. 228). In perceiving the difference between the "man who touched Anna" and his "new self," Will recognizes the perverse cruelty of his action, even the psychological dissociation inherent in it. But the fact that he likes the new self best is ambiguous. In retrospect both character and author seem to consider the cruelty necessary to Will's final independence from Anna. Whereas Tom's suffering turns inward and leads to his idealization of Lydia, his merging with her, Will's is directed outward in an insidious compulsion to dominate women and leads to his freedom. Thus, while both responses advance the theme by pointing the way to the rainbow, they also suggest a different problem. Tom's masochism and Will's sadism are actually counterparts, but Lawrence regards sadism as a partner to accompany the vital self or its release, and masochism as a manifestation of a character's reduction.

The alteration in Will's relation to Anna after the town encounter reflects the causal connection between the two events and clarifies the author's attitude respecting cruelty and the vital self:

> And she roused him profoundly, violently even before he touched her. The little creature in Nottingham had been but leading up to this. They abandoned in one motion the moral principle, each was seeking gratification pure and simple. . . .
> This was what their love had become, a sensuality violent and extreme as death. They had no conscious intimacy, no tenderness of love. It was all the lust and the infinite, maddening intoxication of the senses, a passion of death. . . .
> But still the thing terrified him. Awful and threatening it was, dangerous to a degree, even whilst he gave himself to it. It was pure darkness, also. All the shameful things of the body revealed themselves to him now with a sort of sinister, tropical beauty. All the shameful, natural and unnatural acts of sensual voluptuousness which he and the woman partook of together, created together, they had their heavy beauty and their delight. . . .
> And gradually, Brangwen began to find himself free to attend to the outside life as well. His intimate life was so violently active, that it set another man in him free. (Pp. 232–235)

The causal connection between the encounters is stated in the first sentence and their positive effect upon Will in the last. Though it is difficult to discover precisely what the abandoned moral principle in the first paragraph means, it obviously has to do with the broken marital restraints and the abnormal kind of sexuality they engage in after the Nottingham trip. Not only are

natural and unnatural acts referred to in the third paragraph, but the images and phrases "a passion of death,"
"tropical beauty," "heavy beauty," "sensual voluptuousness," and "violent and extreme as death" occur throughout the passage and emphasize the perverseness of the
sexual explorations. Will is apparently released from
marital bondage by the very abnormality of the sexual
relationship that "set another man in him free," and his
sense of freedom is expressed as a positive achievement.
Sadism and perversity are theoretically a part of the process leading to the vital self, and Lawrence once more
permits the means to justify the ends. He will pursue
this overripe "African way" of sexual expression more
fully in practically every novel from *Women in Love* to
Lady Chatterley's Lover.

In *The Rainbow*, the womb imagery that describes
Will's struggle to gain an identity links his self-division,
which is evident before and after his trip to Nottingham,
to the prior oedipal split in Tom: "But he was struggling
in silence. It seemed as though there were before him a
solid wall of darkness that impeded him and suffocated
him and made him mad. He wanted her to come to him,
to complete him, to stand before him so that his eyes did
not, should not meet the naked darkness. Nothing mattered to him but that she should come and complete him.
For he was ridden by the awful sense of his own limitation. It was as if he ended uncompleted, as yet uncreated
on the darkness, and he wanted her to come and liberate
him into the whole" (pp. 175–176). To be sure, the connection between the "solid wall of darkness" and the
womb appears tenuous, but the image recurs in this novel
and in Lawrence's other work. And, as I have stated, the
imagery is fully developed in *Women in Love*, where
Birkin is released as Gerald Crich is imprisoned in the
womb. Like Tom (and Paul Morel), Will experiences the
same sense of fear, attraction, and dependence upon the
mystery of darkness long before marrying: "It was as
if he ended uncompleted, as yet uncreated on the dark-

ness, and he wanted her to come and liberate him into the whole." Together with feeling suffocated before the wall of darkness, his being uncreated on the darkness surely suggests oedipal enclosure.

Moreover, the parallel is too obvious to miss between Will's suffocation and Tom's 'drowning after his reduction by Lydia and her "subtle sense of the Great Absolute" (p. 99). Both characters react with the same or similar responses to similar experiences, and in one instance fear of reduction by the wife can be related to an oedipal tie with the mother. Will expresses the same fear and hopes initially for the same solution to his problems as Tom: liberation through woman. Therefore, since the one accomplishment that distinguishes the characters is Will's independence from women, the only means of differentiating between them is sexual. Will's achievement is greater than Tom's only because he succeeds in overcoming incestuous merging with his wife, whereas Tom does not. The surrounding context, then, supports the view advanced and suggests that Will's fear of enclosure can be interpreted in totally opposed ways: as part of the theme preparing for his release from the womb or as a manifestation of the Oedipus complex.

Quite understandably, the Ursula section reveals the formal weakness, Lawrence's inability to account for the sexual materials through his theory of consciousness, at its worst. Since the last part of the novel is the climax of the dual movement toward self-exploration and self-transcendence, Ursula's psychic discontinuity becomes much more apparent. The ever-widening split between the known and the vital self in each succeeding generation of Brangwens clarifies the sexual problem that produces the split and exposes the lapse in form. Within context, Ursula's lesbianism announces the absolute necessity for self-transformation by revealing the almost complete rupture between her conscious and unconscious modes of experiencing. American versions of the text based upon the Huebsch edition have generally obscured this aspect of the work through excisions, the most extensive of which is probably this: "Ursula lay still in her mistress's arms, her forehead against the beloved, maddening breast. 'I shall put you in,' said Winifred. But Ursula twined her body around her mistress."[6]

Despite the excision of this passage, Ursula's relationship with Miss Inger is almost self-evident and is clearly within the framework of the light imagery:

> Suddenly Ursula found a queer awareness existed between herself and her class-mistress, Miss Inger. The latter was a rather beautiful woman of twenty-eight, a fearless-seeming, clean type of modern girl whose very independence betrays her sorrow. She was clever, and expert in what she did, accurate, quick, commanding. . . .
>
> The summer term came, and with it the swimming class. Miss Inger was to take the swimming class. . . . How lovely she looked! Her knees were so white and strong and proud, and she was as firm-bodied as Diana. . . . Ursula could see the head put back, the water flickering upon the white shoulders, the strong legs kicking shadowily. And she swam blinded with passion. Ah, the beauty of the firm, white cool flesh! . . .
>
> She swam on eagerly, not wanting to win, only wanting to be near her mistress, to swim in a race with her. They neared the end of the bath, the deep end. Miss Inger touched the pipe, swung herself round, and caught Ursula round the waist in the water, and held her a moment. (Pp. 335–337)

Miss Inger is "modern," "firm-bodied as Diana," and emphatically "white" and intellectual, all typical, according to Lawrence, of the frigid, one-sided nature of modern woman and contemporary society. The marriage of Miss Inger and Tom Brangwen dramatically reinforces the author's view of perverse modernism. Insofar as Ursula is engaged in the lesbian relationship, she, too, possesses the same qualities as her mistress, for she is the product of the same decadent milieu. Thus, with respect to the author's purpose, her coming together with

6. Harry T. Moore, *The Intelligent Heart: The Life of D. H. Lawrence*, p. 209.

Winifred Inger illustrates the deviant part of Ursula's nature, the socially formed, known self she has yet to overcome.

However, when Lawrence fails to relate Ursula's liaison with Miss Inger to her affair with Skrebensky and then proclaims Ursula's victory over him, the novel unravels too completely. Given his qualities as a character, the fiasco with Skrebensky is not so much his fault as Lawrence makes it appear:

> As the dance surged heavily on, Ursula was aware of some influence looking in upon her. Something was looking at her. Some powerful, glowing sight was looking right into her, not upon her, but right at her. Out of the great distance, and yet imminent, the powerful, overwhelming watch was kept upon her. And she danced on and on with Skrebensky, while the great, white watching continued, balancing all in its revelation.
>
> "The moon has risen," said Anton, as the music ceased, and they found themselves suddenly stranded, like bits of jetsam on a shore. She turned, and saw a great white moon looking at her over the hill. And her breast opened to it, she was cleaved like a transparent jewel to its light. She stood filled with the full moon, offering herself. Her two breasts opened to make way for it, her body opened wide like a quivering anemone, a soft, dilated invitation touched by the moon. . . .
>
> But hard and fierce she had fastened upon him, cold as the moon and burning as a fierce salt. Till gradually his warm, soft iron yielded, yielded, and she was there, fierce, corrosive, seething with his destruction, seething like some cruel, corrosive salt around the last substance of his being, destroying him, destroying him in the kiss. And her soul crystallised with triumph, and his soul was dissolved with agony and annihilation. So she held him there, the victim, consumed, annihilated. She had triumphed: he was not any more. (Pp. 317–320)

As with Anna, the Brangwen women generally, and Lydia Lensky and her "Great Absolute," the light imagery reveals Ursula's deviant character, her known self. Remove this known self, the thesis goes, and you remove the perversion. The fact that Lawrence attributes her problems to this cause is no longer open to question. Ursula's quandary, its manifestations, and the solution proposed are the same as for Tom and, especially, Will Brangwen. For this reason there is finally no difference at all between Ursula's "destroying him, destroying him in the kiss," attributed to her dominating will, and the "wild beasts," "like the flash of fangs," of her unconscious. All the psychic manifestations of the abnormality are derived from the same source. The escape from the self, the attempt to go beyond the unconscious, the rejection of consciousness, the quest for self-identity, and the rainbow itself originate in the threat of oedipal enclosure. While the womb imagery relates this threat to the formal design of the work, the vital self upon which release from the womb depends is itself permeated with many of the same elements Lawrence associates with destructive mind. In this sense, the formal imbalance in *The Rainbow* stems from the author's assertion that normative ends follow from non-normative means, an idea that, in the novels following *Women in Love*, becomes almost obsessive.

VI

Dissolution and Reassertion
Women in Love

The most formally satisfactory of Lawrence's novels, *Women in Love* can be fruitfully approached through its tie to *The Rainbow*, through the imagery associated with the social criticism and with the Gerald–Gudrun relationship in particular. These comments do not mean that the symbolism is superimposed, but simply that its origin in *The Rainbow* illuminates its use and clarifies its significance in *Women in Love*. The process begun earlier, the transference of the light imagery from the possessive woman or mother surrogate to society, machine civilization, and traditional religious values, is now complete and forms part of the dramatic structure. That is to say, in *The Rainbow* the process of symbolic development is inductive, leading from the psychic nature and viewpoint of particular characters to general assertions concerning the nature of man and society. But in *Women in Love* the social criticism and the light imagery accompanying it are deductively formulated, they implicitly determine the characters' psychology and their relationships, and they provide the external organization of the work, the central mechanism of thematic and character control.

Because of their common imagery, the formal and interpretive problems of the two novels are similar. In a different and far broader context, the light imagery of *Women in Love* reflects the same transfer of consciousness from woman to the social order that is evident in *The Rainbow*. The source of this projection, Lawrence's insistence upon the mutual exclusiveness of the known and the vital selves, is likewise ultimately responsible for a certain lack of coherence in the work. More immediately, once the reader perceives the similarity in theme and image, otherwise obscure elements in *Women in Love* stand forth illuminated, and its complexity of design can be more truly appreciated. The intensity of Birkin's response to Hermione, for example, which according to Eliseo Vivas is dramatically successful but not to be understood in context, now becomes clear.[1] Since Hermione functions symbolically as the possessive woman eager to assimilate him, Birkin feels his very existence threatened. His ambiguous connection with Gerald Crich is also clarified. To be sure, the brotherhood Birkin proposes certainly has a homosexual aspect reinforced by his view of star polarity and his generally violent reactions to women. But the light imagery indicates that Birkin to some extent realizes his problem, in part overcomes it, and does attempt to save Gerald from the same reduction that threatens him. To understand the Birkin–Gerald relationship, then, is to approach it through the imagery that informs *The Rainbow* and the earlier novels.

Such an approach will be original enough to shed new light on the work without departing altogether from existing criticism. Agreement with some of Vivas' conclusions need hardly include acceptance of his critical apparatus, but his essential insight into *Women in Love* is preliminary to my own. Birkin's relationship with Ursula is not normative;[2] Birkin does engage in deviant and implicitly homosexual practices, and he does feel the strong pull of the "African way";[3] and *The Rainbow*, *Women in Love*, and *Lady Chatterley's Lover* do reveal "a profound emotional disorder, an obdurate major disharmony, informed with genius as the substance of their drama."[4] However, Vivas is led astray by his vehement

1. Eliseo Vivas, *D. H. Lawrence: The Failure and the Triumph of Art*, pp. 103–4.
2. Vivas, *The Failure and the Triumph*, p. 266.
3. Vivas, *The Failure and the Triumph*, p. 267.
4. Vivas, *The Failure and the Triumph*, p. 270.

attack against F. R. Leavis and by his assumption that
Lawrence wishes to exemplify the Birkin–Ursula relationship as normative, *ipso facto*, without qualification. He
somewhat sarcastically suggests that the marriage cannot be called "a norm in the sense that it is the expression of the average—unless Mr. Leavis is in possession
of statistics to which he does not refer, such as those
provided by the late Dr. Kinsey, showing that a significant percentage of the male population constituted by
the world of *Women in Love* suffers from the same frustration and indulges in the same erotic practices (the
African way?) that Birkin indulges in."[5] Vivas quite
unintentionally puts his finger on the very point Lawrence is making, for not only does a significant percentage of the male population suffer from Birkin's
torment, but all the characters do, male and female. The
difference is that, given the universality of the problem,
only Birkin and Ursula search for a solution to the "African way." The word *normative* refers only to the ends
they seek, not to their relationship per se. Vivas is reductive and considers the case against the novel proved
simply because Birkin is homosexual.

The valid argument for Vivas' "obdurate major disharmony" is not really within the scope of his own
moralistic approach to the work at all, but depends upon
a very different viewpoint and upon several alternative
assumptions. Birkin's homosexuality is a symptom rather
than a source of the interpretive problem, and only Lawrence's theory of consciousness embedded in the light
imagery can validate Vivas' criticism, or criticism like it,
within the framework of *Women in Love*. Since this imagery reflects the defect in Lawrence's thought that has
been observable throughout these works, the social criticism that emanates from it is also distorted and vitiated.
The continuing formal problem—the *sine qua non* of the
novels—results from Lawrence's attempt to show the
vital self emerging from Birkin's character, his known

5. Vivas, *The Failure and the Triumph*, p. 267.

self. But the greater achievement of *Women in Love* is in large measure the outcome of the author's willingness to subordinate the psychic quest to an examination of the social ills that necessitate the quest.

Lawrence's purpose in demonstrating Birkin's way as the only alternative to Gerald's clearly includes the social theme as part of the argument for individual wholeness: "He [Gerald] was ready to be doomed. Marriage was like a doom to him. He was willing to condemn himself in marriage, to become like a convict condemned to the mines of the underworld, living no life in the sun, but having a dreadful subterranean activity. . . . It was a committing of himself in acceptance of the established world, he would accept the established order, in which he did not livingly believe, and then he would retreat to the underworld for his life. This he would do. The other way was to accept Rupert's offer of alliance, to enter into the bond of pure trust and love with the other man, and then subsequently with the woman. If he pledged himself with the man he would later be able to pledge himself with the woman: not merely in legal marriage, but in absolute mystic marriage."[6]

In this passage, the thesis that the personal–sexual relationships of the characters are socially determined is neatly joined to the view of Gerald as modern man victimized by the social order. The way out of the dilemma, of course, is to escape the socially conditioned self through woman to the transcendent, impersonal "I" beyond. Marriage is essential because it theoretically assures the stability necessary for the leap into star equilibrium in which man and woman can sexually engage one another without losing their separate identities. The result of this achievement is fulfillment of the self, arrival at individuality, contact with life itself, and self-transformation. All of this process supposedly enables the man and woman in their temporal state to experience the sexual act without fear of "the horrible

6. D. H. Lawrence, *Women in Love*, p. 345.

merging, mingling self-abnegation of love" (p. 193). At the same time, the man-and-man relationship prevents the possibility of merging, assures an external connection with the outside world, and assists in maintaining psychic balance.

In retrospect, it is apparent that Gerald's rejection of Birkin's offer determines the dramatic outcome of the novel. Gerald cannot accept the proposal because he is equated with the established order, and because he is so identified, he dies in the womb-locked valley of the Tyrol while Birkin is released to life or the possibility of attaining it. Certainly one might conclude that the scales are weighted against Gerald and the social order from the beginning, that Birkin is merely the instrument of Lawrence's point of view, and that the author's interference with the tale creates an unresolved ambiguity. The Birkin–Gerald relationship is clearly untenable, yet Birkin's insistence upon it is vague. The reader never discovers why Birkin's assertion that only the personal connection with himself will save Gerald should be valid, nor does Lawrence ever adequately explain how brotherhood will save Gerald. Vivas' argument is understandable: Birkin and Lawrence are deviants, the Birkin–Ursula relationship is not normative, and the work suffers from a profound emotional disorder. But, as I have suggested, such untested generalities are unacceptable on the basis of the evidence Vivas submits.

Starting with the hypothesis that all the characters in *Women in Love* suffer from acute dissociation of sensibility, it becomes clear that psychological reintegration is no longer possible for them, and complete divorce between reason and emotion, mind and body, is imminent. As a result, the characters become mental or physical in basic nature and are symbolically presented accordingly. The emotional disorder perceived by Vivas, therefore, is actually the novel's *donnée*, and it functions to justify Lawrence's extremely radical views of self and society. The split evident in Hermione's emotional and mental processes, for example, is also present in the remaining characters: "There always seemed an interval, a strange split between what she seemed to feel and experience, and what she actually said and thought" (p. 131). Since, with the possible exception of Ursula, the characters are dissociated, they are inevitably victimized by their own consciousness, are reduced to observing their own animal functions (p. 35), and are continually preyed upon by the will to destroy or be destroyed. This is the context in which Birkin and Ursula are labeled "normative." They alone try to overcome their society and the human automatons it produces, to arrive at mutual understanding and tolerance, and to transform themselves.

Moreover, the very factors that condition Birkin's pursuit of star equilibrium with Ursula involve his ambiguous admission of homosexuality. Following Vivas, one must either grant the validity of the conclusion, which it is impossible to do, or one must use the conclusion as final proof of Birkin's homosexuality, which he does not deny. Birkin's association with the bohemian set of the Café Pompadour; his appearance in Halliday's apartment while Halliday and Libidnikov stand naked before the fire; his admission to Ursula that his relationship with Hermione was perverse and morally depraved; the nature of his sexual explorations with Ursula; and, above all, the symbolic significance of his wrestling bout with Gerald—all point toward Birkin's awareness of his own deviance. Birkin's possession of the facts about himself is unquestionable, then, but questionable, certainly, is his interpretation of them, his view that consciousness must be destroyed in order to free the vital self. This difference in what is sure and what is unsure offers the only way in which the contradiction between means and ends in *Women in Love* can be accounted for without violating the fundamental integrity of the character and without reducing the novel to absurdity. Insofar as it exists, the formal problem follows from Lawrence's assertion that a healthy self can emerge from an unhealthy one and that Birkin's desire for star polarity is not an abnormal expression of his dissociated sensibility. Even here, though, Lawrence is aware of the latter possibility, as the work and the letters attest.

Birkin notes the following conflict and possible contradiction between his quest for star equilibrium and his own psychological nature: "The next day, however, he felt wistful and yearning. He thought he had been wrong, perhaps. Perhaps he had been wrong to go to her [Ursula] with an idea of what he wanted. Was it [star equilibrium] really only an idea, or was it the interpretation of a profound yearning? If the latter, how was it he was always talking about sensual fulfilment. The two did not agree very well" (p. 245). This explicit statement relates to Birkin's self-division and suggests a possible contradiction between what he knows to be true of himself and what he would like to be true. Thus, Birkin's problem as a character involves his will to accept the facts about himself and his simultaneous attempt to transcend the facts. He clearly realizes that two unreconciled selves exist in him, and in the process of the novel he reasons out his response to the problem through the doctrine of star polarity.

But his reasoning concerning the mutual exclusiveness of the two selves and how the known self can be overcome is weak. Lawrence endeavors to show the human validity of Birkin's marriage with Ursula and the sterility of Gerald's bondage to Gudrun. The contrasting relationships illustrate the necessity for the new norm (star polarity) that Birkin advocates. Nevertheless, if Birkin's conception of the norm is really "the interpretation of a profound yearning," which neither he nor the author understands, an entirely different view of star polarity than the one recommended becomes possible. I hope to show that Birkin's view of the man–woman relationship is conditioned by an existing oedipal problem concealed in the doctrine of star polarity. For this reason both the conception of love and the social criticism extending from Birkin's norm are questionable.

The author's own awareness of a possible lack of coherence between the social criticism of the novel and Birkin's view of love is apparent from his letter to Edward Garnett of January 29, 1914: "I feel that this second half of *The Sisters* is very beautiful, but it may not be sufficiently incorporated to please you. I do not try to incorporate it very much . . . but I want to write to live, and it must produce its flowers, and if they be frail or shadowy, they will be all right if they are true to their hour. It is not so easy for one to be married. In marriage one must become something else. And I am changing now one way or the other."[7] Obviously referring to *Women in Love* in an incipient stage of composition, the letter suggests the lack of thematic incorporation that is to some extent true of the finished product as well, though the novel is the most incorporated work Lawrence ever wrote.

Granted the relevance of the letter and the separability of the themes, moreover, a crucial area of the novel is illuminated. The difficulty inherent in the personal as distinct from the social theme is suggested when Lawrence mentions his own marriage. Like the author, Birkin is confronted with the challenge of becoming something else through his relation to Ursula, and the aim, implicit in the letter, is self-transformation: "And I am changing now one way or the other." A study of the symbolism that describes star polarity will reveal that Birkin will never achieve the transformation he desires because it is impossible to separate his two selves psychologically. Whereas Lawrence would not have the vital and the known self in any way connected, the reader of *Women in Love* cannot understand one except through the other. Yet, to approach the two selves in this way requires a series of psychological assumptions that the novel does

7. D. H. Lawrence, *The Collected Letters of D. H. Lawrence*, Harry T. Moore, ed., I, 263–64.

not permit, but against which it makes no provision.

The symbolism that manifests the ultimate divergence between the reader's expectations and the author's purpose is of two sorts: the light imagery paralleling and controlling the external organization of the work and the womb imagery associated with a character's attaining or his failure to attain star equilibrium. Underlying the dramatic structure and its extension into social criticism, the womb or dark symbolism determines how the light imagery will be applied, whether a character will be released to the vital self or assimilated by the possessive woman. Since both kinds of imagery together unite the two major themes with their psychic expression through the characters, Schorer's outline of the dramatic structure is a useful preliminary to extended analysis:

> We have a group of "free" characters, and a group of "bound" characters. The free characters are limited to four, the four who actively seek out their fate through the plot movement; the rest are all fixed in their social roles, and in rigid social scenes, and, except perhaps for Hermione and the elder Criches, are caricatures whose fate is sealed before the outset. These have all taken the way of death, and therefore they exist at the level of the social personality alone, and they are characterized by means of the familiar technique of caricature, maximum selection. But the free characters, the four, are compounded of a double drive, and it is here that the method of characterization is new and unfamiliar. They have their social existence and they have their psychic existence; the first is inevitably an expression of the second, but in the second lies the whole motivation. As two take the way of death, their social role becomes more and more important ("Civilized society is insane," reflects Constance Chatterley). And as two others take the way of life, their social role becomes less important, ceases, in fact, to exist. This has been Birkin's ambition and struggle throughout, the need to isolate himself on the cliff of self-responsibility, outside society yet not outside human relationship.[8]

8. Mark Schorer, "Women in Love," in Frederick J. Hoffman

Respecting the symbolism, the point implicit in Schorer's comments is that each of the four free characters reacts differently to the stimuli of contemporary civilization (consciousness) upon him. The imagery relates the psychological dissociation of the characters to modern society and at the same time to Lawrence's conception of human nature. The character's response to his environment, his action in the plot, determines whether he will be totally assimilated to the social machine as Gerald and Gudrun are, or will be released to the pristine unconscious beyond it as Birkin and Ursula hope to be. The effect of the light imagery upon the character, then, will decide whether he is reduced or released from the womb, whether he will find a satisfactory sexual bond with women, and whether he will achieve star polarity. In this sense, though the light and dark imagery operate as diametrically opposed principles in the work, they do not have totally opposed functions. Together they suggest a cause-and-effect relationship between a character's place in the social hierarchy and his loss of spontaneity.

As I have suggested, *Women in Love*, unlike the first section of *The Rainbow*, does not present a gradual and synthetic development of the imagery. The texture of the novel is dramatic and analytic rather than lyrical and descriptive, and the application of the symbolism is sporadic and pervasive rather than clustered and evolving. *The Rainbow* unfolds as a progressive clarification of the rainbow symbol itself, but the imagery of *Women in Love* is conceptually static and subordinate to the dramatic plan of the novel noted by Schorer. As the determinant or psychic equivalent of the external organization, the light imagery reflects the cause of the characters' bondage to the social order and is really part of the novel's *donnée*. It links the abstract quality of consciousness generally to the deadness of the social

and Harry T. Moore, eds., *The Achievement of D. H. Lawrence*, p. 168.

milieu and to the individual trapped within it. The bound character most typical of the modern sensibility, of course, is Hermione Roddice, one of those from whom Birkin must free himself. Birkin's self-liberation and Ursula's later submission to his love ethic differentiate him from Gerald, who is destroyed by Gudrun. Gudrun's role, as distinct from Ursula's, is to demonstrate the catastrophic effects of industrialism and self-division upon Gerald's (and modern man's) sexual nature.

Though Gudrun, like Birkin, ultimately rejects society as constituted, her rejection is only a manifestation of the next phase of social dissolution represented by Loerke, with whom she departs at the end. On the plane of social criticism, then, the death of Gerald, the god of the machine, ushers in the age of the machine-god in whose image human beings are inverted, to whom all bow down, and by whom all are worked. Loerke says: " 'Certainly. What is man doing when he is at a fair like this? He is fulfilling the counterpart of labour—the machine works him instead of he the machine. He enjoys the mechanical motion of his own body' " (p. 415). But on the personal or sexual level of the novel Gerald dies because he has failed to separate himself from Gudrun, whose departure with Loerke introduces a new industrial norm, the mechanization of sexual impulse as a desired condition of existence. Gerald's assimilation by Gudrun, his reduction to the womb, describes the ultimate effect of this process upon him, and Lawrence's evaluation of the social order he represents is expressed in the sexual degradation Gerald is forced to undergo. In this manner the dramatic structure and the symbolism function together to project a vision of social and personal corruption beyond reform.

Gerald obviously fails to separate himself from Gudrun because of his rejection of brotherhood with Birkin, which would have guaranteed his individual identity. Underlying the dramatic structure, the womb imagery defines and clarifies the problem of sexual individuation and accounts for Gerald's and the free characters' difficulties psychically rather than socially. This symbolism is counterpointed against the light imagery, is likewise the product of the psychological dissociation, and describes the effects of mechanical mind upon the individual's sexual life. It is used either to indicate the character's sexual reduction through the deliberate assimilation of his inner life or to suggest his release from bondage and to subsequent growth. Thus, while the womb imagery is related to and parallels the social symbolism, its primary function is to expose the sexual basis of the character's personality; to determine his social fate as victim or victimizer; and to illustrate the extent of his destruction or release from his individual consciousness as distinct from that conceptually represented by society. Since evaluation of the novel in terms of this symbolism depends upon the contention that the imagery is a manifestation of dissociated sensibility, the idea of dissociation must first be more firmly established.

By Chapter VI, "Crême De Menthe," Lawrence's doctrine that modern civilization is the product of this discontinuity and that the vital self is desiccated by usurping consciousness is fully evident. The significance of the African statue over which Birkin ponders long after its initial introduction suggests one of the two ways available to the modern individual for responding to his psychic split:

> He remembered her: her astonishing cultured elegance, her diminished, beetle face, the astounding long elegant body, on short, ugly legs, with such protuberant buttocks, so weighty and unexpected below her slim long loins. She knew what he himself did not know. She had thousands of years of purely sensual, purely unspiritual knowledge behind her. It must have been thousands of years since her race had died, mystically; that is, since the relation between the senses and the outspoken mind had broken, leaving the experience all in one sort, mystically sensual. Thousands of years ago, that which was imminent in himself must have taken place in these Africans: the good-

ness, the holiness, the desire for creation and productive happiness must have lapsed, leaving the single impulse for knowledge in one sort, mindless progressive knowledge through the senses, knowledge arrested and ending in the senses, mystic knowledge in disintegration and dissolution, knowledge such as the beetles have, which live purely within the world of corruption and cold dissolution. (Pp. 245–246)

Except for the word *mystical*, which seems to be ambiguous throughout Lawrence's fiction, the statement referring to Birkin's ruptured sensibility is clear: "The relation between the senses and the outspoken mind had broken." This process, moreover, is not only imminent in Birkin, but is immediately afterward associated with modern society as a whole: "There is a long way we can travel, after the death-break: after that point when the soul in intense suffering breaks, breaks away from its organic hold like a leaf that falls. We fall from the connection with life and hope, we lapse from pure integral being, from creation and liberty, and we fall into the long, long African process of purely sensual understanding, knowledge in the mystery of dissolution" (p. 246). The editorial "we" emphasizes Lawrence's participation in Birkin's observation and suggests that the entire vision of social and personal decay embodied in the novel is intended as a comment on life outside the work as well. And as an examination of the light and dark imagery will reveal, the "African way" of sensual dissolution represented by the statue is only the psychological counterpart of the destructive ice-and-snow consciousness of the north, represented by Gerald, Gudrun, and Hermione.

This relationship becomes clear if Birkin's comment upon Hermione's mentality is linked to his description of the African statue and then to his own tacit admission of perversion to Ursula. In observing her "own animal functions, to get a mental thrill out of them" (p. 35), Hermione forms a conceptual contrast to the mystically sensual African statue: " 'It is all purely secondary— and more decadent than the most hide-bound intellectualism. What is it but the worst and last form of intellectualism, this love of yours for passion and the animal instincts? Passion and the instincts—you want them hard enough, but through your head, in your consciousness. . . . You've got that mirror, your own fixed will, your immortal understanding, your own tight conscious world, and there is nothing behind it. There, in the mirror, you must have everything' " (p. 35). North and south, mind and body, merely signify the predominance of the mental or the sensual in a character after psychological dissociation has occurred. Hermione is associated with the north, mind, and consciousness, because she observes her animal functions, and the African statue means the south, body, and sensuality because she mystically indulges and merges with them. Since her mind is a mirror with nothing beyond it, Hermione displaces and perverts her unconscious impulses by sublimating them. The African woman, on the other hand, lacks whatever awareness is necessary to assure the normal growth of her sexual nature. Her inner distortion is evident in her grotesque appearance, the outward sign of her sensual decadence. As a result, her knowledge "arrested and ending in the senses" turns in upon itself and regresses. Taken together, the two are counterparts, the antithetical expressions of a single psychic process that originates in a common source.

The notion that the mind perverts whatever healthy impulses the characters possess is confirmed by continued references to consciousness as a mirror or reflector. In the Pompadour Café, for example, "the faces and heads of the drinkers showed dimly through the haze of smoke, reflected more dimly, and repeated ad infinitum in the great mirrors on the walls, so that one seemed to enter a vague, dim world of shadowy drinkers humming within an atmosphere of blue tobacco smoke. There was, however, the red plush of the seats to give substance within the bubble of pleasure" (p. 54). The mirrors that reflect only the faces and heads of the habitués magnify their one-sided natures and support the view of the African and Nordic ways as different aspects of the same psychological process. The scene afterward in Halliday's apartment demonstrates that the sexual nature of the customers is African, though their mentality is Nordic. The idea of an endless repetition of the same pleasures reflected in the mirrors enhances the aura of decadence evoked by this microcosmic picture of stunted humanity and the superficiality of it all as a transparent bubble of pleasure.

In addition, previous criticism has noted the contrast between blue, a transparent cold color associated with all the cerebral people in the room—with Gerald, Halliday, Minette, and later with Gudrun—and the more opaque and impenetrable red identified with Ursula.[9] In a different context, the substance of red contrasted to the insubstantial lightness of blue tobacco smoke evidences how thoroughly deliberate Lawrence is in subordinating the most minute descriptive detail to the total symbolic design. Of all the characters, Ursula alone is neither Nordic nor African and therefore not self-divided; the customers in the café are self-divided and therefore both Nordic and African. Clearly, the African way is the sexual consequence of the psychic split—the perversity underlying Nordic mentality—and the connection between the two is dramatically reinforced by the appearance of the bohemians, Halliday and Libidnikov, standing naked before the fire in Halliday's apartment; by Gerald's gradual reduction to a childlike reflection of Gudrun's will and ultimately his death; and by Ursula's immediate reaction against the mountains and snow of the Tyrol.

The light imagery objectifies Ursula's response and explains her otherwise unaccountable feelings: "Ursula went out alone into the world of pure, new snow. But the dazzling whiteness seemed to beat upon her till it

9. Robert L. Chamberlain, "Pussum, Minette, and the Africo-Nordic Symbol in Lawrence's *Women in Love*," *Publications of the Modern Language Association*, 78 (1963), 407–16.

hurt her, she felt the cold was slowly strangling her soul. Her head felt dazed and numb. . . . 'I hate the snow, and the unnaturalness of it, the unnatural light it throws on everybody, the ghastly glamour, the unnatural feelings it makes everybody have' " (p. 425). The unnatural feelings are the consequence of the unnatural light, and the dazzling whiteness of the snow strangling her soul creates the tension between the assimilating pull of consciousness upon her and the inner necessity of maintaining the separate integrity of her vital self. By the end of the novel, only she and Birkin have resisted assimilation, rejected consciousness, and freed themselves from the social order—the necessary prerequisites for gaining star equilibrium and a healthy sexual relationship.

Birkin's sense of corruption, the product of a similar pull, is especially evident when Ursula relates the foulness of his sex life to his spirituality, again emphasizing the tie between the Nordic and African ways: " 'You truth-lover! You purity-monger! It *stinks*, your truth and your purity. It stinks of the offal you feed on, you scavenger dog, you eater of corpses. You are foul, *foul*— and you must know it. . . . What you are is a foul, deathly thing, obscene, that's what you are, obscene and perverse. You, and love! You may well say, you don't want love. No, you want *yourself*, and dirt and death—that's what you want. You are so *perverse*, so death-eating. And then —.' . . . A clearer look had come over Birkin's face. He knew she was in the main right. He knew he was perverse, so spiritual on the one hand, and in some strange way, degraded on the other. But was she herself any better? Was anybody any better?" (pp. 299–300). In spite of the self-justifying "Was anybody any better?", the passage clearly shows how aware Birkin is of his abnormality, and the link he observes between perverseness and spirituality indicts the mental life as the cause of his degradation. While Ursula's outburst lacks a dramatic frame of reference within the novel—there is no way for her to know at this point how degraded Birkin is—her response is still within the pattern of the light imagery. And, as in *The Rainbow*, the identity worked out in that novel between the possessive woman (the "spiritual bride" [p. 298] as Ursula calls her), the known self, and the social order forms the *donnée* of *Women in Love*, which focuses more directly upon the problem of sexual abnormality and the social milieu.

As in *The Rainbow*, the proposed solution to the problem involves the simultaneous rejection of consciousness and of society. This rejection, in turn, leads to a complete rupture of the already fragmented sensibility and defines the process of Birkin's quest for wholeness of being. The only way he can hope to attain the integral being he seeks is by destroying the old and creating new centers of consciousness directly related to the wellsprings of his life. Only thus can the broken circuit within himself be healed. In his puritanical willingness to reduce Birkin's search to a lewd enjoyment of perversity, Vivas fails to perceive that the destination of the quest is not Africa. Though that continent may be explored to obliterate what Freud would consider the superego, Birkin's is the only way, according to Lawrence, in which inner decay can be overcome and wholeness achieved. Birkin's quest for renewal may be misdirected, but the intellectual integrity of the quest per se and its artistic fulfillment in the work can scarcely be questioned. What Birkin wants is a way out of the decadence, not a way to it. Any attempt to reduce his search to the African way, therefore, almost misses the point.

However, Birkin's view of impersonal star equilibrium with Ursula as the only alternative to the African way is specious precisely because it is the outcome of his discontinuity, a sign of the very fragmentation in modern life he hopes to overcome. His readiness to act upon this concept ultimately saves the pair from the fate of Gerald and Gudrun, but star equilibrium itself is conditioned by the neurosis that Birkin shares with all the other characters and particularly with Gerald. As I have claimed, Lawrence's achievement in *Women in Love* is to present the personal (Freudian) and impersonal or transcendent (vital) selves existing side by side, unreconciled and diametrically opposed. The problem arises with the author's suggestion that star equilibrium is the way out of the dilemma, and it is compounded when he damns Gerald for not accepting this solution. Since Birkin and Ursula do not realize star equilibrium in *Women in Love*, but do predicate future actions upon it, Gerald is condemned on behalf of a principle that is not dramatically embodied in the novel. The concept does not operate except abstractly, as a neurotically conditioned value judgment imposed upon one set of characters a priori. Gerald's assimilation to Gudrun, his imprisonment in the mountain womb of the Tyrol, and his death are the symbolic instruments that carry out the judgment. Birkin's release, on the other hand, is founded upon the assumption that he and Ursula alone, in the future, will be able to cut the Gordian knot of consciousness and live solely within the vital self.

The conclusion to this endeavor appears in the extreme alienation of the leadership novels, *Aaron's Rod*, *Kangaroo*, and *The Plumed Serpent*. The only way in which Lawrence can finally surmount the antagonism between the two selves is to insist that the sexual abnormalities that condition the psyche are not really abnormalities at all. Though he does not shrink from such an assertion in *Lady Chatterley's Lover*, the issue is more squarely faced in *Women in Love*. In this respect, *Women in Love* is also a much different work from *The Rainbow*, in which the goals of the quest seem more optimistically attainable, and in which no possible contradiction between the means and ends of the quest is discerned. To repeat, the great merit of *Women in Love* is that Lawrence perceives more clearly than in any of his works the contradiction inherent in Birkin's search: "Was it [star equilibrium] really only an idea, or was it the interpretation of a profound yearning? If the latter, how was it he was always talking about sensual fulfillment? The two did not agree very well" (p. 245). The possibility of Birkin's known self becoming confused with the psychic goals of his search is admitted.

It is clear that Birkin's quest for integral being is the product of psychic disturbance, that the disturbance leads him to reject encroaching intellect and the social order alike, and that the only alternative to the African way is the discovery through marriage of a new self. The following passage illustrates the nature of this self, suggests the conditions under which its further development is possible, presents the argument for a new, reintegrated personality, and introduces the womb symbolism that underlies the light imagery:

> There was a darkness over his mind. The terrible knot of consciousness that had persisted there like an obsession was broken, gone, his life was dissolved in darkness over his limbs and his body. . . .
>
> They drifted through the wild, late afternoon in a beautiful motion that was smiling and transcendent. His mind was sweetly at ease, the life flowed through him as from some new fountain, he was as if born out of the cramp of a womb. . . .
>
> He drove on in a strange new wakefulness, the tension of his consciousness broken. He seemed to be conscious all over, all his body awake with a simple, glimmering awareness, as if he had just come awake, like a thing that is born, like a bird when it comes out of an egg, into a new universe. . . .
>
> She recalled again the old magic of the Book of Genesis, where the sons of God saw the daughters of men, that they were fair. And he was one of these, one of these strange creatures from the beyond, looking down at her, and seeing she was fair. . . .
>
> She traced with her hands the line of his loins and thighs, at the back, and a living fire ran through her, from him, darkly. It was a dark flood of electric passion she released from him, drew into herself. She had established a rich new circuit, a new current of passional electric energy, between the two of them, released from the darkest poles of the body and established in perfect circuit. . . .
>
> Nothing more was said. They ran on in silence. But

with a sort of second consciousness he steered the car towards a destination. For he had the free intelligence to direct his own ends. His arms and his breast and his head were rounded and living like those of the Greek, he had not the unawakened straight arms of the Egyptian, nor the sealed, slumbering head. A lambent intelligence played secondarily above his pure Egyptian concentration in darkness. (Pp. 301–310)

Coming after Ursula's acceptance of Birkin's proposal and the red opal engagement ring, this description is perhaps the most coherent statement in Lawrence's fiction of the ends involved in the hero's search. The anxiety that lends impetus to the quest is clearly related to the womb imagery in the second paragraph, Birkin's delivery from "the cramp of a womb." Having been released from the anxiety, he is at least momentarily free of his obsessive concerns. The first paragraph establishes the lapsing out of mental awareness as the precondition of release and renewal, and the second suggests the ultimate identity between Birkin's point of view and the author's as well as the necessary reason for renewal. Birkin's theoretical emancipation and Gerald's gradual imprisonment within the womb illustrate Lawrence's theory of consciousness in action. The hypothesis that Birkin and Gerald are counterparts endowed with the same psychological problem derives from the dramatic resolution of the theory. What happens to Gerald would have happened to Birkin had he not solved the riddle of incestuous merging through the love ethic.

The third and fourth paragraphs show the immediate result of Birkin's experience: rebirth, new awareness, and paradisaical innocence. The meaning of the word *conscious* in the second sentence of the third paragraph, as distinct from *consciousness* in the first sentence, connotes what Lawrence terms *phallic consciousness* in *Fantasia*, the at-oneness of integral being with itself, the rediscovery of the Paradise within. The final two paragraphs could have been directly transposed from *Fantasia*. They establish the concept of developing new centers and circuits of consciousness as the final goal of the psychic quest. These centers develop from the loins (solar plexus) up the spinal column (lumbar ganglion) to the lambent intelligence playing "secondarily above his pure Egyptian concentration in darkness." Consciousness is now re-created, immediately bound to and a reflection of the physical-unconscious life beneath it. Thus, psychological dissociation is theoretically overcome and the perfect circuit between man and woman in star equilibrium made possible. Lawrence's purpose of justifying the Birkin–Ursula relationship on this basis, his assertion that star polarity is the solution to Birkin's sexual problems, is now established beyond doubt, and it includes the earlier doctrine that mental consciousness alone is responsible for sexual abnormality. The evolution of this view has been in a direct line from Lawrence's first novel and explicitly related to the womb image since *The Trespasser.*

In the face of such evidence, Maxim's discussion of Birkin's letter with Halliday in the Pompadour as an attempt to reconcile psychic opposites (light and dark) is not reason for assuming this to be the author's over-all purpose in the work. Since Maxim has never read the letter, his comment is mere hearsay: " 'Isn't that the letter about uniting the dark and the light—and the Flux of Corruption?' asked Maxim, in his precise, quick voice" (p. 374). Neither the direct quotation from the letter given afterward by Halliday nor a detailed examination of the theory of consciousness and psychic renewal validates Maxim's comment. On the contrary, any attempt to reconcile light and dark ends in the assimilation of one by the other, in the incestuous merging and destructive decay that the whole plan of the novel envisions. In urging this solution to the problem, Maxim ironically damns himself, for he identifies himself thereby with the forces of corruption.

And by following out Maxim's solution in effect, Gerald is destroyed, and his failure with Gudrun of course documents Birkin's success with Ursula. As Birkin's counterpart, Gerald suffers from the same sexual dilemma and is the product of the same psychic discontinuity: "He had found his most satisfactory relief in women. After a debauch with some desperate woman, he went on quite easy and forgetful. The devil of it was, it was so hard to keep up his interest in women nowadays. He didn't care about them any more. A Pussum was all right in her way, but she was an exceptional case, and even she mattered extremely little. No, women, in that sense, were useless to him any more. He felt that his *mind* needed acute stimulation, before he could be physically roused" (p. 225). According to Lawrence, the displacement of Gerald's natural feelings by mental sensationalism constitutes the process of his reduction in the struggle with Gudrun.

The gradual stages of his reduction are implicitly related to the underlying womb imagery through the color white, and the theme is immediately struck with Gudrun's initial description of him: "Gudrun lighted on him at once. There was something northern about him that magnetised her. In his clear northern flesh and his fair hair was a glisten like sunshine refracted through crystals of ice. And he looked so new, unbroached, pure as an arctic thing" (pp. 8–9). The end of the novel is anticipated in the reference to ice and the arctic North at the beginning, and Gudrun's polar relation to Gerald, made possible by his own undeveloped and thwarted inner life, is implied. His appearance, "so new, unbroached, pure as an arctic thing," suggests at once his infantilism and his susceptibility to the influence of the possessive woman. Gudrun "lights" on him, and Gerald's hair, "like sunshine refracted through crystals of ice," shows his readiness to be assimilated, a process typical of Lawrence's passive male. Recalling Siegmund's transformation to an image of Helena, the scene anticipates Gerald's similar fate with Gudrun.

Further, the nature of the relationship is reinforced

by the tie to his parents, especially to his father whose death, like Gerald's own, reflects a similar inner sterility conveyed through the same light imagery: " 'Ay,' she [Mrs. Crich] said bitterly at length, speaking as if to the unseen witnesses of the air. 'You're dead.' She stood for some minutes in silence, looking down. 'Beautiful,' she asserted, 'beautiful as if life had never touched you— never touched you. God send I look different. I hope I shall look my years when I am dead. Beautiful, beautiful,' she crooned over him. 'You can see him in his teens, with his first beard on his face. A beautiful soul, beautiful—' Then there was a tearing in her voice as she cried: 'None of you look like this when you are dead! Don't let it happen again.' . . . Then there came in a low, tense voice: 'if I thought that the children I bore would lie looking like that in death, I'd strangle them when they were infants, yes—' (p. 327). Gerald's being less touched by life than his father and more inherently dead intensifies the irony of the scene. His reduction is not simply to a bearded adolescent but to an imprisoned fetus, and the allusion to him as a baby in the previous passage suggests the very thing is happening that Mrs. Crich fears most. The regressive adolescence in the father appears as an a priori condition of existence in the lives of the children, the quality of whiteness previously ascribed to Gerald alone now evident in the father's "beautiful soul." The father's death, then, is symbolically related to the progressive decay of the capacity to live in the generation following him, a drying up of unconscious wellsprings.

In addition, Mrs. Crich's description of her husband, "beautiful as if life had never touched you—never touched you," is distinctly reminiscent of Mrs. Morel's appearance in death in *Sons and Lovers* and of the exact language Paul uses to portray her. The similarity between the two scenes is too striking to be accidental: "She lay like a maiden asleep. . . . The mouth was a little open as if wondering from the suffering, but her face was young, her brow clear and white as if life had never

touched it."[10] The almost identical use of the clause, "as
if life had never touched it" (or "you"), the comparison
of the characters to adolescents, and the obvious contempt in Mrs. Crich's voice support the view that Paul's
sorrow at his mother's death conceals half-recognized or
unperceived contempt for her. The later short story, "The
Rocking Horse Winner," in which the mother is directly
and bitterly responsible for the death of her son (also
named Paul), is further indication of Lawrence's evolving
attitude toward mothers and their influence on their sons.

The presentation of Gerald in Chapter Four, "Diver," confirms the initial view of him and again includes
Gudrun's direct observtaion:

> Suddenly, from the boat-house, a white figure ran
> out, frightening in its swift sharp transit, across the old
> landing-stage. It launched in a white arc through the air,
> there was a bursting of the water, and among the smooth
> ripples a swimmer was making out to space, in a centre
> of faintly heaving motion. The whole otherworld, wet and
> remote, he had to himself. He could move into the pure
> translucency of the grey, uncreated water. . . .
>
> And she stood motionless gazing over the water at
> the face which washed up and down on the flood, as he
> swam steadily. From his separate element he saw them
> and he exulted to himself because of his own advantage,
> his possession of a world to himself. He was immune and
> perfect. He loved his own vigorous, thrusting motion, and
> the violent impulse of the very cold water against his
> limbs, buoying him up. . . .
>
> He was happy, thrusting with his legs and all his
> body, without bond or connection anywhere, just him-
> self in the watery world. (Pp. 39–40)

A movement of descent abruptly followed by a bursting
of the water and a making out to space creates the momentary illusion in which water and space blend together,
suggesting the increasingly interchangeable relationship
between Gerald's conscious (space) and unconscious
(water) natures.

The inference that water represents the unconscious

10. D. H. Lawrence, *Sons and Lovers*, p. 399.

is perhaps indicated in context by the act of diving down itself; by the reference to a center of faintly heaving motion; by the notion of water presented as uncreated; by the slight opposition of Gerald's whiteness to the gray of the water; and by the apparent contrast between water as an isolated and alien otherworld and the less alien, observing life on shore. Outside of context, Lawrence has earlier used water imagery in *The Rainbow*, and Birkin's throwing stones at the reflection of the moon in the pond also substantiates his use of the water imagery. Conversely, the initial impression of Gerald is strengthened by the reference to him as a white figure, by the white arc he makes as he dives through the air, and by his isolated immunity and perfection in the water. Thus, the comparison of uncreated water to space and pure translucency at the beginning of the passage may also suggest the diver's swimming out to be a form of enclosure within the watery world at the end. His isolation, without bond or connection, implies the way in which his inner life has been cut adrift and assimilated to the known self before the action proper of the novel begins.

The ultimate reductiveness of this process is evident from the last part of the passage: "He loved his own vigorous, thrusting motion, and the violent impulse of the very cold water against his limbs, buoying him up." Gerald's fragmentation derives from the same source as that of Hermione, whom Birkin has accused of observing her own animal functions "to get a mental thrill out of them" (p. 35). Gerald's loving (observing) his own thrusting motion and his playing in the water parallels the narcissistic regressiveness in Hermione, and the image introduced—a baby's uncoordinated kicking about —anticipates his complete future decay. As a child of light, like Siegmund before him, Gerald never develops beyond this point, and the terrible price to be paid for this erosion of his capacity to feel is immanent in the image of his face washing up and down on the flood. The smallness of the mental life (head or face) contrasts with the immensity of the flood (unconscious) about to engulf him and the social order he represents. The scene at Breadalby, in which the heads of Hermione's house guests, including that of Gerald, are compared to seals' heads while swimming, and the drowning of Gerald's sister in "Water-Party" are further evidences of the well-wrought pattern in the work that relates dramatic action and social theme to the underlying psychic drama. Consciousness, the cause of personal and social corruption alike, is objectified in the vision of destruction that constitutes the novel as a whole, and Gerald's inner dissolution is part of a universal process that incorporates figures in the social scale so diverse as Sir Joshua and Halliday.

Since the hypothesis that the womb imagery conditions Lawrence's theory of consciousness, accounts for the conception of star equilibrium, and underlies the dramatic structure of the work is broadly sweeping, another concrete example of its use would be reassuring before pursuing the process of Gerald's reduction further. At the very beginning of the novel, the narrator describes Ursula's outer life as "suspended, but underneath, in the darkness, something was coming to pass. If only she could break through the last integuments! She seemed to try and put her hands out, like an infant in the womb, and she could not, not yet" (p. 3). Clearly, Birkin and Ursula's expected release from the womb forms the symbolic counterpoint to Gerald's imprisonment within it, and their success in breaking through will theoretically be due to the emergence of the vital self. Juxtaposed against this passage, the image previously discussed—Gerald in the water "without bond or connection," the umbilical cord cut—may anticipate the paradoxical and ironic outcome of his reduction, his rebirth in consciousness. The process of Gerald's reduction, however, is not so immediately clear as Birkin's renewal, and it is much more allusively and gradually presented.

Gerald's further regression from baby to fetus begins with his response to the primitive statuary in "Crème De Menthe": "But there were several statues, wood-carvings from the West Pacific, strange and disturbing, the carved natives looked almost like the foetus of a human being. One was a woman sitting naked in a strange posture, and looking tortured, her abdomen stuck out. The young Russian explained that she was sitting in child-birth, clutching the ends of the band that hung from her neck, one in each hand, so that she could bear down, and help labour. The strange, transfixed, rudimentary face of the woman again reminded Gerald of a foetus, it was also rather wonderful, conveying the suggestion of the extreme of physical sensation, beyond the limits of mental consciousness" (p. 67). Since African sensualism is the opposite face of Nordic reduction in consciousness, the reference to "physical sensation, beyond the limits of mental consciousness" clearly indicates the dynamics of psychological dissociation at work in Gerald. His repulsion and even stronger attraction toward the statue is very similar to, though less sophisticated than Birkin's, and for Gerald as well the statue represents "one of his soul's intimates" (p. 245). Associating the statue with a fetus, he unwittingly confronts his fate. The fact that the woman is engaged in childbirth, moreover, relates his emotional identification of the statue with Minette to the beginning of his assimilation to Gudrun.

As the mental thrill Gerald derives from looking at the statue mirrors the delight the woman takes in her own suffering, his sensual involvement with Minette is more openly sadistic. Like the statue, Minette is pregnant, and his sexual enjoyment of her is based upon her own will to gain pleasure from being violated: "Minette lay in her bed, motionless, her round, blue eyes like stagnant, unhappy pools. He could only see the dead, bottomless pools of her eyes. Perhaps she suffered. The sensation of her inchoate suffering roused the old sharp flame in him, a mordant pity, a passion almost of cruelty.

. . . She seemed to flow back, almost like liquid, from his approach, to sink helplessly away from him. Her inchoate look of a violated slave, whose fulfilment lies in her further and further violation, made his nerves quiver with acutely desirable sensation. After all, his was only the will, she was the passive substance of his will. He tingled with the subtle, biting sensation. And then he knew, he must go away from her, there must be pure separation between them" (p. 72). As a violated slave, Minette arouses Gerald's cruelty, but his power over her is illusory: "After all, his was only the will, she was the passive substance of his will." He implicitly acts according to her tacit command, and their relationship of victim–victimizer can easily be reversed, as the later coupling of Gudrun and Gerald against Minette and Halliday reveals. The possibility of the reversal of the roles is the reason why he must leave, and this reason for departing, this wish for pure separation, illuminates the psychology behind the conception of star equilibrium. Polarity must be maintained to avoid the victimization that Gerald's tie to Gudrun illuminates so well. The basis of star equilibrium in Birkin's fear of incestuous merging, however, has still to be shown.

Gerald's discovery of Minette and the statue, then, anticipates his fate with Gudrun, his tie to her gradually approximating and surpassing Halliday's bondage to Minette. Both men are victims, and the comparison of Halliday to a broken Christ, "like a Christ in a Pietà" (p. 70), is echoed in the description of Gerald at the moment of his death: "It was a half-buried crucifix, a little Christ under a little sloping hood at the top of a pole. He sheered away. Somebody was going to murder him. He had a great dread of being murdered. But it was a dread which stood outside him like his own ghost" (p. 465). The desire to victimize conceals the wish for victimization as its final, most degrading expression and is the psychological concept that underlies Lawrence's use of womb imagery. Finding the crucifix in the snow at the end merely completes the psychological action implicit in Gerald's response to Minette and the strange but wonderful sense of fear and titillation he experiences in looking upon the African statue.

In this manner, Gerald's unguarded admission of his fear to Minette binds the beginning and the end of the work together and establishes the basis of his tie to Gudrun: " 'Oh! And weren't you ever afraid?' 'In my life? I don't know. Yes, I'm afraid of some things—of being shut up, locked up anywhere—or being fastened. I'm afraid of being bound hand and foot' " (p. 59). Evident in his fear of being locked up, the womb imagery suggests the nature of Gerald's neurosis, the cause of his wish to be victimized, and subsequently determines his relationship with Gudrun as a fight to the death, ending in his complete subjugation to her will: "He opened his eyes, and looked at her. She greeted him with a mocking, enigmatic smile in which was a poignant gaiety. Over his face went the reflection of the smile, he smiled, too, purely unconsciously. That filled her with extraordinary delight, to see the smile cross his face. She remembered that was how a baby smiled" (p. 409). The image of Gerald as a baby unconsciously reflecting Gudrun's smile of radiant delight (p. 409) explicitly clarifies the meaning of the imagery used to signify the reductive process that has been in progress since the chapter entitled "Diver." The imagery shows that he is not only a symbolically static character but a regressive one and that the umbilical cord previously cut is reestablished as Gudrun's assimilating mind. His smile is a mirror of hers, and her radiant delight at his subjection masks the sadistic will behind the smile, the agent of light compelling the reduction.

The outcome of this fastening to Gudrun, Gerald's paradoxical rebirth in consciousness, leads directly to his final enclosure in the mountain-womb of the Tyrol:

"Oh, but this—!" she cried involuntarily, almost in pain. In front was a valley shut in under the sky, the last huge slopes of snow and black rock, and at the end, like the navel of the earth, a white-folded wall, and two peaks glimmering in the late light. Straight in front ran the cradle of silent snow, between the great slopes that were fringed with a little roughness of pine trees, like hair, round the base. But the cradle of snow ran on to the eternal closing-in, where the walls of snow and rock rose impenetrable, and the mountain peaks above were in heaven immediate. This was the centre, the knot, the navel of the world, where the earth belonged to the skies, pure, unapproachable, impassable. . . .

Gerald bent above her and was now looking out over her shoulder. Already he felt he was alone. She was gone. She was completely gone, and there was icy vapour round his heart. He saw the blind valley, the great cul-de-sac of snow and mountain peaks under the heaven. And there was no way out. The terrible silence and cold and the glamorous whiteness of the dusk wrapped him round, and she remained crouching before the window, as at a shrine, a shadow. . . .

The passion came up in him, stroke after stroke, like the ringing of a bronze bell, so strong and unflawed and indomitable. His knees tightened to bronze as he hung above her soft face, whose lips parted and whose eyes dilated in a strange violation. In the grasp of his hand her chin was unutterably soft and silken. He felt strong as winter, his hands were living metal, invincible and not to be turned aside. His heart rang like a bell clanging inside him. (Pp. 390–391)

Gerald's movement toward the womb, the symbol at once of death, consciousness, and machine civilization, is marked by three stages, each involving a shift in narrative perspective. This device permits Lawrence to apprehend Gudrun, Gerald, and the mountain simultaneously through the single act of perception binding them symbolically together, and it permits the reader to determine that the movement toward the womb described is in fact illusory because Gerald has long ago been imprisoned.

The first paragraph presents the scene from Gudrun's narrative point of view and intimately identifies it with her, for the side of the mountain is an image of her body. The navel is mentioned explicitly as "a white-folded wall" from which no exit is possible; the two peaks are like breasts; and "the great slopes that were fringed with a little roughness of pine trees, like hair," form the focal point, "the centre, the knot, the navel of the world," the image of a gigantic vulva. Conversely, the walls of snow and ice that rise impenetrable to heaven and the fading together of earth and sky suggest Gerald's imprisonment within the womb, associated with Gudrun through her description of it. Since heaven and earth, sky and snow, are in effect interchangeable and inter-penetrate each other, the assimilative process begun in "Diver" is almost complete. Only Gerald's death is re-quired—or his paradoxical rebirth—for a cradle of silent snow awaits the natal hour. Moreover, Birkin has pre-viously used the word *knot* to describe his release from the known self: "The terrible knot of consciousness that had persisted there like an obsession was broken, gone" (p. 301). Lawrence's repetition of the word in this con-text, Gerald's victimization and ultimate destruction through his failure to reject consciousness as Birkin did, and the womb imagery describing the similar psycho-logical problems of each character all suggest Gerald's function as Birkin's counterpart.

The shift in viewpoint in the second paragraph from Gudrun to Gerald carries with it his subliminal identifi-cation of her with the mountain. Gudrun's fuguelike lapsing out from his awareness at the beginning of the paragraph and her re-entrance at the end fuse "the icy vapour round his heart" with "the glamorous whiteness of the dusk" as connecting links between characters and mountain. Thus her "crouching before the window, as at a shrine," not only indicates the sacred purity of the scene to her, but reinforces the identification process taking place. The mountain, Gerald, and Gudrun share the common qualities of whiteness, icy desolation, and lifelessness. Gerald's complete reduction to an inanimate object in the third paragraph, "a bronze bell . . . strong as winter," follows from this identification, since the image unites the notions of consciousness expressed in "winter" and the mechanical reduction implicit in "bronze bell." The fact that Loerke's statue of the naked girl sitting on a horse is made of green bronze (p. 420) also connects Gerald's alteration with the next phase of universal dissolution that Loerke heralds, the dehumanization of mankind to an adjunct of the machine. Green bronze, or living (green) metal, is an ironic contradiction in terms and may echo the irony inherent in Gerald's rebirth.

The intervening stages of reduction of course parallel the mechanical dehumanization that constitutes the social vision of the work according to which Gerald's failure to transform himself can be measured. The extent of his degradation, for example, can be gauged in the contrast between Loerke's statue and his own efforts to mechanize his horse by compelling it to endure the noise of an approaching train in "Coal-Dust." In both cases the horses are symbols of man's vital nature under the dominion of an exploiting will. But whereas Gerald's horse is natural, real, and merely broken, Loerke's is debased, something created out of green bronze, and the young girl on the horse is one whom Loerke "loved and tortured and then ignored" (p. 422). In fact, Gerald's failure to survive his degradation is his greatest virtue and, in a sense, the point of Lawrence's social criticism. As the symbol of modern man, he is not, like Loerke, ultra-modern and beyond humanity, and his death is a tribute to a conception of humanity no longer possible in the coming age. Gerald's very inability to become like Loerke measures the degree of the author's sympathy for him and shows the positive, humanistic side of the apocalyptic vision embodied in the work. The scenes in which Gudrun and Gerald force the submission of Bismarck the rabbit, another symbol of the vital unconscious subjugated; in which Gudrun compels the cattle in the field to break and run in terror; in which Gudrun and Winifred Crich, her art pupil, paint the "looliness" of Looloo, Winifred's dog; and in which Gerald subdues the miners to his mechanical will—are all part of the decomposition, universal and personal, that culminates in the vision of death at the foot of a crucifix in the Tyrol.

In this respect, *Women in Love* is the most nearly complete and angry denunciation of the debased Protestant ethic and the spirit of capitalism since *Moby Dick*; it is approached in this century only by Dos Passos' *U.S.A.* In each work the fundamental relationship perceived between certain features of Protestantism, capitalism, and the mechanized debasement of the human spirit lies behind and gives emphasis to the social criticism. Though philosophically debatable, the association between these elements is considered historically valid by Max Weber:

> One of the fundamental elements of the spirit of modern capitalism, and not only of that but of all modern culture: rational conduct on the basis of the calling, was born—that is what this discussion has sought to demonstrate—from the spirit of Christian asceticism. . . .
>
> The Puritan wanted to work in a calling; we are forced to do so. For when asceticism was carried out of monastic cells into everyday life, it did its part in building the tremendous cosmos of the modern economic order. This order is now bound to the technical and economic conditions of machine production which to-day determine the lives of all the individuals who are born into this mechanism, not only those directly concerned with economic acquisition, with irresistible force. Perhaps it will so determine them until the last ton of fossilized coal is burnt. In Baxter's view the care for external goods should only lie on the shoulders of the "saint like a light cloak, which can be thrown aside at any moment." But fate decreed that the cloak should become an iron cage. . . .
>
> No one knows who will live in this cage in the future, or whether at the end of this tremendous development entirely new prophets will arise, or there will be a great rebirth of old ideas and ideals, or, if neither, mechanized petrification, embellished with a sort of compulsive self-importance. For of the last stage of this cultural development, it might well be truly said: "Specialists without

spirit, sensualists without heart; this nullity imagines that it has attained a level of civilization never before achieved."[11]

However, the causal connection asserted in the work between the sexual nature of the characters and social decay collapses when the rationale behind Gerald's failure with Gudrun is related to Birkin's success with Ursula. Birkin would have it, and Lawrence obviously agrees, that Gerald's regression, his enclosure in the womb, is a manifestation of the Oedipus complex that involves his complete emotional dependence upon the mother surrogate, Gudrun. But Lawrence's view of the Oedipus complex is conditioned by a one-sided view of experience that leads him to misinterpret the intrapsychic processes upon which his view depends. Throughout the fiction, usurping mind is always responsible for a character's sexual dilemma, and in *Women in Love* Gerald's reduction and Birkin's release from the womb serve two distinct purposes, both related to the author's theory of consciousness. The womb imagery explains that society and the known self must be rejected on behalf of the vital self and that the vital self can only be attained through star equilibrium. Since the second assumption is of particular importance in gauging Lawrence's achievement in the work, the connection between the womb imagery and star equilibrium needs to be established and explained as a basis for critical evaluation. The following four pasages, taken from Chapter Nineteen, "Moony," Chapter Twenty-three, "Excurse," and Chapter Sixteen, "Man to Man," suggest the significance of this relationship by linking Birkin's quest for star equilibrium to the psychological motivations of the quest.

In "Moony," Birkin's act of stoning the moon reflected in the pond (the vital self) establishes the identity between the moon image and consciousness and their emasculating hold over him:

11. Max Weber, *The Protestant Ethic and the Spirit of Capitalism* (New York, 1958), pp. 180–82.

And his shadow on the border of the pond was watching for a few moments, then he stooped and groped on the ground. Then again there was a burst of sound, and a burst of brilliant light, the moon had exploded on the water, and was flying asunder in flakes of white and dangerous fire. Rapidly, like white birds, the fires all broken rose across the pond, fleeing in clamorous confusion, battling with the flock of dark waves that were forcing their way in. The furthest waves of light, fleeing out, seemed to be clamouring against the shore for escape, the waves of darkness came in heavily, running under towards the centre. But at the centre, the heart of all, was still a vivid, incandescent quivering of a white moon not quite destroyed, a white body of fire writhing and striving and not even now broken open, not yet violated. It seemed to be drawing itself together with strange, violent pangs, in blind effort. It was getting stronger, it was re-asserting itself, the inviolable moon. And the rays were hastening in in thin lines of light, to return to the strengthened moon, that shook upon the water in triumphant reassumption. (P. 239)

Associated first with Lettie in *The White Peacock*, with Helena in *The Trespasser*, and with Anna, Ursula, and women generally in *The Rainbow*, the moon now forms the immovable core of Birkin's mind. While its oedipal nature, its connection with the mother surrogate and the possessive woman, need not be insisted upon here, the inherent weakness in Lawrence's handling of the light imagery as a partial projection of the hero's fantasy becomes clear once more.

Birkin's unsuccessful attempt to destroy the white center and to replace it with the vital self is evident in the struggle of the dark and light waves. The light waves are initially deflected from the center of the pond outward, but again usurp the center in "triumphant reassumption" at the end. Since the middle of the pond is a center and the conflict in the pond is waged by light and darkness, the inference that the pond represents the vital unconscious struggling to free itself seems clear. The moon *in* the pond implies Birkin's view of con-

NOVELS OF D. H. LAWRENCE

sciousness, a cancerous, poisonous virus so far sunk into the vital self that it cannot be uprooted without destroying the entire organism. On this basis Birkin's personality is obviously an androgynous compound of the masculine dark and feminine light. It is clear, therefore, that Lawrence must be aware of his hero's homosexuality, since this problem is implicitly associated with the known self and the light imagery. Birkin fights against this self in order to overcome his personal conflict, and his failure to do so suggests his supreme awareness of it.

His identification of the moon and consciousness with the mother surrogate is also clear from his reaction to Hermione in "Man to Man": "It filled him with almost insane fury, this calm assumption of the Magna Mater, that all was hers, because she had borne it. Man was hers because she had borne him. A Mater Dolorosa, she had borne him, a Magna Mater, she now claimed him again, soul and body, sex, meaning, and all. He had a horror of the Magna Mater, she was detestable. She was on a very high horse again was woman, the Great Mother. Did he not know it in Hermione. Hermione, the humble, the subservient, what was she all the while but the Mater Dolorosa, in her subservience, claiming with horrible, insidious arrogance and female tyranny, her own again, claiming back the man she had borne in suffering. By her very suffering and humility she bound her son with chains, she held him her everlasting prisoner" (p. 192). Seen against the background of the previous scene, this passage furnishes the justification for Birkin's psychological reasoning.

His own consciousness is shown to be a self-alienating force that exists within him, forming and molding his response to women, but Hermione (and Ursula) are accused of being tyrannical mother surrogates apart from him, since this is the nature of Woman. Birkin does not discover that the psychic mechanism transferring the image of whiteness from his own mind to woman's is projection. For him, the result of the projection alone is real, the Magna Mater. His lack of perception is the reason why the last two lines of the passage suggest the neurotic source of Birkin's conception of women to be an aspect of his own mother fixation, without theoretically negating the claims Lawrence continues to make for the vital self: "By her very suffering and humanity she bound her son in chains, she held him her everlasting prisoner." Though *her* and *son* refer immediately to Man and Woman, the context, with its specific reference to Hermione, clearly implies the particular relevance of the generalization to Birkin as son. His highly emotional and irrational response to Hermione is understandable in view of the imagery.

Consequently, by "Excurse" all signs point to fear of incestuous merging as the cause of Birkin's treatment of women: "No doubt Ursula was right. . . . He knew that his spirituality was concomitant of a process of depravity, a sort of pleasure in self-destruction. . . . And was not Ursula's way of emotional intimacy, emotional and physical, was it not just as dangerous as Hermione's abstract spiritual intimacy? Fusion, fusion, this horrible fusion of two beings, which every woman and most men insisted on, was it not nauseous and horrible anyhow, whether it was a fusion of the spirit or of the emotional body? Hermione saw herself as the perfect Idea, to which all men must come: and Ursula was the perfect Womb, the bath of birth, to which all men must come! Why could they not remain individuals, limited by their own limits? Why this dreadful all-comprehensiveness, this hateful tyranny? Why not leave the other being free, why try to absorb, or melt, or merge?" (p. 301). The crucial statement is Birkin's admission of depravity and his almost simultaneous attack upon Ursula's emotional intimacy and Hermione's abstract spiritual intimacy. Inherent in the rhetoric, the self-justifying and untrue accusation that Birkin's fear of fusion is Ursula's fault, though "every woman and most men" insist upon it, is self-evident. If Hermione poses the ultimate threat of a fusing, assimilating consciousness, Ursula represents the very real possibility of Birkin's Brangwenesque engulfment within the perfect womb. In whatever direction he proceeds then, toward consciousness or away from it, Birkin encounters the same image of ever-present, ever-threatening enclosure. His fear of being shut up, imprisoned, or fastened upon is the same as Gerald's and derives from the same source. The assertion previously made, that Gerald is Birkin's counterpart, a dramatic projection of one side of Birkin, has substance, for it is part of Lawrence's symbolic technique.

Birkin's whole notion of star equilibrium follows as an expression of his obsessive fear of oedipal imprisonment, and for this reason his solution to the problem of the man–woman relationship is neurotically conditioned: "In the old age, before sex was, we were mixed, each one a mixture. The process of singling into individuality resulted into the great polarisation of sex. The womanly drew to one side, the manly to the other. But the separation was imperfect even then. And so our world-cycle passes. There is now to come the new day, when we are beings each of us, fulfilled in difference. The man is pure man, the woman pure woman, they are perfectly polarised. But there is no longer any of the horrible merging, mingling self-abnegation of love. There is only the pure duality of polarisation, each one free from any contamination of the other" (p. 193). Blended with the discourse is the essential but unrelated and unperceived source of the love ethic proposed: "But there is no longer any of the horrible merging, mingling self-abnegation of love." In failing to anticipate and to explain the presence or absence of any link between the "duality of polarisation" and "the horrible merging . . . of love," Lawrence is again open to criticism. Together with the man–and–man relationship he advocates, Birkin's view of sexual polarity can be considered a form of homosexual misogyny. His dismissal of physical and spiritual love as mere merging in favor of the star equilibrium of the new day, as if all history were leading up to this union, is at best naïve.

The contradiction between the claims made on behalf of the new love ethic and the physical and psychological facts of Birkin's experience begins to emerge. As in *The Rainbow*, the psychic nature of the character does not lead him to his goals but away from them. The essential criticism of *Women in Love* is not primarily that there is a cleavage between the social criticism rendered and the view of human relationships proposed, nor that Lawrence is once more distorting the picture of psychic processes he presents by insisting upon their universal truth, nor that Birkin's relation with Gerald conceals a homosexual desire for the African way, although these assertions are plausible in themselves. The primary shortcoming of *Women in Love* lies in the author's willingness to admit the most perverse and damaging facts about Birkin while at the same time expecting the reader to accept Birkin's philosophy. The links between means and ends, between admissions made and goals espoused, and between the character's known and vital selves are not coherently joined.

Nevertheless, the formal imbalance is much less intrusive than in *The Rainbow* and the achievement far greater. Lawrence is not so interested in exploring and affirming the vital self as he is in simply demanding it. In effect, Birkin realizes his abnormality when he asks Ursula to accept the facts about him, "to give herself up so much that she could take the last realities of him, the last facts, the last physical facts, physical and unbearable" (p. 286). His problem is not really one of coming to self-knowledge, but of adopting an attitude toward knowledge already possessed. On the one hand, he wants Ursula to accept the facts about him in order to accept his own human condition and limits: "Ursula watched him as he talked. There seemed a certain impatient fury in him, all the while, and at the same time a great amusement in everything, and a final tolerance" (p. 120). Birkin's tolerance of others is tantamount to self-affirmation. But he is sometimes so morally outraged at his own physical and psychological shortcomings that he lacerates himself, and the self-hatred implicit in the laceration is ultimately inverted to hatred of humanity and to the demand for self-transcendence.

The one sexual encounter of Birkin and Ursula presented in the novel confirms this estimate of his problem and Lawrence's intention by giving the meaning of the facts through the dramatic action:

> When they were alone in the darkness, she felt the strange licentiousness of him hovering upon her. She was troubled and repelled. Why should he turn like this.
>
> "What is it?" she asked in dread.
>
> But his face only glistened on her, unknown, horrible. And yet she was fascinated. Her impulse was to repel him violently, break from this spell of mocking brutishness. But she was too fascinated, she wanted to submit, she wanted to know. What would he do to her? . . .
>
> They might do as they liked—this she realised as she went to sleep. How could anything that gave one satisfaction be excluded? What was degrading? Who cared? Degrading things were real, with a different reality. And he was so unabashed and unrestrained. Wasn't it rather horrible, a man who could be so soulful and spiritual, now to be so—she balked at her own thoughts and memories: then she added—so bestial? So bestial, they two!—so degraded! She winced. But after all, why not? She exulted as well. . . . She was free, when she knew everything, and no dark shameful things were denied her. (Pp. 402–403)

Though Ursula's submission to Birkin proceeds from revulsion to exultation to final acceptance because it will make her free, the act itself is "licentious," "degrading," "horrible," "bestial," "shameful" (p. 403), and implicitly perverse. As in key passages of *Lady Chatterley's Lover*, the sexual act is not directly described, and the specific nature of the perversity is only alluded to. The obvious hint apparent in Ursula's balking at the remembrance of Birkin's former misdeeds perhaps carries the reader outside the text completely. Since there is no evidence of their past relationship in the work, Lawrence is obviously intruding. But Ursula's submission, her female acceptance of male dominion, is part of the star equilibrium theme, and as such it is intended more to indicate the fact of their mutual tolerance, in contrast with Gerald and Gudrun, than to conceal the perversity of their sexual relationship. Both Ursula and Birkin are aware of the corruptness, and Birkin's soulful spirituality provides the tenuous connection between the abnormality of the sexual encounter and Lawrence's theory of consciousness. Birkin will conquer the perversity when he overcomes his mental nature, his known self, and Lawrence's theory provides the only possible explanation for the discrepancy between the means Birkin employs and the normative ends he seeks. According to the dramatic plan of the work, Birkin's perverseness must be considered the product of consciousness alone, or he is unwittingly allowed to trap himself in an unresolvable and unalterable contradiction.

If evaluating the novel were a simple matter of spotting the perversity and concluding from it that Birkin's way is indeed the African way, Vivas would be entirely correct in his assessment. One could even point to Ursula's toleration of Birkin and uncover another essential ambiguity. Her wish to experience "all" is also the African way and seems directly opposed to Birkin's view of sex and star polarity. The objection that this is Ursula's point of view and not Birkin's could be countered by arguing that Birkin's sensibility informs the description. His acceptance of the sexual relationship with Ursula on this basis is in direct contradiction to his polarized view of it: "On the whole, he hated sex, it was such a limitation. It was sex that turned a man into a broken half of a couple, the woman into the other broken half. And he wanted to be single in himself, the woman single in herself. He wanted sex to revert to the level of the other appetites, to be regarded as a functional process, not as a fulfilment. He believed in sex marriage. But beyond this, he wanted a further conjunction, where man had being and woman had being, two pure beings, each constituting the freedom of the other, balancing each other like two poles of one force, like two angels, or two demons" (p. 191). Juxtaposing the previous passage against this, a tendency to blur the distinction between the African way and star equilibrium is clear. Yet Vivas' whole line of argument is centered around the point that Birkin is homosexual and does not know it and that therefore the work is morally false.

I suggest that Birkin is not only aware of his homosexuality, but also of the potential conflict between his quest for star equilibrium and his tendency toward the African way, of the almost unbridgeable gap between the known and vital selves. What he does not recognize is the significance and source of his problem, which can be demonstrated by the use of the word *demons* in the last line of the preceding passage. The notion of star polarity or pure being as demonic is itself a sign of perversion, as is clear in *The Rainbow*. Lawrence's conviction that consciousness is corrupt is partially reflected in his view of the unconscious as destructive (demonic), yet neither he nor Birkin is aware of the implicit relation between the two. Consequently, some confusion arises from the character's, and the author's, inability to accept the truth of his own observations. The fact of abnormality is admitted, but the interpretation of the fact argues away the abnormality. Is Birkin's bond with Ursula only one step in the total process toward psychic renewal and star equilibrium, or is it not at all degrading and therefore not perverse? "What was degrading? Who cared?" (p. 403) asks Ursula. While either tendency is more restrained in *Women in Love* than in *The Rainbow* and *Lady Chatterley's Lover*, both exist.

The restraint in *Women in Love* derives from a clear distinction—never fundamentally violated—between Birkin's knowledge of himself and his ends: "He turned in confusion. There was always confusion in speech. Yet it must be spoken. Whichever way one moved, if one were to move forwards, one must break a way through. And to know, to give utterance, was to break a way through the walls of the prison, as the infant in labour strives through the walls of the womb" (p. 178). Birkin never intimates that he is completely free; the self acknowledged, the self imprisoned in the womb, and the free self proposed are never essentially related to each other or identified, only juxtaposed. The failure of the novel in this respect is its greatest virtue, an act of great integrity on the author's part. Since Lawrence's purpose is not to reconcile opposites but to deny through the mutual exclusiveness of the light and dark imagery the very foundations upon which psychic reintegration is based, the only partially intended effect in the work is a very faithful delineation of the split personality. The end in view, star equilibrium, must therefore be judged in part as a manifestation of the very split Birkin seeks to overcome. The novels after *Women in Love* largely confirm this estimate by showing the self either in dissolution, as in *Aaron's Rod* and *Kangaroo*, or in an already achieved state of fulfillment, as in *The Plumed Serpent* and *Lady Chatterley's Lover*. Never again is the dialectical conflict between decay and renewal centered within a single character. Kate (*The Plumed Serpent*) and Constance Chatterley, the two apparent exceptions to this rule, do not embody the conflict within themselves. They exist primarily to illustrate the author's ideology, and the solution to their problems is superimposed from without.

The thesis and the emotional experiences that condition the self are so obviously irreconcilable that they cannot be presented successfully in a single character. Birkin is Lawrence's last hero to describe and to deal forthrightly with the opposites in himself, and the limit of his objectivity is nowhere more apparent than in his association with Gerald. To begin with, the reader never discovers why Birkin's assertion that brotherhood is essential to the man–woman relationship should be true. On the contrary, his insistence tends to reduce the conception of the vital self to the African way, as Vivas asserts: "His craving for the African way and his need for a friendship with Gerald, made impossible by the latter's death, give the lie to Birkin's religion of love and Lawrence's intention."[12] But Vivas is right only in the broadest sense and only in the context of Lawrence's theory of consciousness with its distorted view of psychic processes.

The wrestling bout in the chapter entitled "Gladiatorial" shows Lawrence's lucid handling of the Birkin–Gerald relationship within this context:

> So the two men entwined and wrestled with each other, working nearer and nearer. Both were white and clear, but Gerald flushed smart red where he was touched, and Birkin remained white and tense. He seemed to penetrate into Gerald's more solid, more diffuse bulk, to interfuse his body through the body of the other, as if to bring it subtly into subjection, always seizing with some rapid necromantic foreknowledge every motion of the other flesh, converting and counteracting it, playing upon the limbs and trunk of Gerald like some hard wind. It was as if Birkin's whole physical intelligence interpenetrated into Gerald's body, as if his fine, sublimated energy entered into the flesh of the fuller man, like some potency, casting a fine net, a prison, through the muscles into the very depths of Gerald's physical being. . . .
>
> The normal consciousness, however, was returning, ebbing back. Birkin could breathe almost naturally again. . . .
>
> Birkin laughed. He was looking at the handsome figure of the other man, blond and comely in the rich robe, and he was half thinking of the difference between it and himself—so different; as far, perhaps, apart as man from woman, yet in another direction. But really it was Ursula, it was the woman who was gaining ascendance over Birkin's being at the moment. Gerald was becoming dim again, lapsing out of him. (Pp. 262–266)

12. Vivas, *The Failure and the Triumph*, p. 268.

According to the author's use of light imagery, which recurs throughout the novels, the wrestling bout must exemplify incestuous merging. In the first paragraph, both men are white, and Birkin penetrates and subjugates Gerald, "casting a fine net, a prison, through the muscles into the very depths of Gerald's physical being." In a sense, then, Birkin desires the same tie with Gerald that he eschews with women, whose predatory aspect he now assumes. The encounter is a homosexual one in which Birkin takes the active, consciously depraved role.

But through his use of the light imagery, Lawrence shows his awareness of the homosexuality, since perversity of any kind in the novels is always designated by the color white to indicate its psychological source. Thus, in spite of the distortion in his whole line of thought, Lawrence's awareness here seems unquestionable, for Birkin's normal consciousness returns (in the second paragraph), along with Ursula, who gains ascendance over him as Gerald lapses out. The clue to the significance of Ursula's ascendancy is implicit in the word *normal*. If Birkin means *white-consciousness* by this word, then Ursula is obviously to be considered the possessive woman who will enthrall him. But her ascendancy is not the connotation, because Birkin laughs as he returns to balance; he is glad because his restoration anticipates a healthy relationship with Ursula, to whom he now turns. The implication is that the tie with Gerald dominates one side of him only, whereas the bond with Ursula is more firmly and deeply rooted. My own view of the scene, then, is that Birkin endeavors to overcome his homosexual tendencies after having initially yielded to them. On the one hand, the idea of sexuality in relation to psychic processes that governs the novel and the conception of Birkin's character suggests that certain aspects of his problem go beyond the manifestations he realizes. On the other hand, Lawrence's use of the light imagery clearly establishes his artistic purpose of freeing Birkin from Gerald.

Corroborating evidence exists in the total plot movement away from the Birkin–Gerald relationship; in the womb imagery used to indicate the cause of Gerald's failure and Birkin's unqualified success; and in two chapters or drafts Lawrence deleted from the finished work —"The Wedding Chapter" and "Prologue."[13] This passage from "Prologue" announces the explicitly homosexual nature of their tie: "Birkin and Gerald felt take place between them, the moment they saw each other, that sudden connection which sometimes springs up between men who are very different in temper. There had been a subterranean kindling in each man. Each looked towards the other, and knew the trembling success. . . . Yet there remained always, for Birkin and for Gerald Crich, the absolute recognition that had passed between them then, the knowledge that was in their eyes as they met at the moment of parting. They knew they loved each other, that each would die for the other."[14]

The ramifications of the tie, in accordance with Birkin's view of women, is also suggested: "All the time, he recognized that, although he was always drawn to women, feeling more at home with a woman than with a man, yet it was for men that he felt the hot, flushing, roused attraction which a man is supposed to feel for the other sex. Although nearly all his living interchange went on with one woman or another, . . . and practically never with a man, yet the male physique had a fascination for him, and for the female physique he felt only a fondness, a sort of sacred love, as for a sister."[15] To be sure, it is entirely speculative to advance an hypothesis one way or another concerning the deletions, but both the novel and the omitted chapters

13. George H. Ford, "An Introductory Note to D. H. Lawrence's Prologue to *Women in Love*," *Texas Quarterly*, 6 (1963), 92–111; and "The Wedding Chapter of D. H. Lawrence's *Women in Love*," *Texas Studies in Literature and Language*, 6 (1963), 134–47.

14. Ford, "Prologue," 98.

15. Ford, "Prologue," 107–8.

agree in one essential: Lawrence's awareness of Birkin's known self. Therefore, Vivas' charge that the relationship with Gerald is proof of Birkin's homosexuality is in itself irrelevant. Not only does Birkin admit it, but the thesis of the novel reflects the attempt to transcend the condition through the creation of a new personality. The validity of the assertion that because Birkin is homosexual the work fails is at best questionable.

Nevertheless, the fact finally remains of Birkin's insistence upon the intrinsic connection between brotherhood and star equilibrium: " 'Having you [Ursula] I can live all my life without anybody else, any other sheer intimacy. But to make it complete, really happy, I wanted eternal union with a man too: another kind of love,' he said. . . . 'You can't have it, because it's false, impossible,' she said. 'I don't believe that,' he answered" (pp. 472–473). To repeat, following Vivas' approach to *Women in Love*, the conclusion must be granted or it must be used as final proof of Birkin's homosexuality. Yet, in either instance, the probability of coming to a valid literary and moral evaluation of the novel and its ideology on this basis alone is slight. My agreement with one of Vivas' conclusions concerning the "obdurate major disharmony" has led me to question the assumptions and methods by which he reached his judgments.

VII

The Leadership Motif
Aaron's Rod,
Kangaroo,
The Plumed Serpent

In embodying a sociopolitical program as a theoretical extension of the vital self, *Aaron's Rod, Kangaroo,* and *The Plumed Serpent* represent various points of departure from *Women in Love* and share several of its assumptions. One assumption is that the dissociation of sensibility or split in the modern world makes any reconciliation of psychic opposites impossible, the assertions of Lawrence's vitalist (Jungian) critics notwithstanding. Another is that the known self, the source of self-division, must be uprooted before a new society based upon Lawrence's gradually altering conception of the vital self can be formed. In addition, the male primacy so necessary to the man–woman relationship in star polarity is now extended to include a similar tie between men. The new association is not founded upon brotherhood, however, but upon leadership and the power urge, the submission of the inferior male will to the higher. From this view of male primacy new social norms will evolve, rooted in individual "maleness" rather than in existing "feminine" institutions. As a group, then, the leadership novels are governed by the same *idées fixes* that control *Women in Love,* are subject to the same sort of criticism, and because of his increasing dependence upon autobiographical realism, conceptualization, and prophetic assertion, they reveal Lawrence's art in precipitous decline.

The theme of *Aaron's Rod* is anticipated early in *Women in Love* when Gerald Crich shows Birkin a newspaper article he is reading: " 'Isn't it funny, what they

do put in newspapers,' he said. 'Here are two leaders'—
he held out his *Daily Telegraph*, 'full of the ordinary
newspaper cant—' he scanned the columns down—'and
then there's this little—I dunno what you'd call it, essay,
almost—appearing with the leaders, and saying there
must arise a man who will give new values to things,
give us new truths, a new attitude to life, or else we
shall be a crumbling nothingness in a few years; a
country in ruin—' "[1] And as in *Women in Love*, the
theme can be divided into two not entirely related parts,
the dissolution of Aaron, who represents the postwar
European, and the way of new political leadership offered
by Lilly in exchange for Aaron's pledge of allegiance to
the superior man. Because Aaron initially refuses the
pledge, he succumbs, his "rod" breaks, and the thesis is
implicitly proved: a social organism that is governed by
abstract, mechanical laws and that reduces the individual
to sexual impotence must be replaced by vital, personal,
male leadership.

The tie between Aaron and Lilly, which expresses
the leadership idea, parallels the blood brotherhood
theme centered around Gerald and Birkin. Like Gerald's,
Aaron's relations to women, first with his wife Lottie
and then with the Marchesa, end in catastrophe because
he cannot live within the dark core of his being, to which
Lilly alone can lead him. He, too, is the product of the
split, falls victim to the possessive woman, and is sexually
assimilated. And again as in *Women in Love*, Lawrence
posits interchangeability between sexual reduction and
social decay, culminating this time in the anarchistic
bombing of the Florentine café where Lilly, Aaron, and
friends are assembled: "Here was a blow he [Aaron]
had not expected. And the loss was for him symbolistic.
It chimed with something in his soul: the bomb, the
smashed flute, the end."[2]

The theme of social (and personal) dissolution repre-

1. D. H. Lawrence, *Women in Love*, p. 46.
2. D. H. Lawrence, *Aaron's Rod*, p. 276.

sented by Aaron is then linked by contrast to the idea of potential renewal as enunciated by Lilly: " 'But listen. I told you there were two urges—two great life-urges, didn't I? There may be more. But it comes on me so strongly, now, that there are two: love and power. And we've been trying to work ourselves, at least as individuals, from the love-urge exclusively, hating the power-urge, and repressing it. And now I think we've got to accept the very thing we've hated. . . . Power—the power-urge. The will-to-power—but not in Nietzsche's sense. Not intellectual power. Not mental power. Not conscious will-power. Not even wisdom. But dark, living, fructifying power. Do you know what I mean?' " (p. 288). Though he does stop short of full commitment to Lilly and the power motive, the questing Aaron gradually realizes his need to submit to a greater male soul in principle, and Lawrence demonstrates his thesis through the plot movement, the character relationships, and the governing symbolism. In admitting his need, Aaron differs from Gerald, is saved from further deterioration, and forms the dramatic counterpart to Lilly. He is the old, known, conscious self in decay as Lilly is the new, power-motivated, vital self rising from dissolution.

The formal problem of *Aaron's Rod* is also familiar and follows from the author's view of the characters, his inability to explain other than conceptually why the conflict between man and woman should inevitably lead to the leader-cum-follower relationship among men.[3] The reader may grant the social criticism that emanates from the sexual dilemma, for the sake of the argument, but he can hardly help noticing that the psychological basis of the criticism is merely superimposed upon the characters rather than embodied in them. All the male characters are compelled to agree, for example, that the individual disintegration manifested in the general social decay is caused by woman's refusal to submit sexually

3. D. H. Lawrence, *The Collected Letters of D. H. Lawrence*, Harry T. Moore, ed., II, 1045.

to man: " 'But can't there be a balancing of wills?' said
Lilly. 'My dear boy, the balance lies in that, that when
one goes up, the other goes down. One acts, the other
takes. It is the only way in love. And the women are
nowadays the active party. Oh yes, not a shadow of
doubt about it. They take the initiative, and the man
plays up. Nice manly proceeding, what!' cried Argyle.
. . . 'What was yours [your experience with women]?'
asked Lilly. 'Mine was the same. Mine was the same, if
ever it was,' said Aaron. 'And mine was extremely
similar,' said Argyle with a grimace. 'And yours, Lilly?'
asked the Marchese anxiously. 'Not very different,' said
Lilly" (pp. 237–238). Yet there is no attempt at all as is
made in *Sons and Lovers, The Rainbow,* and *Women in
Love,* to present the woman's point of view or to show
the dynamics of the thesis that evolves from the various
conflicts of the persona.

In addition, the same symbolic identity between the
known self, the possessive woman, and social decay
universalizes the idea of the male relationship as the
only possible solution to the sexual problem: "But no!
If he [Aaron] had to give in to something: if he really
had to give in, and it seemed he had: then he would rather
give in to the devilish little Lilly than to the beastly
people of the world. If he had to give in, then it should
be to no woman, and to no social ideal, and to no special
institution. No!—if he had to yield his wilful independence, and give himself, then he would rather give himself to the little, individual *man* than to any of the rest.
For to tell the truth, in the man was something incom-
prehensible, which had dominion over him, if he chose
to allow it" (p. 280). But even if the connection between
social decay and sexual failure is the novel's *donnée,* the
male tie cannot be critically accepted as the basis for a
new social order. Lawrence never demonstrates why the
leadership ideal should not be considered a homosexual
manifestation of the failure between man and woman.

The scene in a London pension in which Lilly massages Aaron's body will illustrate Lawrence's views, for it establishes Lilly's conceptual value as a representative of the life principle associated with male leadership. As a piece of realism the scene is incredible, and since Lawrence does not create characters at once symbolically and realistically convincing, the reader has to reject the integrity of the male relationship proposed. This technical breakdown, in turn, points to the larger problem of form, the reasons for the author's unconvincing assertion of the leadership ideal as a valid way to a social and potentially political program. The reasons are to be found in the symbolism and its relation to Aaron's discontinuity. While the imagery illuminates Aaron's motives for seeking fulfillment elsewhere than in consciousness, woman, and existing social institutions, it also prevents conditional assent to the solutions offered. By the very fact of his split, Aaron's semisubmission to Lilly is the consequence, not the solution to his personal difficulties.

The symbolism to describe Aaron and parallel the development of plot and theme is essentially a rehash of the light imagery applied to Gerald Crich in *Women in Love*, and it is predicated upon the character's self-division: "Thoughts something in this manner ran through Aaron's subconscious mind as he sat in the strange house. He could not have fired it all off at any listener, as these pages are fired off at any chance reader. Nevertheless, there it was, risen to half-consciousness in him. All his life he had *hated* knowing what he felt. He had wilfully, if not consciously, kept a gulf between his passional soul and his open mind. In his mind was pinned up a nice description of himself, and a description of Lottie, sort of authentic passports to be used in the conscious world" (p. 159). Aaron's dissociation is clear from the "gulf between his passional soul and his open mind," and his awareness of it is suggested in the preceding sentence, in the splintering of the psychological barriers that block him. The narrator's intrusion into the scene, however, and the addressing of pages to the reader indicate that Lawrence is not really interested in the character, only in the formulation of his problem, a measure of the author's growing weariness and lack of serious aesthetic endeavor. The affinity of writer and persona(s) is not concealed, and the characters become direct extensions of Lawrence's personal, untransmuted state of mind. Lilly's sense of messianic betrayal is another instance of the deficiency of art in the work. Since the motivation of his feeling is not objectively rendered within the scope of the novel, the necessary aesthetic distance between author and work is violated, and the distinction between autobiography and art is increasingly blurred. The psychic split ascribed to Aaron and somewhat less openly to Lilly seems applicable to Lawrence as well.

Consequently, the assertions conveyed through the imagery lack credibility, and the disproportion between means and ends is sometimes so evident that the reader's interest is seldom sufficiently challenged. One assertion involves Aaron's reduction by his wife—the cause, he says, of his leaving her: "He had a certain horror of her. The strange, liquid sound of her appeal seemed to him like the swaying of a serpent which mesmerises the fated, fluttering, helpless bird. She clasped her arms round him, she drew him to her, she half roused his passion. At the same time she coldly horrified and repelled him. . . . He could see himself as the fascinated victim, falling to this cajoling, artful woman, the wife of his bosom" (p. 122). One may conclude that an unstated connection exists between Aaron's final, if tentative, acceptance of Lilly's rule and his victimization by Lottie, the conceptual denouement of the predatory woman. As "woman, and particularly as mother" (p. 154), she is in the long line of development from Lettie Beardsall, Helena, Mrs. Morel, Miriam, and Anna Brangwen, and she shares with them the wish to be "the centre of creation, . . . the first great source of life and being, and also of culture" (p. 154). Since the unstated relationship alone explains the novel's lack of unity, a biographical connection between the author, the symbolism, and the major characters must be assumed. The immediate effect, of course, is to subvert the thesis. Lilly and Aaron are too personally related to Lawrence to exist independently; and their comments upon woman cannot be accepted as impersonally motivated, objectively rendered, and historically accurate, which the novel demands.

Aaron's tie to the Marchesa clarifies the formal problem by arguing that the cause of the passive male's reduction is still attributed to his mental nature. As with Lottie, Aaron's relation to the Marchesa ends in his victimization: "She was absolutely gone in her own incantations. She was absolutely gone, like a priestess utterly involved in her own terrible rites. And he was part of the ritual only, God and victim in one. God and victim. . . . He was aware of the strength and beauty and god-likeness that his breast was then to her—the magic. But himself, he stood far off, like Moses' sister Miriam. She would drink the one drop of his innermost heart's blood, and he would be carrion. As Cleopatra killed her lovers in the morning. Surely they knew that death was their just climax. They had approached the climax. Accept then" (pp. 264–265). The supreme threat to his masculinity posed by the Marchesa is self-evident, reveals the nature of his personal problem, and fully accounts for the general outburst in the novel against women. The complete reversal of sexual roles implicit in the comparison of Aaron to Miriam suggests the source of his conflict in the divided self; the association of death with the feminization process can be observed as early as *The White Peacock*. Cyril's incestuous motive in that work, his desire to merge with Lettie, is not conceptually different from Aaron's identification with Miriam, his biblical sister. From this perspective also, the author's unwillingness to explore the characters' psychology prevents him from integrating the sexual and leadership themes more fully.

This being the case, the reader is free to reject the cause-and-effect relationship that Lawrence establishes between Aaron's assimilation to the Marchesa and the social criticism as arbitrary: " 'The ideal of love, the ideal that it is better to give than to receive, the ideal of liberty, the ideal of the brotherhood of man, the ideal of the sanctity of human life, the ideal of what we call goodness, charity, benevolence, public spiritedness, the ideal of sacrifice for a cause, the ideal of unity and unanimity—all the lot—all the whole beehive of ideals—has all got the modern bee-disease, and gone putrid, stinking. And when the ideal is dead and putrid, the logical sequence is only stink. Which, for me, is the truth concerning the ideal of good, peaceful, loving humanity and its logical sequence in Socialism and equality, equal opportunity or whatever you like. By this time he stinketh —and I'm sorry for any Christus who brings him to life again, to stink livingly for another thirty years: the beastly Lazarus of our idealism' " (p. 271). The emotional extremism of this passage implies the neurosis that conditions it. In *Aaron's Rod* Lawrence uses an historical period of disillusionment and destruction to embody an entirely personal and incoherent vision of decay and renewal.

Missing from the novel, as from *Kangaroo* and *The Plumed Serpent*, is any stated connection between the self in decay (Aaron–Somers–Kate) and the self reborn (Lilly–Kate–Don Ramón). The question of how one self derives from the other is simply assumed, and the characters are divided into two types, each lacking human complexity and the tool of the author's ideology. Those reborn are even more abstract, one-dimensional and brutalized than those in quest. The reader is asked to accept at face value the assertion that the dissolving self can be fully renewed only when the existing order of things is overcome. He is not expected to search for the obvious connection between the two selves; nor to inquire too closely into the psychological basis of the new order to understand the characters; nor, above all, to perceive that the only evidence of character motivation is not unrelated to fear of homosexual surrender or misogyny. These novels stimulate response as "thought-adventures," as essays about problems that are inherent in Lawrence's earlier work, or as art less interesting in its achievement than in the neurosis that dominates it.

The ethical outcome of Lawrence's endeavor to build a new society is the betrayal of the fundamental moral assumption posited in all the preceding novels, the integrity of the individual. This value is repeated by Lilly: " 'Why, I'll tell you the real truth,' said Lilly. 'I think every man is a sacred and holy individual, *never* to be violated. I think there is only one thing I hate to the verge of madness, and that is *bullying*. To see any living creature *bullied*, in *any* way, almost makes a murderer of me. That is true. Do you believe it—?' " (p. 273). But, like the later Carlyle in *Past and Present* (especially in "Captains of Industry," "The Nigger Question," and "Shooting Niagara and After?"), Lawrence tends to solve the problem of individual integrity in the novels subsequent to *Aaron's Rod* by denying the value of the other person. The leader completes himself through the social order, which he embodies, only by dominating the lesser individuals who comprise it, by bullying them on behalf of the dark gods. As a result, the concept of the vital self becomes a mere instrument of repression used to justify brutal and inhuman ends.

Like *Aaron's Rod*, *Kangaroo* involves the anti-hero's search for renewal, but it is even less unified. Somers' relation to his wife Harriet, undoubtedly a satire of the man and the mask, establishes the difference for him between the mundane, married reality and the quest for the ideal of lordship and mastery. Yet his connection with Kangaroo is part of a serious attempt to arrive at a political position that has nothing to do with his marriage. The major themes of the novel do not cohere, and Somers' ultimate rejection of Kangaroo and the diggers led by Jack Callcott is not really political. The diggers are not repudiated because they are fascistic, but because they are common and would indirectly perpetuate the existing social order. Somers does not in theory disdain the use of force so long as it is directed against the *status quo*, and his temporary support of the socialist Willie Struthers is simply expedient: "Mastership is based on possessions. To kill mastership you must have communal ownership. Then have it, for this superiority based on possession or money is worse than any of the pretensions of Labour or Bolshevism, strictly. Let the serpent swallow itself. Then we can have a new snake. The moment Labour takes upon itself to be its own boss, the whole show is up, the end has begun."[4] The ends justify the means, and Somers' commitment is to a whole new order different from any represented by Jack Callcott, Struthers, or Kangaroo.

But Somers' willingness to obtain his obscure social and political goals by force suggests that he, too, falls victim to the same postwar mentality he would escape. It is not insignificant, nor indicative of artistic decline only, that *Kangaroo* and *Aaron's Rod* are more firmly rooted in their historical period than any of the other novels. Justifying their social schemes by the necessity of the times, Somers and Lilly reflect the times: "It was in 1915 the old world ended. In the winter of 1915–1916 the spirit of the old London collapsed; the city, in some way, perished, perished from being a heart of the world, and became a vortex of broken passions, lusts, hopes, fears, and horrors. The integrity of London collapsed, and the genuine debasement began, the unspeakable baseness of the press and the public voice, the reign of

4. D. H. Lawrence, *Kangaroo*, p. 309.

that bloated ignominy, *John Bull*. No man who has really consciously lived through this can believe again absolutely in democracy" (p. 220). The will to power equated with the dark self of Somers' quest is often almost an inverted expression of everything symbolized by John Bull. In reacting against his age, Somers actually represents it, and the dark gods are invoked to vindicate his position. Partly in consequence—since his identification with Somers is scarcely disguised—Lawrence's viewpoint hardens, earlier theories become dogmas, and artistic sensibility is lost in a plethora of argumentation.

Together with his artistic decline, the defects in the author's theory of consciousness suggest why Somers' rejection of Kangaroo, the Christ-like upholder of a dead *status quo*, on behalf of the dark gods is unconvincing. The product of a tired and entirely mechanical application of the light imagery, Kangaroo, like Aaron, is a simple foil to Somers' (and Lawrence's) pronouncements: " 'No,' he said, in a slow, remote voice. 'I know your love, Kangaroo. Working everything from the spirit, from the head. You work the lower self as an instrument of the spirit. Now it is time for the spirit to leave us again; it is time for the Son of Man to depart, and leave us dark, in front of the unspoken God: who is just beyond the dark threshold of the lower self, . . . whom I fear while he is my glory. And the spirit goes out like a spent candle' " (p. 134). The absolute distinction between the known and the vital self, the self "beyond the dark threshold of the lower self," continues to provide the theoretical basis upon which the Lawrentian hero acts. In addition, the known self, in this case Kangaroo, has been automatically identified with traditional Christianity and the social system that have been rejected by each hero since *The Rainbow*.

The basis for rejecting Kangaroo, then, can be inferred from the concepts associated with him and from Somers' own victimized sexual attraction to him: "Richard, curled narrow in his chair like a snake, glanced up at the big man projecting over him. A sort of magnetic effusion seemed to come out of Kangaroo's body, and Richard's hand was almost drawn in spite of himself to touch the other man's body. He had deliberately to refrain from laying his hand on the near, generous stomach of the Kangaroo, because automatically his hand would have lifted and sought that rest. But he prevented himself, and the eyes of the two men met. . . . 'Ah, well,' he said, 'I can see there is a beast in your eyes, Lovat, and if I can't conquer him then—woe-betide you, my dear. But I love you, you see.' 'Sounds like a threat,' laughed Somers" (pp. 134–135). Here, as elsewhere, the hero transfers his own response to the other person, holds him responsible for his own perversity, associates the mental life with religion, society, and humanity generally, and on this basis repudiates the whole lot. In this respect, the formal problem of *Kangaroo* is similar to that of *Women in Love* and *Aaron's Rod*. Somers' condemnation of the existing order of things is based ultimately upon the misinterpretation of a personal dilemma asserted as a norm in the work.

More than any other novel, *Kangaroo* raises the issue of the legitimacy of the vital self and the hero's pursuit of it. The reader has already observed the Freudian elements that are entangled with this self, and now the will to power fully identified with it suggests a radical alteration in the nature of the quest, from the evidence presented in *Sons and Lovers* and *The Rainbow*. Dominated by neurosis, Somers is dehumanized by his search and glorifies the very process of his dehumanization as self-fulfilling. His attempt to locate the source of being beyond consciousness and "the dark threshold of the lower self" leads to a despairing journey outside the limits of humanity: "In the sperm whale, intense is the passion of amorous love, intense is the cold exultance in power, isolate kingship. With the most intense enveloping vibration of possessive and protective love, the great bull encloses his herd into a oneness. And with the intensest vibration of power he keeps it subdued in awe, in fear. These are the two great telepathic vibrations which rule all the vertebrates, man as well as beast. Man, whether in a savage tribe or in a complex modern society, is held in unison by these two great vibrations emitted unconsciously from the leader, the leaders, the governing classes, the authorities. First, the great influence of shadow of power, causing trust, fear, and obedience: second, the great influence of protective love, causing productivity and the sense of safety" (p. 306).

The qualities shared by the animal and human worlds indicate the direction of the quest and determine how the new self and the new order are to be defined. Using Leviathan or Moby Dick to express an apparent reconciliation between love and power, Somers arrives at the edge of the nonhuman, conveyed there by his insistence upon the primacy of trust, fear, and obedience. The assertion of the power urge as the essential characteristic of the vital self comes close to reducing the concept to mere animalism and evidences how illusory any acceptance of the quest along the integrative lines set forth by the vitalist (Jungian) critics would be. Controlled by the sexual problem, the journey can end only in a reduction much worse than the one endured by Aaron or Gerald Crich. And while the ideology of the vital self is made more tentative by his humorous departure from Australia with Harriet as "two gentle kangaroos" (p. 437), Somers' thoughts are thoroughly opposed to the meekness of his actions. He does not think of a gentle, reconciled self, but of a self beyond good and evil, beyond consciousness, and beyond humanity.

The Plumed Serpent concerns the savage tribe, where the "two great telapathic vibrations" form the basis of Lawrentian society. In attempting to clarify the relation of protective love and power to the vital self and to show the significance of their human embodiment, the novel illustrates the full emergence of the leadership thesis that is implicit in Lawrence's fiction subsequent to the creation of *Women in Love*. From the assertion of brotherhood in the earlier work, the notion evolves of the leader's dominion over men as a condition of the man–woman relationship and of the proposed social organization. Taken together, the three main characters, Kate, Cipriano, and Don Ramón, formulate the doctrine. The wholeness of being represented by the characters is at once the result and the expression of a society that is organically rooted in the superior male individual. Within the triangle, each character is bound by his specific symbolic function: the potentially active body of life beneath the old mentality (Kate); the unconscious male source of the power urge (Cipriano); and the spiritual reflection of this source in possessive and protective love (Don Ramón). Ramón's love can be considered a mirror or a dualistic manifestation of the power urge, a refinement of it by a kind of consciousness that is directly related to the unconscious as its object. This relation contrasts with the dissociated sensibility that has been cut off from the life source and is represented here by Ramón's wife Carlota and, originally, by Kate.

Kate's thematic function is to illustrate the process by which the older, "white" European mind is gradually initiated into the "life of the new day," when the veil of the older life-form will be torn away and replaced by "phallic consciousness."[5] Her sexual submission to Cipriano, as John Vickery indicates, is the last part of her three-stage initiation. The first stage presents Kate, a European in Mexico City who is dissatisfied with modern life there; the second stage, her introduction to the world of Cipriano and Don Ramón; the final stage, her submission and emergence as the goddess "Malintzi."[6] "In brief," Vickery says, "the three stages of

5. D. H. Lawrence, *Studies in Classic American Literature*, p. 16.
6. John B. Vickery, "*The Plumed Serpent* and the Eternal Paradox," *Criticism*, 5 (1963), 129–31.

Kate's sexual initiation are counterpointed by a shift in her consciousness from the rational to the intuitive and in Lawrence's style from the satiric to the mythopoeic."[7] As the questing character in search of new life, then, Kate's submission to Cipriano exemplifies the superimposed connection between the fulfillment of her quest and the thesis of mastery.

Though her final departure from Mexico leaves the issue of her submission formally unresolved, Kate does affirm the personal changes wrought by her experience: "The moment she had admitted the necessity [of returning to England], she realised it was a certain duplicity in herself. It was as if she had two selves, one, a new one, which belonged to Cipriano and to Ramón, and which was her sensitive, desirous self: the other hard and finished, accomplished, belonging to her mother, her children, England, her whole past. This old accomplished self was curiously invulnerable and insentient, curiously hard and 'free.' In it, she was an individual and her own mistress. The other self was vulnerable, and organically connected with Cipriano, even with Ramón and Teresa, and so was not 'free' at all."[8] The problem that this concluding scene suggests, the affirmation of the vital self by a character who remains split throughout, merits further discussion.

Since *The Plumed Serpent* marks the partial return of Lawrence's creative power in a context that expresses mythopoeically his formerly enunciated doctrine, the obvious novelistic failure may be overlooked. The book may be disregarded as primarily a novel for, given the rationale of form, motivation, probability, and character delineation, it is a disappointment. Don Ramón in breechclouts is incredible; Kate's submission to Cipriano unlikely; the external trappings of myth, Aztec brutality, and peasant costumes hardly an objective correlative for the central thesis and the nature of the principal charac-

7. Vickery, "*The Plumed Serpent*," p. 131.
8. D. H. Lawrence, *The Plumed Serpent*, p. 429

ters. The significant aspect of the work, however, is Lawrence's endeavor to formulate the relationship between the vital self, the hero's mastery over man and woman, and the social and political goals espoused as organic. The attempt involves him in several inconsistencies that expose the contradictions inherent in the doctrine and reveal the author in partial retreat from his own thesis.

The problem within this framework centers around Ramón's conflicting attitudes toward the vital self and humanity. Not knowing whether to escape, accept, or redefine and perhaps obliterate human nature, his commitment to a vital self based upon mastery and manhood is fundamentally ambiguous. Formally, at least, the ideas of mastery and manhood and the psychological processes they include are synonymous: " 'And Mexico!' he [Ramón] said. 'Mexico is another Ireland. Ah no, no man can be his own master. If I must serve, I will not serve an idea, which cracks and leaks like an old wine-skin. I will serve the God that gives me my manhood. There is no liberty for a man, apart from the God of his manhood. Free Mexico is a bully, and the old, colonial, ecclesiastical Mexico was another sort of bully. When man has nothing but his *will* to assert—even his good-will—it is always bullying. Bolshevism is one sort of bullying, capitalism another: and liberty is a change of chains" (p. 69). Ramón's hatred of bullying suggests that his view of mastery ought to be limited to power over himself, the condition of self-fulfillment. In giving up his own will and liberty to serve the God of his manhood, he ought to abandon thoughts of dominating others as well, for bullying is a form of tyranny representative of the world Ramón rejects. Since the words *idea*, *liberty*, *ecclesiastical*, *Bolshevism*, *capitalism*, and *will* all share the same connotation of mental consciousness, they in effect define this world and tell us that manhood and mastery must originate elsewhere.

But the nature of its source, an unconscious, virtually inhuman force to which he is fatalistically bound,

pushes Ramón over a precipice and gives quite a different connotation to *mastery*: "The will of God! She [Kate]
began to understand that once fearsome phrase. At the
centre of all things, a dark, momentous Will sending out
its terrific rays and vibrations, like some vast octopus.
And at the other end of the vibration, men, created men,
erect in dark potency, answering Will with will, like
gods or demons" (p. 385). The inhuman actions committed in the name of the god extend the meaning of the
word from self-possession to dominion and tyranny over
others. On behalf of the god, Ramón assents to Cipriano's
murder of the rebels in the conquered church, celebrates
the rites of Quetzalcoatl there, declares the death of
Christ and Christianity, and asserts the right of his
political-social-"religious" dictatorship over men and
women of inferior being. The nonhuman origin of the
power thus reflects the extent to which Ramón is dehumanized, but made potent by it.

In this manner, he theoretically fulfills his manhood
and is reborn through direct participation in the godhead:

> And tense like the gush of a soundless fountain, he
> thrust up and reached down in the invisible dark, con-
> vulsed with passion. Till the black waves began to wash
> over his consciousness, over his mind, waves of darkness
> broke over his memory, over his being, like an incoming
> tide, till at last it was full tide, and he trembled, and fell
> to rest. Invisible in the darkness, he stood soft and re-
> laxed, staring with wide eyes at the dark, and feeling the
> dark fecundity of the inner tide wash over his heart, over
> his belly, his mind dissolved away in the greater, dark
> mind, which is undisturbed by thoughts.
> He covered his face with his hands, and stood still,
> in pure unconsciousness, neither hearing nor feeling nor
> knowing, like a dark sea-weed deep in the sea. With no
> time and no World, in the deeps that are timeless and
> wordless. . . . Only in the heart of the cosmos man can
> look for strength. And if he can keep his soul in touch
> with the heart of the world, then from the heart of the
> world new blood will beat in strength and stillness into
> him, fulfilling his manhood. (Pp. 192–193)

In *The Plumed Serpent* Lawrence presents the quest as more nearly achieved than in any other novel except *Lady Chatterley's Lover*, and the goal of the quest, the unconscious "undisturbed by thoughts," as more exclusively identified with manhood and power. But the legitimacy of the vital self is again open to serious doubt, since evading the disturbing thoughts is in effect the condition of self-fulfillment. And though a kind of archetypal lapsing back into the life source is apostrophized, the comparison with the collective unconscious that Jungian critics might invite is misleading.

In the first place, Lawrence's view of the vital self is a form of self-deception, the basis of which is everywhere apparent in the link between Ramón's escapism and his previously unfortunate sexual experiences: " 'But which woman can I meet in the body, without that slow degradation of ravishing, or being ravished, setting in? If I marry a Spanish woman or a dark Mexican, she will give herself up to me to be ravished. If I marry a woman of the Anglo-Saxon or any blond northern stock, she will want to ravish me, with the will of all the ancient white demons. These that want to be ravished are parasites on the soul, and one has revulsions. Those that want to ravish a man are vampires. And between the two, there is nothing" (p. 272). As in the preceding novels, the vital self and the over-all view of human completeness they advance are a manifestation of the hero's psychic split, a product of his sexual torment. For Ramón the parasites and the vampires, the Minettes and the Gudruns, are sisters under the skin, and though he is presented as a fulfilled man, he yet considers himself a potential victim of the possessive woman.

The fear of domination determining Ramón's notions of mastery and maleness leads him in two opposite directions at once. He seeks to compel obedience to the lordship principle invested in him, but he also wishes to escape from the humanity that grants the obedience and, implicitly, from the very lordship principle he professes:

" 'One must disentangle oneself from persons and per-
sonalities, and see people as one sees trees in the landscape. People in some way *dominate* you. In some way
humanity dominates your consciousness. So you must
hate people and humanity, and you want to escape. But
there is only one way of escape: to turn beyond them,
to the greater life' " (p. 249). Consciousness is again the
ostensible factor that precipitates Ramón's flight into the
nonhuman, upon which the concept of the vital self now
rests. Conditioning the flight, however, is not the will to
dominate, but the fear of being dominated. Fear, not the
dark gods, is the primary reality for Don Ramón, and it
renders concocted and forced the notion of mastery in its
relation to the vital self.

Consequently, his union with the sources of life
as lord of the two ways does not ring true, and the par-
able of Quetzalcoatl whose embodiment Ramón is, or
seeks to be, is ambiguous: " 'But I, I am lord of two ways.
I am master of up and down. I am as a man who is a
new man, with new limbs and life, and the light of the
Morning Star in his eyes. Lo! I am I! The lord of both
ways. Thou wert lord of the one way. Now it leads thee
to the sleep. Farewell! So Jesus went on towards the
sleep. And Mary the Mother of Sorrows lay down on the
bed of the white moon, weary beyond any more tears.
And I, I am on the threshold. I am stepping across the
border. I am Quetzalcoatl, lord of both ways, star between day and the dark' " (p. 227). The function of the
passage is undoubtedly to demonstrate Ramón's wholeness, which is ambiguously assumed throughout the
work. Like Quetzalcoatl, he apparently reconciles the
opposites within himself: earth and air, up and down,
light and dark, body and mind. Thus, Ramón may be
represented as lord of the two ways, an integrated man.

Nevertheless, the kind of integration that has occurred (after mental consciousness is destroyed and
phallic consciousness takes its place) illustrates Lawrence's rejection of the Jungian view and his limited

grasp of it. The statement "I am on the threshold" echoes "the dark threshold of the lower self" leading to the "unspoken God" (p. 134) of *Kangaroo*, and the quest toward the nonhuman in that novel is, certainly, diametrically opposed to psychic integration. More immediately, the old mentality has died with Mary, the mother surrogate, "on the bed of the *white* moon" and with Jesus, the eternal victim, whom Ramón, like all other Lawrentian heroes, has rejected. As another representative of the predatory woman, Carlota is also repudiated, and Kate gains a new identity only insofar as she, too, disavows the mental life and the will to victimize. It is repeated again and again that "white" and "red" blood do not mix; that the way of Jesus and modern European civilization is finished; and that Ramón represents a new way. Ramón's role as representative of the new way explains his tie to his cosmic, nonhuman origin, and its effect upon him suggests that the kind of wholeness to which Lawrence refers is created by and reflects the primal source alone. Only in this way can the new day be understood and the idea of a society constructed upon the leadership principle be related to it.

The entire thematic background of the novel up to this point indicates how explicitly Lawrence has rejected Jungian integration as part of a fulfilled Ramón. Were it otherwise, Ramón could not achieve manhood at all, but would succumb like Jesus to the Virgin Mother, to the probing instrument of consciousness. For this reason the idea of protective love, like the power urge, must be considered a reflection of the life source or of phallic consciousness. Made manifest in the relationship with Teresa, his new-found ability to love is the final dramatic proof of his rebirth. The point to be repeated is not that Lawrence regards the process of renewal as a reconciliation of opposites, but as a new growth of an entirely different kind, originating in the primal source and in harmony with it.

Yet, toward the end of the novel, this view is sud-

denly contradicted and another notion of the reintegrative process introduced:

> The Mexicans were still this. That which is aboriginal
> in America still belongs to the way of the world before
> the Flood, before the mental-spiritual world came into
> being. In America, therefore, the mental-spiritual life of
> white people suddenly flourishes like a great weed let loose
> in virgin soil. Probably it will as quickly wither. A great
> death come. And after that, the living result will be a
> new germ, a new conception of human life, that will arise
> from the fusion of the old blood-and-vertebrate conscious-
> ness with the white man's present mental-spiritual con-
> sciousness. The sinking of both beings, into a new
> being. . . .
>
> She knew more or less what Ramón was trying to
> effect: this fusion! She knew what it was that made
> Cipriano more significant to her than all her past, her
> husbands and her children. It was the leap of the old,
> antediluvian blood-male into unison with her. And for
> this, without her knowing, her innermost blood had been
> thudding all the time. (P. 415)

One point of view excludes mental consciousness because it threatens the vital self; the other, almost Jungian
viewpoint would fuse "the old blood-and-vertebrate consciousness with the white man's mental-spiritual consciousness" to form a new being.

The presence late in *The Plumed Serpent* of what
amounts to the Jungian concept of integration is difficult
to underestimate. Though he has rejected it many times
previously, this is the first time that Lawrence has seriously entertained the notion in his fiction, and his acceptance of Jung would immediately contradict the
thesis, the organic connection proposed in the work between a sociopolitical program and the vital self. As a
result, the entire psychological process that culminates
in the author's identification of mental consciousness,
Christianity, the possessive woman, and the existing
social order would be unraveled and exposed. The presence of the Jungian concept here, then, suggests a
genuine doubt about the soundness of the vital self chal-

lenging Lawrence's final acceptance of it. In another connection, Kate's reference to her husbands at the end of the passage may have arisen from Lawrence's too closely associating her with Frieda (and himself with Ramón). Up to this point, Kate has had only one husband, Joachim, dead before the story proper begins, so that the author's participation in the characters' quest makes him personally responsible for the thematic confusion.

Since the Jungian theory does not evolve from the Lawrentian, the passage quoted is obviously not planned, though perhaps not accidental either. Ramón maintains the primacy of maleness, mastery, and the cosmic life force to the end, and Kate also rejects the Jungian hypothesis soon after she has made the previous statement: "And as it was in the love-act, so it was with him [Cipriano]. She could not *know* him. When she tried to know him, something went slack in her, and she had to leave off. She had to let be. She had to leave him, dark and hot and potent, along with the things that *are*, but are not known. The presence. And the stranger. . . . It was his impersonal presence which enveloped her. She lived in his aura, and he, she knew, lived in hers, with nothing said, and no personal or spiritual intimacy whatever. A mindless communion in the blood" (p. 423). The means of the characters' renewal, the "mindless communion in the blood," negates the participation of mental consciousness in the renewal process. "She could not *know* him." He is.

The known and the vital selves are irreconcilable, and at the conclusion, in a passage already cited, the conflict in Kate continues: "It was as if she had two selves, one, a new one, which belonged to Cipriano and Ramón, and which was her sensitive, desirous self: the other hard and finished, accomplished, belonging to her mother, her children, England, her whole past. This old accomplished self was curiously invulnerable and insentient, curiously hard and 'free.' In it, she was an individual and her own mistress. The other self was vulnerable, and organically connected with Cipriano, even with Ramón and Teresa, and so it was not 'free' at all" (p. 429). The striking contrast between the old accomplished self and the new emphatically supports the view of the vital self as the product of a psychic split, not of reintegration, as the vitalist critics suggest. The old self is associated with Kate's "mother, her children, England, her whole past," and it is "hard," "insentient," and "free." This self is developing in *The White Peacock* and *The Trespasser*, emerging in *Sons and Lovers*, and is at least momentarily transcended, according to Lawrence, in *The Rainbow* and *The Plumed Serpent*. Isn't this what Lawrence refers to as the "mental-spiritual" self, or the known, Freudian self? It belongs, after all, "to her mother, her children, England, her whole past." Omitting the "her children," there is a reverberation here, an echo of the entire dialectic in the novels, of the unsuccessful though unremitting effort to surmount the facts of experience.

The other self, which Lawrence posits variously as the vital self, the unknown self, the unconscious self, is organic and related to Cipriano, Ramón, and Teresa. This self is "vulnerable," "sensitive," "desirous," not "free," and not mental, though its presence is experienced. Hasn't this self appeared, as well, in *Sons and Lovers*, *The Rainbow*, *Women in Love*, and in greatly modified form in *Aaron's Rod*, *Kangaroo*, and *The Plumed Serpent*? One concept of self is diametrically opposed to the other in the novels and in the passage cited. The Freudian self must be uprooted for the vital self to emerge, yet Kate's departure from Mexico with the knowledge of psychological dissociation implicit in her precipitous retreat shows Lawrence's final unwillingness to cut the Gordian knot completely. Kate's retreat qualifies her acceptance of the vital self; her return to the old world almost cancels out her intellectual rejection of that world; and her attitude toward submission to the male principle is never wholly formulated. The two selves continue to exist side by side in unresolved conflict, and the presence of the Jungian concept in a key passage la.e in the work probably reveals the author's own dissatisfaction with Lawrentian theories.

The significance of the two mutually exclusive principles standing opposite each other is unquestionable. If the "self" under consideration in the novel is only one self whose parts are represented by the characters, the sudden intrusion of the Jungian view signifies Lawrence's partial withdrawal from the extreme ideological and psychological positions that culminate in *The Plumed Serpent*. While he never retracts his theory of consciousness, the presence of an opposing viewpoint is indirect evidence that the author recognizes the inhumanity of the lordship ideal and the kind of self it helps to create. Thus, even though the work presents an extreme and brutalized view of the vital self, it also contains the seeds that modify this perspective in *Lady Chatterley's Lover*. Lawrence's correspondence with Witter Bynner over his reconsidered view of the leadership ideal merely confirms what is already implicit in the novel: "I sniffed the red herring in your last letter a long time: then at last decide it's a live sprat. I mean about *The Plumed Serpent* and the 'hero.' On the whole, I think you're right. The hero is obsolete, and the leader of men is a back number. After all, at the back of the hero is the militant ideal: and the militant ideal, or the ideal militant, seems to me also a cold egg. We're sort of sick of all forms of militarism and militantism, and *Miles* is a name no more, for a man. On the whole I agree with you, the leader-cum-follower relationship is a bore."[9]

Still, the basic criticisms of the work remain. Lawrence's attitude toward humanity is ambiguous and contradictory, and his notion of the vital self is inconsistent

9. Lawrence, *Letters*, II, 1045.

and unrelated to the sexual problems that condition its inception. As a result of the brutal actions committed in the name of the vital self, the work is not unified, and the reader is sometimes aesthetically and morally repelled. Contrary to Lawrence's assertions, the love ethic and the sociopolitical program advocated lead away from rather than toward human wholeness. Caught in the crossfire of conflicting and uncertain aims, Ramón scarcely knows whether to accept, escape, or obliterate humanity in the struggle to overcome his limitations. But the possibility that the vital self is a cul-de-sac is seriously though obliquely considered; the neofascistic ideal of the leader is no longer glorified; and the affirmation of the inhumanly brutal, the devil's compact between the will to power and the expectation of self-fulfillment, is finally moderated if not disowned.

VIII

The Search for Limits
Lady Chatterley's Lover

Unlike the leadership novels in its overly schematized structure, dependence upon plot, and bawdy humor, *Lady Chatterley's Lover* is a deceptively simple, dogmatically defiant, profanely perfect affirmation of life according to Lawrentian principles. It marks an ostensible return to conventional novelistic form, an effort to establish and to remain within well-designated limits, and, above all, a more disciplined attempt at credible characterization to convey the doctrine. Yet the center of interest, which contributes something new to the Lawrence canon, derives from the leadership works, from the conception of the vital self as power urge and protective tenderness. In *Lady Chatterley's Lover*, Lawrence's primary concern is with protective tenderness, which makes his brief description of the novel's theme somewhat misleading: "For England it is a very shocking novel: shocking! But that's because they are fools. It is really a novel contrasting the mental consciousness with the phallic consciousness."[1] In spite of the continuing contrast between these two kinds of reality, the handling of mental consciousness in the work is often perfunctory and occasionally boring. Lawrence has lost interest in it except as a frame of reference, and the analysis of phallic consciousness alone creates the reader's interest and reflects the author's own central preoccupations. The relationship of Constance and Mellors is in fact an outgrowth of the dualistic conception of the vital self he formulated earlier.

At least on the primary level, however, the sub-

1. D. H. Lawrence, *The Collected Letters of D. H. Lawrence*, Harry T. Moore, ed., II, 1047.

ordination of love-as-protective-tenderness to love-as-power-urge constituting the earlier definition of phallic consciousness is now reversed. Lawrence establishes the Constance–Mellors relationship as an illustration of achieved wholeness of being in which both partners to the marriage are humanly fulfilled. As part of the attempt to show this wholeness, Lawrence underplays Mellors' role; the action of the novel springs from Constance's decisions, not from his. "The story of *Lady Chatterley's Lover*," Schorer writes, "is among the simplest that Lawrence devised: Constance Chatterley, the frustrated wife of an aristocratic mine owner who has been wounded in the war and left paralyzed and impotent, is drawn to his gamekeeper, the misanthropic son of a miner, becomes pregnant by him, and hopes at the end of the book to be able to divorce her husband and leave her class for a life with the other man."[2]

In addition, the theme of male leadership is for the most part held in abeyance, and positive political and social preachings are eschewed. Though remaining an outsider, the hero affirms his life within the context of the existing social order, in spite of it, to be sure, but not quite beyond its all-encompassing confines. The ambiguity of Mellors' social position more than any other factor gives *Lady Chatterley* its tone of pathos and persuasiveness and turns the novel into a positive humanistic accomplishment in spite of the doctrine. Viewed obliquely, it is altogether possible to interpret the book according to the notions of vitalist criticism, as the one novel after *Women in Love* in which the preacher and the artist are reconciled, in which assertion and experience square, and in which the hero emerges as an essentially unified person. There is a new sense of warmheartedness and a laying aside of the militant ideal.

But where the doctrine does predominate the work becomes unnecessarily polemical, and the characters are

2. Mark Schorer, "On *Lady Chatterley's Lover*," *Evergreen Review*, I (1957), 160.

often sacrificed to the superimposed thesis. Society, for example, is still associated with all the antilife forces of the industrial order. As the antilife character, Clifford Chatterley tends to be little more than a blooded abstraction, and Mellors and Constance perform equally schematized functions. Like Gerald Crich and Siegmund, Clifford is ultimately reduced by the possessive woman, Mrs. Bolton, and Mellors is simply juxtaposed against him, his symbolic counterpart, the "vitalist" hero. He is the embodiment of the unconscious life-force as Constance, who moves gradually from one world to the other, is of the character in quest. Partly as a result of this schematic and mechanical handling of the characters, *Lady Chatterley's Lover* represents a final formalization of Lawrence's thematic concerns into an almost ossified structural pattern. The formalization is accompanied by a tentative, but not an essential alteration in the direction of his thought.

Julian Moynahan's structural analysis clarifies the nature of this change and suggests the interpretive problem involved:

> *Lady Chatterley's Lover* dramatizes two opposed orientations toward life, two distinct modes of human awareness: the one abstract, cerebral, and unvital; the other concrete, physical, and organic. . . .
>
> The novel's structural method involves a simple juxtaposition of the two modes; its narrative method combines explicit interpretative comment by a narrator who from the beginning makes clear his sympathy for the vitalist viewpoint together with lucid and objective renderings of characters, situations, and settings. Furthermore, there is a sort of synecdochic method employed in the narration. Wragby Hall and the industrial village of Tevershall are realized in themselves but come also to stand for entire industrial, social, and even spiritual orders dominant in twentieth-century England. Sir Clifford Chatterley sums up a modern habit of mind as well as a ruling class in transition from one type of economic proprietorship to another. In contrast, the gamekeeper, Oliver Mellors, not only follows but represents the organic way of

life, and the wood in which he lurks is a spatial metaphor of the natural order, or, what Lawrence frequently called "the living universe."[3]

An examination of Mellors' viewpoint within this framework will reveal that he does not represent the organic view of life at all, but is the product of a psychic split, a fact the vitalist critics of Lawrence do not deem intrinsically important. And while Lawrence himself juxtaposes the two modes in order to indicate why the mechanical world of Clifford and Wragby should be rejected, he does not consider the consequence of this rejection upon the vital self. It is demonstrable, I believe, that the conflict between the opposed principles produces a split within the vital self, which is evident in the dual view of love as power urge and as protective tenderness. Lawrence's claim in the work is that the split can be overcome through the vital self if only consciousness is held in abeyance. The outcome suggests that this cannot happen without further psychic displacement.

The leadership novels demonstrate that the author's view of love based upon the power urge is perverse—a result of Lawrence's theory of consciousness as it affects the vital self. Thus, since the order of the two modes is merely reversed in *Lady Chatterley's Lover*, love based upon protective tenderness must also be perverse, a product of the split within the vital self. To put the matter more directly, Mellors' love for Constance cannot be vital because the doctrine that determines their relationship conceals an unenforceable distinction between love as protective tenderness and as power urge, the components of the vital self from which Lawrence derives his definition of love. One part of the definition negates the other, a claim the leadership novels have abundantly validated. In *Lady Chatterley's Lover*, while the will to power is for the most part held in check, the vital self presented through the sexual intimacies of Mellors and

3. Julian Moynahan, *The Deed of Life: The Novels and Tales of D. H. Lawrence*, pp. 140–41.

Constance remains substantially unchanged. Assertions to the contrary notwithstanding, Constance is indeed "raped into fulfillment," and she does not "use her head as well as her body to escape unwholesome circumstances."[4] The work is acceptable as an affirmation of life, but hardly as the deed of life, a profanely perfect expression of achieved wholeness of being.

The sombre tone of discord and catastrophe struck at the beginning anticipates the dissociation-of-sensibility theme as the cause of the disunity and Lawrence's solution to this problem as the only one possible: "Ours is essentially a tragic age, so we refuse to take it tragically. The cataclysm has happened, we are among the ruins, we start to build up new little habits, to have new little hopes. It is rather hard work: there is now no smooth road into the future: but we go round, or scramble over the obstacles. We've got to live, no matter how many skies have fallen."[5] The author at once establishes himself as omniscient, identifies himself explicitly with his age, and introduces the wasteland theme through such words as *cataclysm*, *ruins*, *tragic*, and *obstacles*. But the tone of muted despair is immediately countered by determined affirmation: "We've got to live, no matter how many skies have fallen." The rest of the novel is a descriptive and prescriptive analysis of the cataclysm and a possible way to survive it.

The causes of the wasteland emerge initially in the background description of the young sisters, Constance and Hilda, as free and rootlessly intellectual: "So they had given the gift of themselves, each to the youth with whom she had the most subtle and intimate arguments. The arguments, the discussions were the great things: the love-making and connection were only a sort of primitive reversion and a bit of an anti-climax. One was less in love with the boy afterwards, and a little inclined to hate him, as if he had trespassed on one's privacy and

4. Moynahan, *The Deed of Life*, p. 144.
5. D. H. Lawrence, *Lady Chatterley's Lover*, p. 1.

inner freedom" (p. 3). The disorientation implicit in the contrast between the discussions and the love-making and connection is then immediately linked to the contemporary social context.

Connie's description of Wragby after her marriage establishes this relationship, for shaking off "the old and sordid connections" (p. 4) of the instinctual life leads directly to the "mechanical anarchy" (p. 16) of the contemporary scene, which Wragby represents. Connie's known self, her freedom and egotistical sense of intellectual superiority, is on the verge of collapse, and the impression of individual dissolution blends with the dreariness of the house to suggest the problem inherent in the times and in the self: "No warmth of feeling united it organically" (p. 16). The descriptive analysis has been made. The prescription to follow shows Mellors offering the only possible alternative to mechanical anarchy through a way of life that is diametrically opposed to freedom and intellectuality.

That which is responsible for the personal displacement, social decay, and sexual impotence is soon introduced. Tommy Dukes speaks for the author, diagnoses the problem of the cast of characters assembled at Wragby, and prepares the reader for Mellors' viewpoint when he says: " 'I wasn't talking about knowledge. . . . I was talking about the mental life,' laughed Dukes. 'Real knowledge comes out of the whole corpus of the consciousness; out of your belly and your penis as much as out of your brain and mind. The mind can only analyse and rationalise. Set the mind and the reason to cock it over the rest, and all they can do is criticise, and make a deadness. I say *all* they can do. It is vastly important. My God, the whole world needs criticizing today. . . . But, mind you, it's like this; while you *live* your life, you are in some way an organic whole with all life. But once you start the mental life you pluck the apple. You've severed the connection between the apple and the tree: the organic connection' " (p. 41). The severed connection leads either to a glorification of the mental life and destructiveness or to the attempted recovery of wholeness of being in a new way.

Himself a prime example of the victimized male, the "mental-lifer," Dukes's statement of belief anticipates the new way that is illustrated through the Mellors–Constance relationship, and it implies the impossibility of regaining organic unity through Jungian means, which intrude at the end of *The Plumed Serpent*: " 'But you do believe in something?' 'Me? Oh, intellectually I believe in having a good heart, a chirpy penis, a lively intelligence, and the courage to say "shit!" in front of a lady.' 'Well, you've got them all' said Berry. Tommy Dukes roared with laughter. 'You angel boy! If only I had! If only I had! No; my heart's as numb as a potato, my penis droops and never lifts its head up, I dare rather cut him clean off than say "shit!" in front of my mother or my aunt . . . they are real ladies, mind you; and I'm not really intelligent, I'm only a "mental-lifer" ' " (p. 43). The contrast between what Dukes is and what he would like to be again illustrates the complete break in him between the two modes of awareness, and the reader's attention is focused upon the emerging thesis. His statement, "I believe in having a good heart, a chirpy penis, a lively intelligence, and the courage to say 'shit!' in front of a lady," forms the philosophical core of the work, and it echoes Lawrence's own view of the centers of consciousness he expressed in the *Fantasia*.

Almost identical with Dukes's comments, Mellors' statement of belief shows that the author's use of four-letter words actually embodies his conception of the known and the vital self: " 'But what *do* you believe in?' she [Constance] insisted. . . . 'Yes, I do believe in something. I believe in being warm-hearted. I believe especially in being warm-hearted in love, in fucking with a warm heart. I believe if men could fuck with warm hearts, and the women take it warm-heartedly, everything would come all right. It's all this cold-hearted fucking that is death and idiocy'" (pp. 240–241). The contrast between "warm-hearted fucking" and "cold-hearted fucking" is essentially a profanely humorous way of stating the difference between modes of awareness, between sex in the head and in the solar plexus. Suggesting the wellsprings of his inner being, Mellors' very dialect reveals the nature of the vital self in contrast to the highly conceptualized, social speech used by others and at times by himself. Thus Mellors' way is diametrically opposed to the mental life and all it stands for, including its verbal expression. His dialect is the voice of the vital self as cultivated English is the language of consciousness.

Dramatically rendered through the opposition of Mellors and Clifford, the antagonism of these two principles is explicitly stated in a dialogue between Constance and Dukes: "'A woman wants you to like her and talk to her, and at the same time love and desire her; and it seems to me the two things are mutually exclusive.' . . . Connie considered this. 'It isn't true,' she said. 'Men can love women and talk to them. I don't see how they can love them *without* talking, and being friendly and intimate. How can they?' 'Well,' he said, 'I don't know. What's the use of my generalising? I only know my own case. I like women, but I don't desire them. I like talking to them; but talking to them, though it makes me intimate in one direction, sets me poles apart from them as far as kissing is concerned. . . . We're all intelligent human beings, and the male and female business is in abeyance. Just in abeyance'" (pp. 62–63). This passage contains the clearest formulation of doctrine in the work and sets the stage for the Constance–Mellors relationship to follow. Consciousness, or talking to women and liking them, is opposed to the unconscious "love and desire her." The two attitudes negate each other: "'I like women,' Tommy Dukes says, 'and *therefore* I don't love them and desire them'" (p. 62). The fact that the "two things don't happen at the same time" (p. 62) in him clinches the reference to psychological dissociation and suggests the only possible alternative to it. Not only Dukes, but all the characters assembled show the same split in one way or another, and the "normal" view of integration is rejected because it will not work. Connie expresses her hope for Jungian reintegration when she remarks that men ought to be able to love women as well as talk to them; the two should not be mutually exclusive.

But they are, and this fact is made clear through the contrast between the Constance–Mellors and the Constance–Clifford relationships. One is a union of phallic consciousness, the other of mental consciousness; one succeeds, the other fails. In the previous description, then, Dukes's suggestion that he knows only his own particular case forms part of the actual generalization made in the work concerning the failure of the integrative process. Dukes feels poles apart from women because the mental life has irreparably damaged his vital self and with it the capacity to maintain a separate male identity. Men and women have fused, have become androgynous reflections of each other, desexed, other-directed mechanisms. Given the universality of the problem and its catastrophic effects, Mellors and Constance's relationship offers the only alternative.

As the preceding passage helps to establish, the counterpointing between Clifford (mechanical mind), Constance (the character in quest), and Mellors (the vital self) is a dialectical one in which Constance moves from one sphere to the other, proving the thesis. With the scales weighted against him from the beginning, the wrongness of Clifford's way ends in his complete reduction by Mrs. Bolton:

> And when she sponged his great blond body, he would say the same: "Do kiss me!" and she would lightly kiss his body, anywhere, half in mockery.
> And he lay with a queer, blank face like a child, with a bit of the wonderment of a child. And he would gaze

on her with wide, childish eyes, in a relaxation of madonna-worship. It was sheer relaxation on his part, letting go all his manhood, and sinking back to a childish position that was really perverse. And then he would put his hand into her bosom and feel her breasts, and kiss them in exaltation, the exaltation of perversity, of being a child when he was a man.

Mrs. Bolton was both thrilled and ashamed, she both loved and hated it. Yet she never rebuffed nor rebuked him. And they drew into a closer physical intimacy, an intimacy of perversity, when he was a child stricken with an apparent candour and an apparent wonderment, that looked almost like a religious exaltation: the perverse and literal rendering of: "except ye become as a little child." —While she was the Magna Mater, full of power and potency, having the great blond child-man under her will and her stroke entirely. (Pp. 340–341)

While critics, notably Eliseo Vivas, have previously discerned the intensity of Lawrence's attack upon Clifford, they have not generally related it to the symbolic frame of reference. Clifford's way is wrong for the reason that the mental life is in itself perverse. Any attempt to use it as an agent in the reintegrative process, according to Lawrence, merely intensifies the perversion by corrupting the vital self. This is truly a revolutionary and extreme view, but it is implicit in the novels from the beginning and merely restated in *Lady Chatterley*.

As the theme, the reasons, and the imagery that describes the male's reduction have already been discussed at length, further analysis is not necessary. The same weakness in the use of the light imagery is evident now as in *Sons and Lovers*—more significance is claimed for it than it can legitimately embody. Such words and phrases as *perversity, child-man, religious exaltation, Magna Mater, full of power and potency, under her will and her stroke*, and *madonna worship* have their roots at least in *The Rainbow*, if not in *The Trespasser*. Perfunctorily and somewhat compulsively, the terminology repeats the associative process that identifies consciousness, the possessive woman, traditional religious values, and the industrial order formulated long ago. In this sense, Clifford is the special victim of the author's conceptualizations, and the one-dimensional, abstract treatment of him also weakens the portrayal of Mellors, his psychic counterpart.

The basis of their opposition is fixed early in the work when Connie's initial response to Wragby as mechanical anarchy is juxtaposed against her impression of the wood: "The wood was her one refuge, her sanctuary. But it was not really a refuge, a sanctuary, because she had no connection with it. It was only a place where she could get away from the rest. She never really touched the spirit of the wood itself . . . if it had any such nonsensical thing. Vaguely she knew herself that she was going to pieces in some way. Vaguely she knew she was out of connection: she had lost touch with the substantial and vital world. Only Clifford and his books, which did not exist . . . which had nothing in them! Void to void" (p. 20). Reminding Constance of her lost wholeness and anticipating her encounters with Mellors, the wood is from the beginning the symbol of the vital self associated with Mellors, of a substantial and vital world complete in itself. The credibility of Mellors as a character, however, is not derived from the background, but from the immediacy of his relation to Constance.

The wood merely enhances Mellors' mystique, his abstract and romantic identification with the spirit of place, as Connie's first encounter with him there confirms: " 'I consider this is really the heart of England,' said Clifford to Connie, as he sat there in the dim February sunshine. . . .'I do! this is the old England, the heart of it; and I intend to keep it intact.' . . . It was only the new game-keeper, but he had frightened Connie, he seemed to emerge with such a swift menace. That was how she had seen him, like a sudden rush of a threat out of nowhere. He was a man in dark green velveteens and gaiters . . . the old style, with a red face and red moustache and distant eyes. He was going quickly down hill" (pp. 47, 51). Clifford's associating the wood with old England and the description of Mellors as being in the old style evoke the symbolic identity between the man, the place, and the nature of the vital self proposed. Perhaps like the Green Knight, Mellors archetypally dresses in green and wears a red mustache, and he signifies potential renewal. The time span of the story proper—between February and late fall, the period of cyclic rebirth, growth, and fruition—is probably significant in this respect as well.

Woven into the archetypal embroidery, the thesis lurks as the sense in which Mellors is a threatening menace. Directed against Connie's free self, his sexual authority demands obedience: " 'Sit 'ere then a bit, and warm yer,' he said. She obeyed him. He had that curious kind of protective authority she obeyed at once. . . . She did not really want to sit, poked in a corner by the fire; she would rather have watched from the door, but she was being looked after, so she had to submit" (p. 99). Stripped of some of its connotations of the power urge and dressed up in dialect, the male principle of the leadership novels once more emerges, disclosing behind the mask of protective authority the assertion of dominion. Connie's extremely ready submission to Mellors here, as elsewhere, conceals his will to power and prevents it from gaining too obvious an ascendancy. To repeat, the same duality that guides Lawrence's conception of the vital self in the leadership novels is also true of *Lady Chatterley's Lover*, and because of the inner fragmentation implicit in the duality, Mellors is not free of the perversity associated with Clifford.

His discontinuity is clear the first time he encounters Constance alone: "He saluted and turned abruptly away. She had wakened the sleeping dogs of the old voracious anger in him, anger against the self-willed female. And he was powerless, powerless. He knew it!" (p. 102). Like Annable and Ramón, Mellors is still the potential victim of the possessive woman, and his with-

drawal to the wood is at once a protest against the conditions of modern life and a response to his own self-
division, which he realizes. Thus Mellors' symbolic
identity with the wood is somewhat misleading, for the
author's actual view of him is potentially contradictory.
Again like Annable and Ramón, his relation to his first
wife, Bertha Coutts, exposes him as the passive male:
" 'And do you think you've always been right with
women?' 'God, no! I let my first wife get to what she
was: my fault a good deal. I spoilt her. And I'm very
mistrustful.' . . . 'And perhaps the women *really* wanted
to be there and love you properly, only perhaps they
couldn't. Perhaps it wasn't all their fault,' she said. 'I
know it. Do you think I don't know what a broken-
backed snake that's been trodden on I was myself!' "
(pp. 238–239). In any ordinary sense, Mellors can scarcely be considered a fulfilled person; even though he is
presented as having attained inner unity before the story
proper begins, he is simply one who has learned to live
outside the center of gravity associated with Clifford and
Tommy Dukes. This is Mellors' claim to our attention,
and his fulfilled relationship with Constance is enlisted
to justify Lawrence's thesis and the hero's life: "For me
it's the core of my life: if I have a right relation with a
woman" (p. 238).

Executing the thesis, however, is another matter.
While the subsequent encounters between them are cal-
culated to demonstrate this right relation as a fulfillment
of the vital self in harmony with the other person, Mellors is never completely free from the social order and
all it represents. Unlike the other Lawrentian heroes
since Paul Morel, he does not attempt to uproot but
merely to evade the known self, and his diatribes against
consciousness unwittingly indicate the extent of his subjection to it. The inconsistency between Mellors' (and
the author's) view of the relationship as fulfilled and his
blunted awareness of personal disturbance accounts for
the discontinuity in the work. Given Lawrence's notion

of organic wholeness, the reader cannot at the same time accept the idea of fulfillment and Mellors' outbursts at what he calls the "Thing." The author cannot maintain both at once, as he seems to do, without negating his thesis and identifying himself wholly with his character.

Thus Mellors' admission that the mental life is a condition of human existence and a never-ending menace to the vital self is crucial:

> He had a sense of foreboding. No sense of wrong or sin; he was troubled by no conscience in that respect. He knew that conscience was chiefly fear of society, or fear of oneself. He was not afraid of himself. But he was quite consciously afraid of society, which he knew by instinct to be a malevolent, partly-insane beast.
>
> The woman! if she could be there with him, and there were nobody else in the world! The desire rose again, his penis began to stir like a live bird. At the same time an oppression, a dread of exposing himself and her to that outside Thing that sparkled viciously in the electric lights, weighed down his shoulders. . . . Driven by desire and by dread of the malevolent Thing outside, he made his round in the wood, slowly, softly. He loved the darkness and folded himself into it. It fitted the turgidity of his desire which, in spite of all, was like a riches; the stirring restlessness of his penis, the stirring fire in his loins! Oh, if only there were other men to be with, to fight that sparkling electric Thing outside there, to preserve the tenderness of life, the tenderness of women, and the natural riches of desire. If only there were men to fight side by side with! But the men were all outside there, glorying in the Thing, triumphing or being trodden down in the rush of mechanised greed or of greedy mechanism. (P. 137)

Clearly a conceptualization of modern industrialism, the "outside Thing" is hardly ambiguous in its further connotation of repressive mind. The Thing is associated in the second paragraph with electric lights weighing down his shoulders and in the third paragraph is contrasted to the darkness in which Mellors enfolds himself. If the symbol is an objective correlative both for the industrial order and for encroaching consciousness, then the differences implicit in the passage between the known and the vital self are clear. The former connotes society, the electric lights, Mellors' fear, and the "malevolent, partly-insane beast," which perhaps echoes Ursula's description of the fangs and terrors of her dream in *The Rainbow*; the latter identifies with the rising penis, "the natural riches of desire," "tenderness," and darkness. Mellors' achievement lies in affirming himself in spite of the Thing, in controlling his anxiety toward it externally, and in refusing to be "trodden down in the rush of mechanised greed or of greedy mechanism." His achievement does not consist of encountering, mastering, or accepting the Thing in himself, for in his exacerbated state of mind it exists outside of him.

And while Mellors can manage his response to the outer world, the response itself is a manifestation of anxiety; it is overemphatic and renders his self-affirmation compulsive and forced. His praise of John Thomas, for example, is not a natural affirmation but a defiant and overly aggressive one, more asserted than real. By the same token, even though Mellors' external control of his anxiety implies a mature recognition of personal limits, it also conceals an ambiguity. As part of the attempt to evade rather than to obliterate the known self, his self-possession distinguishes him, as I have said, from all Lawrentian heroes since Paul Morel. But Mellors still evades himself, and the evasion clarifies the dilemma inherent in his character. He must either accept his limitations and radically modify his view of the vital self or reject his limitations on behalf of the vital self; one precludes the other.

The author's unwillingness to confront the dilemma is evident in the function of the double language: Mellors' use of dialect and conventional English to express his polarities. Though Lawrence would disagree entirely, the idea of the double language itself suggests that both kinds of expression are alike the products of psychic displacement and that they ought to be interdependent rather than separate. For confirmation, all that is necessary is to observe Lawrence's method of dealing with consciousness within the framework established by the dialect: " 'Dunna ax me nowt now,' he said. 'Let me be. I like thee. I luv thee when tha lies theer. A woman's a lovely thing when 'er's deep ter fuck, and cunt's good. Ah luv thee, thy legs, an' th' shape on thee, an' th' womanness on thee. Ah luv th' womanness on thee. Ah luv thee wi' my ba's an' wi' my heart. But dunna ax me nowt. Dunna ma'e me say nowt. Let me stop as I am while I can. Tha can ax me ivrything after. Now let me be, let me be!' And softly, he laid his hand over her mound of Venus, on the soft brown maidenhair, and himself sat still and naked on the bed, his face motionless in physical abstraction, almost like the face of Buddha. Motionless, and in the invisible flame of another consciousness, he sat with his hand on her, and waited for the turn" (p. 247).

Mellors' "tha can ax me ivrything after" recalls Tommy Dukes's comment upon the mutual exclusiveness of loving and talking to women. Both statements suggest the incompatibility of one of the psychic components in the man–woman relationship, and both imply the dissociation of the characters. The major difference is in Mellors' handling of consciousness as it impinges upon him; his "let me be, let me be" is a way of dominating his mental processes so that the vital self, the "another consciousness" of the last sentence, can reassert itself. Implicit in the entire passage is the notion that Mellors can suspend part of his psychic life and live wholly within the vital self. Whether this is the case, however, depends upon the reader's view of the love relationship and how valid an illustration it is of the doctrine. The doctrine rests upon the claims that the mental life can be evaded and that an absolute separation exists between the psychic processes implied by the symbolism. Only in this way, Lawrence suggests, can the problem confronting his characters be solved and Mellors' limitations be accepted without abandoning or essentially modifying the concept of the vital self.

What makes it difficult for the author to present his case convincingly is the implication that Mellors achieves sexual spontaneity and controls his thought processes almost simultaneously: "The quiver was going through the man's body, as the stream of consciousness again changed its direction, turning down-wards. And he was helpless, as the penis in slow soft undulations filled out and surged and rose up, and grew hard, standing there hard and overweening, in its curious towering fashion. The woman too trembled a little as she watched. 'There! Take him then! He's thine,' said the man" (p. 246). This scene in which Mellors turns off the mental lights preparatory to sexual engagement pinpoints one of the difficulties respecting the vital self in *Lady Chatterley's Lover* and in the novels generally. Lawrence would have it that Mellors' erection occurs spontaneously and results automatically in a change in the direction of vital flow, but the compulsive nature of the description suggests a forced spontaneity and a fixation willfully exploited. And if the Constance–Mellors relationship is in fact sodomistic, as several critics maintain, there is a fairly obvious lack of coherence between experience and doctrine.

As the means of conveying the doctrine, the sexual encounters (and the direct terms that describe them) theoretically define and humanize the vital self by equating psychic fulfillment with successful consummation. But the basic assumptions tied to this conception in part negate the thesis, and the view of the vital self presented does not result in protective tenderness. The assumptions are, of course, that the active male and passive female roles are entirely differentiated; that the mental nature prevents psychic and sexual fulfillment; and that no contradiction exists between the dual elements within the vital self, the desire for mastery and for protective tenderness.

Preliminary to examining the two sexual meetings that demonstrate the weakness of Lawrence's viewpoint, a number of secondary assumptions can be granted. Dramatically, the relationship does evolve credibly from Mellors' initially one-sided efforts to comfort and sexually arouse Constance, to her acceptance of him, to the fruition of the relationship when both characters achieve the sexual orgasm together. In addition, given the novel's frame of reference, most passages are neither obscene nor perverse. Depending upon the reader, certain scenes may be aesthetically repulsive, forced, or even exhibitionist, as when Constance encircles Mellors' penis with flowers, orally masturbates him, and glorifies her enslavement generally to Mellors' mystique. Yet even these scenes are credibly rendered from the perspective of dramatic realism and in themselves are affirmations of the life-principle as Mellors conceives it.

The two scenes that illuminate Lawrence's unsatisfactory conception of the vital self are precisely those which reveal Mellors transgressing beyond the human limits of the warm-heartedness he advocates. By violating the spirit of protective tenderness through the compulsion to dominate, he evokes, instead, the inhuman and perverse elements that lie buried within the vital self. The first scene depicts the sexual encounter on the evening before Connie's departure for Europe:

> It was a night of sensual passion, in which she was a little startled and almost unwilling: yet pierced again with piercing thrills of sensuality, different, sharper, more terrible than the thrills of tenderness, but, at the moment, more desirable. Though a little frightened, she let him have his way, and the reckless, shameless sensuality shook her to her foundations, stripped her to the very last, and made a different woman of her. It was not really love. It was not voluptuousness. It was sensuality sharp and searing as fire, burning the soul to tinder.
>
> Burning out the shames, the deepest, oldest shames, in the most secret places. It cost her an effort to let him have his way and his will of her. She had to be a passive,

consenting thing, like a slave, a physical slave. Yet the
passion licked round her, consuming, and when the sensual
flame of it pressed through her bowels and breast, she
really though [thought] she was dying: yet a poignant,
marvellous death.

She had often wondered what Abélard meant, when
he said that in their year of love he and Heloise had passed
through all the stages and refinements of passion. The
same thing, a thousand years ago: ten thousand years
ago! The same on the Greek vases, everywhere! The refinements of passion, the extravagances of sensuality! And
necessary, forever necessary, to burn out false shames and
smelt out the heaviest ore of the body into purity. With
the fire of sheer sensuality.

In the short summer night she learnt so much. She
would have thought a woman would have died of shame.
Instead of which, the shame died. Shame, which is fear:
the deep organic shame, the old, old physical fear which
crouches in the bodily roots of us, and can only be chased
away by the sensual fire, at last it was roused up and
routed by the phallic hunt of the man, and she came to the
very heart of the jungle of herself. She felt now, she had
come to the real bed-rock of her nature, and was essentially shameless. She was her sensual self, naked and
unashamed. She felt a triumph, almost a vainglory. So!
That was how it was! That was life; that was how oneself
really was! There was nothing left to disguise or be
ashamed of. She shared her ultimate nakedness with a
man, another being. (Pp. 288–289)

This passage has been cited by G. Wilson Knight,
among others, to indicate the essentially sodomistic nature of the sexual encounters.[6] Prior to, but less specifically than Knight, Eliseo Vivas also makes this charge.
He links the third paragraph to Mellors' marriage with
Bertha Coutts and infers that his bond with Constance
is also perverted and sodomistic, "the Italian way" of
Benvenuto Cellini.[7] It is not really necessary to prove or
disprove either critic to suggest that neither has granted

6. G. Wilson Knight, "Lawrence, Joyce, and Powys," *Essays
in Criticism*, 11 (1961), 403.

7. Eliseo Vivas, *D. H. Lawrence: The Failure and the Triumph
of Art*, pp. 133–34.

Lawrence more than a cursory and superficial insight into the sexual problem he deals with here. Vivas' conclusion that one relationship is perverse because the other was can be dismissed, since he does not examine Mellors' sexual explorations with Constance in detail. Nor does he consider Mellors' admission of "buggery"[8] with Bertha Coutts at all significant. Yet the whole Mellors–Constance relationship is based upon the assertion that the unconscious source of it makes their union a healthy one and therefore different in kind from Mellors' tie to Bertha. Vivas does not grant Lawrence his initial argument, and so the criticism is not valid. Knight's remarks, on the other hand, are not confirmed, because the passage is too vague to be considered explicitly sodomistic and the criticism too exact.

Nevertheless, neither criticism is without foundation. In the first sentence of the first paragraph, Lawrence introduces a distinction between tenderness and sensual passion, suggesting his awareness that the scene does not on the face of it cohere with his stated thesis. The thesis is, to repeat, that the right relationship of man and woman is one in which individual human significance emerges as a result of mutual success in the sexual encounter. The perverseness of the scene is thus implicitly admitted: "It was not really love. It was not voluptuousness. It was sensuality sharp and searing as fire, burning the soul to tinder."

While not specifying the exact nature of the encounter to illustrate the sensuality, the second, third, and fourth paragraphs do define the sense in which this word is used. The reference to Abélard and Heloise, with their stages and refinements of passion, in the third paragraph, for example, suggests that Mellors is deliberately exploiting the perversely titillating. This conclusion is justified in the same paragraph by Constance's thought that men and women had acted so "ten thousand

8. John Sparrow, "Regina v. Penguin Books Ltd.," *Encounter*, 18 (1962), 36.

years ago," and in the fourth paragraph by the belief that "the phallic hunt of the man" kills shame and fear. The nature of the hunt is implied by Connie's sense of dishonor and by her enduring rather than enjoying the process, as is evident in the second paragraph. Since previous sexual engagement with Mellors has not made her ashamed, the phallic hunt "in the most secret places" must be considered perverse: "It cost her an effort to let him have his way and his will of her. She had to be a passive, consenting thing, like a slave, a physical slave."

That the hunt can be sodomistic, then, as well as many other things is apparent and intended to be so by the description. But to accuse Mellors of sodomy or other perverse acts while he is knowingly engaged in them, and to criticize the work on this basis alone is in a sense irrelevant. Lawrence is asserting throughout the passage that the source of perversity is the mental life and that the very violence of the perverse act burns out consciousness, releases the vital self from bondage, and leads to protective tenderness. The perversity is justified because Constance comes to the "real bed-rock of her nature" thereby.

The central significance of this episode to the work as a whole is now clear, for through this particular engagement, more than any other, Constance theoretically attains ultimate womanhood. Like the Ursula of *Women in Love*, she arrives at her essential self via the African way, and the necessity of her becoming a slave in order to win an identity is not only pronounced here but emphatically stressed elsewhere as the only road to womanhood: "No, no, she would give up her hard bright female power; she was weary of it, stiffened with it; she would sink in the new bath of life, in the depths of her womb and her bowels that sang the voiceless song of adoration. It was early yet to begin to fear the man" (p. 156).

With her submission, however, the power urge comes obliquely into play and with it Lawrence's effort to justify Mellors' perversity by saying it makes a woman out of her. Consequently, the author's suggestion that Constance comes to the jungle at the heart of her self by submitting to Mellors; that her submission is a positive good and leads to real knowledge of her self; and that it permits her to share "her ultimate nakedness with a man" is not true. Her obedience to him can be considered only a part of Lawrence's strategy in gaining the reader's assent to the same kind of love mastery he proposes in *The Plumed Serpent*. In effect, the ends are supposed to justify the means because the source of perversity is mental consciousness. But, even if the reader were disposed to grant this aspect of the thesis, he would have difficulty doing so without granting the whole. Inseparably welded to the theory of consciousness is the assertion that, in overcoming "the old, old physical fear which crouches in the bodily roots of us," Constance simultaneously wins through to the vital self and submits to the lordship principle in Mellors.

Moreover, the doctrine is conveyed through a highly ambiguous use of the words *shame* and *fear* to describe her submission. At the beginning of the previous scene, *shame* has a connotation of silent moral disapproval. She is *unwilling, startled, frightened,* and ashamed. Yet, by the end of the short night, her sense of shame is reduced to simple physical fear, which also has a double connotation—Connie's fear of her body and her fear of the lordship principle in Mellors. By blurring this distinction, Lawrence can have things both ways at once: that Connie's confronting the physical fear in herself leads to "the real bed-rock of her nature," and that her rising unashamed from the encounter results in her complete submission to Mellors, "a passive, consenting thing." Almost as if by sleight of hand, Lawrence presents the overcoming of physical fear as synonymous with acceptance of the lordship principle. Needless to say, this kind of ambiguity is not valid, for if the reader accepts the nature of the sexual engagement and the affirmation of it as credible, he must also accept the lordship principle that underlies it. In this sense, Mellors' insistence upon her fear and passive obedience suggests a lack of protective tenderness and concern for the other person.

John Sparrow's evaluation of this scene in relation to the work as a whole parallels my own point of view: "In this episode Lawrence is 'false to the rule that he follows so faithfully in every other "sexual" passage in the book—the rule that prescribed a full and frank account of what occurred.' . . . That being so, it is surely a remarkable fact that, at a climax of the book, Lawrence should 'do dirt on' his own sexual creed. . . . Was he ashamed, or was he afraid? Either way (or, perhaps, both ways) he lost his nerve . . . and in the very passage in which he utters his loudest paean in praise of shamelessness . . . shame seems to have overcome him. This failure of integrity, this fundamental dishonesty, not only is interesting as a human trait, but . . . may help to explain the failure of *Lady Chatterley's Lover* as a work of art."[9] Lawrence cannot extend his theory of consciousness and his conception of the vital self to the core of human relationships without appearing reductive.

Mellors' deficiency, his lack of protective tenderness, is nowhere more evident than in the forest scene when he and Constance run naked through the wood and copulate in the rain and mud: "She ran, and he saw nothing but the round wet head, the wet back leaning forward in flight, the rounded buttocks twinkling: a wonderful cowering female nakedness in flight. . . . She gave a shriek and straightened herself, and the heap of her soft, chill flesh came up against his body. He pressed it all up against him, madly, the heap of soft, chilled female flesh that became quickly warm as flame, in contact. The rain steamed on them till they smoked. He gathered her lovely, heavy posteriors one in each hand

9. Sparrow, "Regina v. Penguin Books," pp. 39–41.

and pressed them in towards him in a frenzy, quivering motionless in the rain. Then suddenly he tipped her up and fell with her on the path, in the roaring silence of the rain, and short and sharp, he took her, short and sharp and finished, like an animal" (p. 258). While the affirmation of life and glorification of passion ring true, it is a reductive affirmation that celebrates less the truly human relationship than Mellors' own individual potency. His taking her "short and sharp and finished, like an animal," glorifies animality for its own sake, and it suggests that he is more attracted by the "cowering female nakedness" and the power urge than by protective tenderness.

In gaining such an ascendancy, the will to power precludes and victimizes the very warm-heartedness Lawrence advocates, and the episode goes far beyond the stated thesis of the work. Instead of humanizing the sexual relationship, Lawrence tends to dehumanize it. Instead of eliminating sensuality, he tends to justify it. Instead of overcoming the perverse will to power, he tends to glorify and relate it integrally to the sexual bond as a manifestation of the life principle, the vital self. The cumulative effect of such incidents reflects the degeneration of the vital self into mere animalism and the inversion of tenderness to potential cruelty. In this way, he subverts his thesis, and it is impossible to accept the author's last word on the sexual relationship.

In *Lady Chatterley's Lover* Lawrence's endeavor to reveal the human significance of one mode of awareness apart from the other meets with qualified success only. On the positive side, both the tone and the thesis reflect the struggle in coming to terms with the problems of self, society, and human nature. The author does not altogether reject mental consciousness; for the most part he merely evades it. He admits the necessity of existing in a social order, though as an outsider. The institution is more powerful than the man, and he recognizes the inability of the individual to remain totally outside the social context. Human nature has its limits. But like other Lawrentian heroes, Mellors continues to blame one part of the mind for his woes and to insist upon the opposition of the two modes of awareness. Thus the very limits assigned to human nature are in constant danger of being violated.

The reasons for the danger are part and parcel of the means the author uses to describe, evaluate, and transform psychological processes, for the development in the novels is inseparable from the conflict waged in them between various segments of the self embodied in created characters. As Lawrence becomes aware of conflict (*The White Peacock* and *The Trespasser*), the complexity and power of his art increases (*Sons and Lovers*) until the vital self is in view (*The Rainbow* and *Women in Love*), where insight and expression converge and culminate. With *The Rainbow* an almost exact balance is struck between the old, Freudian, known self and the new, vital antithesis. This balance is upset in the last part of *The Rainbow* and in *Women in Love*—the finest of the novels—by Ursula's and Birkin's dogmatic rejection of the modern world, of which Birkin, at least, is so completely and corruptly a part, and by Birkin's assertion that marriage with Ursula will lead ultimately to a rebirth of personality on a radically new basis.

In *The Rainbow* and *Women in Love*, the vital and the known self also become clearly distinguishable, though not yet completely dissociated. Up to this time Lawrence has been engaged by and large in examining the known self and in making several value judgments upon it. Afterward, he is concerned almost exclusively with asserting the new self over the old through a more or less doctrinaire extension of it into political and social areas. His art betrays at once a rational tentativeness in attempting to describe the separate existence of the vital self and a too strident, morally outraged emotionalism that condemns the interference of the known self in the endeavor. During this phase, the two selves are in effect completely divorced yet inextricably bound together in jarring opposition.

The novels from *Aaron's Rod* through *The Plumed Serpent* are therefore uneven and psychologically unbalanced efforts in contrary directions, a defense and further exploration of the vital self and an attack upon the forces that impede its separate development. This imbalance partially accounts for Lawrence's failure to integrate the symbolism and realism of these works and for the marked disparity between the doctrine and the experience he presents. The disparity is less evident in *Lady Chatterley's Lover*, but the novel is still marred by a conflict of means and ends. While a new sense of tenderness is present, the conventional and schematized form of the book is at odds with the rendering of sexual materials in the lives of the two main characters. The form chosen, perhaps deliberately, blurs the basic purpose.

In interpreting the work, Freudian critics have usually related the formal problem to an abnormality in the author and have reduced the novels to case studies of the neuroses conditioning them. They have disregarded Lawrence's fundamental attempt to render the work objectively through his theory of consciousness, a concept that informs every novel and around which, through the light and dark imagery, all the novels progressively develop. The vitalist critics, on the other hand, while attempting to defend the novels, have not been thorough enough in applying their insights and have not looked in the right direction. Their examination of the primary symbolism has been insufficient, and they have obscured Lawrence's basic purpose and his achievement. By superimposing a Jungian view upon the novels and the psychic processes they include, the vitalists in many respects have been responding as much to the Freudians as to the work, and they, too, have not encountered the author on his own ground. For these and similar reasons a new approach to Lawrence is necessary, especially in our time, and I have suggested what I hope will be the basis for such an approach in this study.

I have now come full circle, and the problem of consciousness in relation to the vital self remains substantially the same. The conception formulated in *Sons and Lovers* to transform experience results in a duality Lawrence never overcomes in his novels. Lawrence's repudiation of Christianity, along with the integrative idea he identifies with it in *The Rainbow*, represents the crucial choice in his work. Consequently, a norm based upon the inviolability of the person and the belief in wholeness through grace[10] is replaced by an eccentricity dependent upon compulsion and force. Still, in *Lady Chatterley* Lawrence comes closer to casting aside his compulsions and accepting duality than in any of his earlier writings. The fact that Mellors cannot quite bring himself to submit, though, leads him defiantly in some parts of the book to the verge of the nonhuman, and his final commitment to this way of life is only narrowly averted. Yet, insofar as the novel celebrates profane human perfection and insofar as this condition is

10. I have asserted in "W. H. Auden: A Reading," *Ball State Monograph Number Eighteen* (1970), that the idea of a psychic split and a view of it is of central and crucial significance in the work of major contemporary artists (Yeats, Eliot, Auden, Joyce, Lawrence). Auden arrives at the very notion of Christianity and its relation to psychic integration that Lawrence rejects, and he succeeds, I believe, in joining Freudian and Jungian psychology to the Christian idea of grace. In an essay entitled "Psychological Dissociation in the Victorian Novel," *Literature and Psychology*, 20 (1970), 63–73, I have also tried to show the roots of the modern problem of duality in the Victorian novel and the relationship between this problem and the evolution of novelistic form. In his adaptation of certain novelistic conventions for the purpose of psychodrama and in his treatment of characters and character relationships, Lawrence is the last (and the greatest) of the Victorians.

achieved, it is revealed primarily through Mellors' acceptance of his human condition: " 'Tha'rt real, tha art! Tha'rt real, even a bit of a bitch. Here tha shits an' here tha pisses: an' I lay my hand on 'em both an' like thee for it. I like thee for it. Tha's got a proper, woman's arse, proud of itself. It's none ashamed of itself, this isna' " (p. 260).

To this extent, *Lady Chatterley's Lover* approximates the wisdom, insight, and profane joy of Crazy Jane:

> A woman can be proud and stiff
> When on love intent;
> But love has pitched his mansion in
> The place of excrement;
> For nothing can be sole or whole
> That has not been rent.

And a whole man is also a moral man in "necessarye coniunction" with himself and with others, "Whiche betokeneth concorde."

Bibliography

WORKS

Aaron's Rod. Toronto: The Phoenix Edition, 1954.

Apocalypse. New York: Viking Press, 1931, 1966.

Assorted Articles. New York: Alfred A. Knopf, 1930.

The Boy in the Bush. With M. L. Skinner. New York: Thomas Seltzer, 1924.

The Collected Letters of D. H. Lawrence. Edited by Harry T. Moore. 2 vols. New York: Viking Press, 1962.

Complete Plays. New York: Viking Press, 1966.

The Complete Poems of D. H. Lawrence. Edited by Vivian de Sola Pinto and F. Warren Roberts. 3 vols. Toronto: The Phoenix Edition, 1957.

The Complete Short Stories of D. H. Lawrence. 3 vols. Toronto: The Phoenix Edition, 1957.

D. H. Lawrence's Letters to Bertrand Russell. Edited by Harry T. Moore. New York: Gotham Book Mart, 1948.

Etruscan Places. New York: Viking Press, 1963.

Kangaroo. Toronto: The Phoenix Edition, 1955; with Introduction by Richard Aldington, New York: Viking Press, 1968.

Lady Chatterley's Lover. New York: Cardinal Edition, 1959.

The Lost Girl. Toronto: The Phoenix Edition, 1957.

The Man Who Died. New York: Alfred A. Knopf, 1950.

Mornings in Mexico and Etruscan Places. Toronto: The Phoenix Edition, 1957.

Phoenix: The Posthumous Papers of D. H. Lawrence. Edited by Edward D. MacDonald. London: William Heinemann, 1936.

The Plays of D. H. Lawrence. London: Martin Secker, 1933.

The Plumed Serpent. New York: Alfred A. Knopf, 1952.

"The Portrait of M. M." In *the noble savage*, edited by Saul Bellow, Keith Botsford, and Jack Ludwig, pp. 178–253. 2d issue. New York: Meridian Books, 1960.

Psychoanalysis and the Unconscious; Fantasia of the Unconscious. New York: Viking Press, 1962.

The Rainbow. Toronto: The Phoenix Edition, 1955.

Reflections on the Death of a Porcupine and Other Essays. Bloomington: Indiana University Press, 1963.

Sea and Sardinia. Introduction by Richard Aldington. New York: Viking Press, 1963.

Selected Literary Criticism. Edited by Anthony Beal. New York: Viking Press, 1956.

Sex, Literature and Censorship. Edited by Harry T. Moore. New York: Twayne Publishers, 1953.

The Short Novels. 2 vols. Toronto: The Phoenix Edition, 1956.

Sons and Lovers. Toronto: The Phoenix Edition, 1956.

Studies in Classic American Literature. New York: Viking Press, 1964.

The Trespasser. Toronto: The Phoenix Edition, 1955.

Twilight in Italy. Toronto: The Phoenix Edition, 1955.

The White Peacock. Toronto: The Phoenix Edition, 1955.

Women in Love. Toronto: The Phoenix Edition, 1954.

BIOGRAPHIES

Carswell, Catherine M. *The Savage Pilgrimage: A Narrative of D. H. Lawrence.* London: Secker & Warburg, 1951.

E. T. (Jessie Chambers). *D. H. Lawrence: A Personal Record.* New York: Knight, 1936.

Lawrence, Frieda. *Not I, but the Wind.* New York: The Viking Press, 1934.

Luhan, Mabel Dodge. *Lorenzo in Taos.* New York: Alfred A. Knopf, 1932.

Moore, Harry T. *The Intelligent Heart: The Life of D. H. Lawrence.* New York: Farrar, Straus, and Young, 1954. Rev. ed., 1962.

Nehls, Edward H., ed. *D. H. Lawrence: A Composite Biography.* 3 vols. Madison: University of Wisconsin Press, 1959.

CRITICISM—BOOKS

Aldington, Richard. *Portrait of a Genius, But . . . .* New York: Duell, Sloan & Pearce, Inc., 1950.

Arnold, Armin, ed. *The Symbolic Meaning: The Uncollected Versions of Studies in Classic American Literature.* New York: Viking Press, 1962.

Auden, W. H. *The Dyer's Hand and Other Essays.* New York: Random House, 1962.

Beach, Joseph Warren. *The Twentieth Century Novel: Studies in Technique.* New York: The Century Company, 1932.

Beal, Anthony. *D. H. Lawrence.* New York: Grove Press, 1961.

Blackmur, R. P. *Form and Value in Modern Poetry.* New York: Doubleday and Company, 1957.

Carter, Frederick D. *D. H. Lawrence and the Body Mystical.* London: Folcroft, 1932.

Cavitch, David. *D. H. Lawrence and the New World.* New York: Oxford University Press, 1969.

Chase, Richard. *The American Novel and Its Tradition.* Garden City, N.Y.: Doubleday and Company, 1957.

Clark, L. D. *Dark Night of the Body: D. H. Lawrence's "The Plumed Serpent."* Austin: University of Texas Press, 1964.

Cornwell, Ethel F. *The "Still Point": Theme and Variations in the Writings of T. S. Eliot, Coleridge, Yeats, Henry James, Virginia Woolf, and D. H. Lawrence.* New Brunswick, N.J.: Rutgers University Press, 1962.

Daleski, H. N. *The Forked Flame: A Study of D. H. Lawrence.* Evanston: Northwestern University Press, 1965.

Draper, Ronald P. *D. H. Lawrence.* New York: Twayne Publishers, 1964.

Fiedler, Leslie A. *Love and Death in the American Novel.* New York: Stein and Day, 1960.

Ford, George H. *Double Measure: A Study of the Novels and Stories of D. H. Lawrence.* New York: Holt, Rinehart and Winston, 1965.

Freeman, Mary. *D. H. Lawrence: A Basic Study of His Ideas.* Gainesville: University of Florida Press, 1955.

Goodheart, Eugene. *The Utopian Vision of D. H. Lawrence.* Chicago: University of Chicago Press, 1963.

Hardy, John E. *Man in the Modern Novel.* Seattle: University of Washington Press, 1964.

Hoffman, Frederick J. *Freudianism and the Literary Mind.* Baton Rouge: Louisiana State University Press, 1945.

————, and Harry T. Moore, eds. *The Achievement of D. H. Lawrence.* Norman: University of Oklahoma Press, 1953.

Hough, Graham. *The Dark Sun: A Study of D. H. Lawrence.* New York: Macmillan, 1957.

Kazin, Alfred. *The Inmost Leaf.* New York: Harcourt, Brace, 1955.

Leavis, F. R. *D. H. Lawrence, Novelist.* New York: Alfred A. Knopf, 1956.

Lewis, R. W. B. *The American Adam.* Chicago: University of Chicago Press, 1955.

Moore, Harry T., ed. *A D. H. Lawrence Miscellany.* Carbondale: Southern Illinois University Press, 1959.

Moynahan, Julian. *The Deed of Life: The Novels and Tales of D. H. Lawrence.* Princeton: Princeton University Press, 1963.

Murry, John Middleton. *Son of Woman: The Story of D. H. Lawrence.* London: Cape, 1931.

Nin, Anais. *D. H. Lawrence: An Unprofessional Study.* London: E. W. Titmus, 1932.

Rolph, C. H., ed. *The Trial of Lady Chatterley.* Baltimore: Penguin Books, Inc., 1961.

Schorer, Mark, ed. *Modern British Fiction.* New York: Oxford University Press, 1961.

Spilka, Mark. *The Love Ethic of D. H. Lawrence.* Bloomington: Indiana University Press, 1955.

————, ed. *D. H. Lawrence: A Collection of Critical Essays.* Englewood Cliffs, N.J.: Prentice-Hall, 1963.

Tedlock, Ernest W., Jr. *D. H. Lawrence, Artist and Rebel.* Albuquerque: University of New Mexico Press, 1963.

Tindall, William York. *D. H. Lawrence and Susan His Cow.* New York: Columbia University Press, 1939.

Tiverton, Father William. *D. H. Lawrence and Human Existence.* New York: Philosophical Library, 1951.

Vivas, Eliseo. *D. H. Lawrence: The Failure and the Triumph of Art.* Evanston: Northwestern University Press, 1960.

————. *The Artistic Transaction and Essays on Theory of Literature.* Columbus: Ohio State University Press, 1963.

Weiss, Daniel A. *Oedipus in Nottingham: D. H. Lawrence.* Seattle: University of Washington Press, 1963.

Widmer, Kingsley. *The Art of Perversity: D. H. Lawrence's Shorter Fictions.* Seattle: University of Washington Press, 1963.

Wilson, Edmund. *The Shock of Recognition.* New York: Doubleday, Doran and Company, Inc., 1943.

CRITICISM—ARTICLES

Abel, Patricia, and Robert Hogan. "D. H. Lawrence's Singing Birds." In *A D. H. Lawrence Miscellany*, edited by Harry T. Moore, pp. 204–14. Carbondale: Southern Illinois University Press, 1959.

Abolin, Nancy. "Lawrence's 'The Blind Man': The Reality of

Touch." In *A D. H. Lawrence Miscellany*, edited by Harry T. Moore, pp. 215–20. Carbondale: Southern Illinois University Press, 1959.

Adelman, Gary. "Beyond the Pleasure Principle: An Analysis of D. H. Lawrence's 'The Prussian Officer'." *Studies in Short Fiction* (Fall, 1963), 8–15.

Aldington, Richard. "The Composite Biography as Biography." In *A D. H. Lawrence Miscellany*, edited by Harry T. Moore, pp. 144–53. Carbondale: Southern Illinois University Press, 1959.

Allott, Kenneth, and Miriam Allott. "D. H. Lawrence and Blanche Jennings." *Review of English Literature*, I, iii, 57–76.

Alvarez, A. "D. H. Lawrence: The Single State of Man." In *A D. H. Lawrence Miscellany*, edited by Harry T. Moore, pp. 342–59. Carbondale: Southern Illinois University Press, 1959.

Appleman, Philip. "D. H. Lawrence and the Intrusive Knock." *Modern Fiction Studies*, 3 (1957), 328–32.

———. "One of D. H. Lawrence's 'Autobiographical' Characters." *Modern Fiction Studies*, 4 (1958), 237–38.

Arnold, Armin. "In the Footsteps of D. H. Lawrence in Switzerland: Some New Biographical Material." *Texas Studies in Literature and Language*, 3 (1961), 184–88.

———. "D. H. Lawrence's First Critical Essays: Two Anonymous Reviews Identified." *Publications of the Modern Language Association of America*, 79 (March, 1964), 185–88.

———. "The Transcendental Element in American Literature: Some Unpublished D. H. Lawrence Manuscripts." *Modern Philology*, 60 (1962), 41–46.

Baldanza, Frank. "D. H. Lawrence's Song of Songs." *Modern Fiction Studies*, 7 (1962), 106–14.

Beach, Joseph Warren. "Impressionism: Lawrence." In *The Twentieth Century Novel: Studies in Technique*, pp. 366–84. New York: Appleton, 1932.

Beebe, Maurice. "Lawrence's Sacred Fount: The Artist Theme of *Sons and Lovers*." *Texas Studies in Literature and Language*, 4 (1962), 539–52.

———, and Anthony Tomasi. "Criticism of D. H. Lawrence: A Selected Checklist with an Index to Studies of Separate Works." *Modern Fiction Studies*, 5 (1959), 83–98.

Beharriel, Frederick J. "Freud and Literature." *Queen's Quarterly*, 65 (1958), 118–25.

Bergler, Edmund, M. D. "D. H. Lawrence's 'The Fox' and the Psychoanalytic Theory on Lesbianism." In *A D. H. Lawrence Miscellany*, edited by Harry T. Moore, pp. 49–55. Carbondale: Southern Illinois University Press, 1959.

Bertocci, Angelo. "Symbolism in *Women in Love.*" In *A D. H. Lawrence Miscellany*, edited by Harry T. Moore, p. 83–102. Carbondale: Southern Illinois University Press, 1959.

Betsky, Seymour. "Rhythm and Theme: D. H. Lawrence's *Sons and Lovers.*" In *The Achievement of D. H. Lawrence*, edited by Frederick J. Hoffman and Harry T. Moore, pp. 138–39. Norman: University of Oklahoma Press, 1953.

Birrell, T. H. "Where the Rainbow Ends: A Study of D. H. Lawrence." *Downside Review*, 69 (1951), 453–67.

Blackmur, R. P. "D. H. Lawrence and Expressive Form." In *The Double Agent*, pp. 103–20. New York: Peter Smith, 1935.

Bloom, Harold. "Lawrence, Blackmur, Eliot and the Tortoise." In *A D. H. Lawrence Miscellany*, edited by Harry T. Moore, pp. 360–69. Carbondale: Southern Illinois University Press, 1959.

Branda, Eldon S. "Textual Changes in *Women in Love.*" *Texas Studies in Literature and Language*, 6 (Autumn, 1964), 306–22.

Chamberlain, Robert L. "Pussum, Minette, and the Africo-Nordic Symbol in Lawrence's *Women in Love.*" *Publications of the Modern Language Association of America*, 78 (1963), 407–16.

Corke, Helen. "D. H. Lawrence as I Saw Him." *Renaissance & Modern Studies* (1960), 5–13.

———. "Portrait of D. H. Lawrence, 1909–1910." *Texas Quarterly*, 5 (1962), 169–77.

Cowan, James C. "The Function of Allusions and Symbols in Lawrence's *The Man Who Died.*" *American Imago*, 17 (1960), 241–53.

Craig, G. Armour. "D. H. Lawrence on Thinghood and Selfhood." *Massachusetts Review*, 1 (1959), 59–60.

Dahlberg, Edward, and Herbert Read. "A Literary Correspondence." *Sewanee Review*, 67 (1959), 177–203, 422–45.

Daleski, H. M. "The Duality of Lawrence." *Modern Fiction Studies*, 5 (1959), 3–18.

Dataller, Roger. "Mr. Lawrence and Mrs. Woolf." *Essays in Criticism*, 8 (1958), 48–59.

Davis, Herbert. "*Women in Love*: A Corrected Typescript." *University of Toronto Quarterly*, 27 (1957), 34–53.

Deakin, William. "D. H. Lawrence's Attack on Proust and Joyce." *Essays in Criticism*, 7 (1957), 383–403.

Draper, R. P. "Authority and the Individual: A Study of D. H. Lawrence's *Kangaroo*." *Critical Quarterly*, 1 (1959), 208–15.

———. "D. H. Lawrence on Mother-Love." *Essays in Criticism*, 8 (1958), 285–89.

Elliott, John R., ed. " 'The Man Who Was Through with the World': An Unfinished Story by D. H. Lawrence." *Essays in Criticism*, 9 (1959), 213–21.

Ellmann, Richard. "Barbed Wire and Coming Through." In *The Achievement of D. H. Lawrence*, edited by Frederick J. Hoffman and Harry T. Moore, pp. 253–67. Norman: University of Oklahoma Press, 1953.

Empson, William. "Lady Chatterley Again." *Essays in Criticism*, 13 (1963), 101–4.

Engel, Monroe. "The Continuity of Lawrence's Short Novels." *Hudson Review*, 11 (1958), 210–19.

Engelberg, Edward. "Escape from the Circle of Experience: D. H. Lawrence's *The Rainbow* as a Modern Bildungsroman." *Publications of the Modern Language Association of America*, 68 (1963), 103–13.

Englander, Ann. " 'The Prussian Officer': The Self-Divided." *Sewanee Review*, 71 (1963), 605–19.

Fahey, William A. "Lawrence's *The White Peacock*." *Explicator*, 17 (1958), item 17.

Fergusson, Francis. "D. H. Lawrence's Sensibility." *Hound and Horn*, 6 (1933), 447–63.

Ford, George H. "An Introductory Note to D. H. Lawrence's Prologue to *Women in Love*." *Texas Quarterly*, 6 (1963), 92–97.

———. "The Wedding Chapter of D. H. Lawrence's *Women in Love*." *Texas Studies in Literature and Language*, 6 (1963), 134–47.

Foster, Richard. "Criticism as Rage: D. H. Lawrence." In *A D. H. Lawrence Miscellany*, edited by Harry T. Moore, pp. 312–25. Carbondale: Southern Illinois University Press, 1959.

Fraiberg, Louis. "The Unattainable Self: D. H. Lawrence's *Sons and Lovers*." In *Twelve Original Essays on Great American Novels*, edited by Charles Shapiro, pp. 175–201. Detroit: Wayne State University Press, 1960.

Gajdusek, Robert E. "A Reading of *The White Peacock*." In

A D. H. Lawrence Miscellany, edited by Harry T. Moore, pp. 183–203. Carbondale: Southern Illinois University Press, 1959.

Goldberg, S. L. "*The Rainbow*: Fiddle-Bow and Sand." *Essays in Criticism*, 11 (1961), 418–34.

Goodheart, Eugene. "Lawrence and Christ." *Partisan Review*, 21 (1964), 42–59.

———. "Lawrence and His Critics." *Chicago Review*, 16 (1963), 127–37.

Green, Martin Burgess. "The Composite Biography as Composition Text." In *A D. H. Lawrence Miscellany*, edited by Harry T. Moore, pp. 154–67. Carbondale: Southern Illinois University Press, 1959.

Gregor, Ian. " 'The Fox': A Caveat." *Essays in Criticism*, 9 (1959), 10–21.

Gurko, Leo. " 'The Lost Girl': D. H. Lawrence as a 'Dickens of the Midlands'." *Publications of the Modern Language Association of America*, 78 (1963), 601–5.

———. "*The Trespasser*: D. H. Lawrence's Neglected Novel." *College English*, 24 (1962), 29–35.

Guttmann, Allen. "D. H. Lawrence: The Politics of Irrationality." *Wisconsin Studies in Contemporary Literature*, 5 (Summer, 1964), 151–63.

Hassall, Christopher. "Black Flowers: A New Light on the Poetics of D. H. Lawrence." In *A D. H. Lawrence Miscellany*, edited by Harry T. Moore, pp. 370–77. Carbondale: Southern Illinois University Press, 1959.

Hoffman, Frederick J. "Lawrence's Quarrel with Freud." In *Freudianism and the Literary Mind*, pp. 149–85. Baton Rouge: Louisiana State University Press, 1945.

———. "From Surrealism to the Apocalypse: A Development in Twentieth Century Irrationalism." *Journal of English Literary History*, 15 (1948), 147–65.

Hogan, Robert. "The Amorous Whale: A Study in the Symbolism of D. H. Lawrence." *Modern Fiction Studies*, 5 (1959), 39–46.

———. "D. H. Lawrence and His Critics." *Essays in Criticism*, 9 (1959), 381–87.

———. "Lawrence's 'Song of a Man Who Came Through'." *Explicator*, 17 (1959), item 51.

Honig, Edwin. "The Ideal in Symbolic Fictions." *New Mexico Quarterly*, 23 (1953), 153–68.

Jarrett, James L. "D. H. Lawrence and Bertrand Russell." In *A D. H. Lawrence Miscellany*, edited by Harry T. Moore, pp. 168–87. Carbondale: Southern Illinois University Press, 1959.

Karl, Frederick R. "Lawrence's 'The Man Who Loved Islands': The Crusoe Who Failed." In *A D. H. Lawrence Miscellany*, edited by Harry T. Moore, pp. 265–79. Carbondale: Southern Illinois University Press, 1959.

Kazin, Alfred. "Lady Chatterley in America." *Atlantic Monthly*, 204 (July, 1959), 33–36.

———. "The Painfulness of D. H. Lawrence." In *The Inmost Leaf*, pp. 98–102. New York: Harcourt, Brace and Company, 1955.

———. "Psychoanalysis and Contemporary Literary Culture." *Psychoanalysis and the Psychoanalytic Review*, 45 (1958), 41–51.

———. "Sons, Lovers and Mothers." *Partisan Review*, 29 (1962), 373–85.

Kessler, Jascha F. "Descent in Darkness: The Myth of *The Plumed Serpent*." In *A D. H. Lawrence Miscellany*, edited by Harry T. Moore, pp. 238–61. Carbondale: Southern Illinois University Press, 1959.

———. "D. H. Lawrence's Primitivism." *Texas Studies in Literature and Language*, 5 (1963), 467–88.

Knight, G. Wilson. "Lawrence, Joyce, and Powys." *Essays in Criticism*, 11 (1961), 403–17.

Knoepflmacher, U. C. "The Rival Ladies: Mrs. Ward's *Lady Connie* and Lawrence's *Lady Chatterley's Lover*." *Victorian Studies*, 4 (1960), 141–58.

Kuo, Carol Haseley. "Lawrence's *The Rainbow*." *Explicator*, 19 (1961), item 60.

Lainoff, Seymour. "*The Rainbow*: The Shaping of Modern Man." *Modern Fiction Studies*, 1 (1955), 23–27.

[Lawrence, D. H.] "Prologue to *Women in Love* (Unpublished)." *Texas Quarterly*, 6 (1963), 98–111.

Leaver, Florence B. "The Man-Nature Relationship of D. H. Lawrence's Novels." *University of Kansas City Review*, 19 (1953), 241–48.

Leavis, F. R. " 'Lawrence Scholarship' and Lawrence." *Sewanee Review*, 71 (1963), 25–35.

———. "The Novel as Dramatic Poem (IV): *St. Mawr*." *Scrutiny*, 17 (1950–1951), 38–53.

———. "The Novel as Dramatic Poem (V): *Women in Love* (I)." *Scrutiny*, 17 (1950–1951), 203–20.

———. "The Novel as Dramatic Poem (V): *Women in Love* (II)." *Scrutiny*, 17 (1950–1951), 318–30.

————. "The Novel as Dramatic Poem (VI): *Women In Love* (III)." *Scrutiny*, 18 (1951–1952), 18–31.

————. "The Novel as Dramatic Poem (VII): *The Rainbow* (I)." *Scrutiny*, 18 (1951–1952), 197–210.

————. "The Novel as Dramatic Poem (VII): *The Rainbow* (II)." *Scrutiny*, 18 (1951–1952), 273–87.

————. "The Novel as Dramatic Poem (VII): *The Rainbow* (III)." *Scrutiny*, 19 (1952–1953), 15–30.

Lidenberger, Herbert. "Lawrence and the Romantic Tradition." In *A D. H. Lawrence Miscellany*, edited by Harry T. Moore, pp. 326–41. Carbondale: Southern Illinois University Press, 1959.

Longeville, Timothy. "The Longest Journey: D. H. Lawrence's *Phoenix*." *Critical Quarterly*, 4 (1962), 82–87.

Merivale, Patricia. "D. H. Lawrence and the Modern Pan Myth." *Texas Studies in Literature and Language*, 6 (Autumn, 1964), 297–305.

Miller, James E., Jr. "Four Cosmic Poets." *University of Kansas City Review*, 23 (1957), 312–20.

Moore, Harry T. " 'The Fox'." In *A D. H. Lawrence Miscellany*, edited by Harry T. Moore, pp. 28–48. Carbondale: Southern Illinois University Press, 1959.

————. "*Lady Chatterley's Lover* as Romance." In *A D. H. Lawrence Miscellany*, edited by Harry T. Moore, pp. 262–64. Carbondale: Southern Illinois University Press, 1959.

————. "Lawrence From All Sides." *Kenyon Review*, 25 (1963), 555–58.

Morris, Wright. "Lawrence and the Immediate Present." In *A D. H. Lawrence Miscellany*, edited by Harry T. Moore, pp. 7–12. Carbondale: Southern Illinois University Press, 1959.

Moynahan, Julian. "*Lady Chatterley's Lover*: The Deed of Life." *Journal of English Literary History*, 26 (1959), 66–90.

————. "Lawrence's 'The Man Who Loved Islands': A Modern Fable." *Modern Fiction Studies*, 5 (1959), 57–64.

Mudrick, Marvin. "The Originality of *The Rainbow*." In *A D. H. Lawrence Miscellany*, edited by Harry T. Moore, pp. 56–82. Carbondale: Southern Illinois University Press, 1959.

Murry, John Middleton. "D. H. Lawrence: Creative Iconoclast." In *A D. H. Lawrence Miscellany*, edited by Harry T. Moore, pp. 3–6. Carbondale: Southern Illinois University Press, 1959.

Myers, Neil. "Lawrence and the War." *Criticism*, 4 (1962), 44–58.

Nehls, Edward. "D. H. Lawrence: The Spirit of Place." In *The Achievement of D. H. Lawrence*, edited by Frederick J. Hoffman and Harry T. Moore, pp. 268–90. Norman: University of Oklahoma Press, 1953.

Newman, Paul B. "D. H. Lawrence and *The Golden Bough.*" *Kansas Magazine* (1962), 79–86.

Nicholes, E. L. "The Symbol of the Sparrow in *The Rainbow* by D. H. Lawrence." *Modern Language Notes*, 64 (1949), 171–74.

Noon, William T. "God and Man in Twentieth-Century Fiction." *Thought*, 37 (1962), 35–56.

Panichas, George A. "F. M. Dostoyevsky and D. H. Lawrence: Their Vision of Evil." *Renaissance & Modern Studies*, 5 (1961), 49–75.

———. "D. H. Lawrence's War Letters." *Texas Studies in Literature and Language*, 5 (1963), 398–409.

Peter, John. "The Bottom of the Well." *Essays in Criticism*, 12 (1962), 226–27.

Pinto, Vivian de Sola. "Poet Without a Mask." *Critical Quarterly*, 3 (1961), 5–18.

Porter, Katherine Anne. "A Wreath for the Gamekeeper." *Shenandoah*, 11 (1959), 3–12.

Raleigh, John Henry. "Morals and the Modern Novel." *Partisan Review*, 25 (1958), 241–64.

Read, Herbert. "On D. H. Lawrence." *Twentieth Century*, 165 (1959), 556–66.

Roberts, F. Warren. "The D. H. Lawrence New Mexico Fellowship Fund Collection [A Checklist, 1950–1960]." *Texas Quarterly*, 3 (1960), 211–16.

Ryals, Clyde de L. "D. H. Lawrence's 'The Horse Dealer's Daughter': An Interpretation." *Literature and Psychology*, 12 (1962), 39–63.

Sale, Roger. "The Narrative Technique of *The Rainbow.*" *Modern Fiction Studies*, 5 (1959), 29–38.

Schorer, Mark. "On *Lady Chatterley's Lover.*" *Evergreen Review*, 1 (1957), 149–78.

———. "Technique as Discovery." *Hudson Review*, 1 (1948), 67–87.

———. "Lawrence and the Spirit of Place." In *A D. H. Lawrence Miscellany*, edited by Harry T. Moore, pp. 280–94. Carbondale: Southern Illinois University Press, 1959.

———. "*Women in Love.*" In *The Achievement of D. H. Lawrence*, edited by Frederick J. Hoffman and Harry T.

Moore, pp. 163–77. Norman: University of Oklahoma Press, 1953.

Shapiro, Karl. "The Unemployed Magician." In *A D. H. Lawrence Miscellany*, edited by Harry T. Moore, pp. 378–95. Carbondale: Southern Illinois University Press, 1959.

Sharpe, Michael C. "The Genesis of D. H. Lawrence's *The Trespasser*." *Essays in Criticism*, 11 (1961), 34–39.

Shonfield, Andrew. "Lawrence's Other Censor." *Encounter*, 17 (1961), 63–64.

Snodgrass, W. D. "Lawrence's Rocking Horse." *Hudson Review*, 11 (1958), 191–200.

Sparrow, John. "Regina v. Penguin Books Ltd." *Encounter*, 18 (1962), 35–43.

Spilka, Mark. "Post-Leavis Lawrence Critics." *Modern Language Quarterly*, 25 (1964), 212–17.

———. "The Shape of an Arch: A Study of Lawrence's *The Rainbow*." *Modern Fiction Studies*, 1 (1955), 30–38.

Stanford, Raney. "Thomas Hardy and Lawrence's *The White Peacock*." *Modern Fiction Studies*, 5 (1959), 19–28.

Steinhauer, H. "Eros and Psyche." *Modern Language Notes*, 64 (1949), 217–28.

Tedlock, E. W., Jr. "D. H. Lawrence's Annotations of Ouspensky's *Tertium Organum*." *Texas Studies in Literature and Language*, 2 (1960), 206–18.

Thody, Philip, "*Lady Chatterley's Lover*: A Pyrrhic Victory." *Threshold*, 5 (1961), 36–49.

Van Ghent, Dorothy. "On *Sons and Lovers*." In *D. H. Lawrence: A Collection of Critical Essays*, edited by Mark Spilka, pp. 16–17. Englewood Cliffs, N.J.: Prentice-Hall, 1963.

Vickery, John B. "*The Golden Bough* and Modern Poetry." *Journal of Aesthetics and Art Criticism*, 15 (1957), 271–88.

———. "Myth and Ritual in the Shorter Fictions of D. H. Lawrence." *Modern Fiction Studies*, 5 (1959), 65–82.

———. "*The Plumed Serpent* and the Eternal Paradox." *Criticism*, 5 (1963), 119–34.

Vivas, Eliseo. "Lawrence's Problems." *Kenyon Review*, 3 (1941), 83–94.

———. "Mr. Leavis on D. H. Lawrence." *Sewanee Review*, 65 (1957), 123–36.

———. "The Substance of *Women in Love*." *Sewanee Review*, 66 (1958), 588–632.

———. "The Two Lawrence's." *Bucknell Review*, 7 (1958), 113–32.

Wagner, Robert D., and F. R. Leavis. "Lawrence and Eliot."
    Scrutiny, 18 (1951), 136–44.
Weiner, S. Ronald. "Irony and Symbolism in 'The Princess'."
    In *A D. H. Lawrence Miscellany*, edited by Harry T.
    Moore, pp. 221–38. Carbondale: Southern Illinois Uni-
    versity Press, 1959.
Welch, Colin. "Black Magic, White Lies." *Encounter*, 16
    (1961), 75–79.
Welker, Robert H. "Advocate for Eros." *American Scholar*,
    30 (1961), 191–202.
Werner, Alfred. "Lawrence and Pascin." *Kenyon Review*, 23
    (1961), 217–28.
Widmer, Kingsley. "Birds of Passion and Birds of Marriage
    in D. H. Lawrence." *University of Kansas City Review*,
    25 (1958), 73–79.
———. "D. H. Lawrence and the Art of Nihilism." *Kenyon
    Review*, 20 (1958), 604–16.
———. "Lawrence and the Fall of Modern Woman." *Modern
    Fiction Studies*, 5 (1959), 47–56.
———. "Our Democratic Heritage: D. H. Lawrence." In *A
    D. H. Lawrence Miscellany*, edited by Harry T. Moore,
    pp. 295–311. Carbondale: Southern Illinois University
    Press, 1959.
———. "The Primitive Aesthetic: D. H. Lawrence." *Journal
    of Aesthetics and Art Criticism*, 17 (1959), 344–53.
Wilde, Alan. "The Illusion of *St. Mawr*: Technique and Vision
    in D. H. Lawrence's Novel." *Publications of the Modern
    Language Association of America*, 79 (1964), 164–70.
Williams, Raymond. "The Law and Literary Merit." *Encoun-
    ter*, 17 (1961), 66–69.
———. "Lawrence and Tolstoy." *Critical Quarterly*, 2 (1960),
    33–39.
———. "Our Debt to Dr. Leavis." *Critical Quarterly*, 1
    (1959), 245–47.
———. "The Social Thinking of Lawrence." In *A D. H. Law-
    rence Miscellany*, edited by Harry T. Moore, pp. 295–
    311. Carbondale: Southern Illinois University Press,
    1959.
———. "Tolstoy, Lawrence and Tragedy." *Kenyon Review*,
    25 (1963), 632–50.
Wright, Raymond. "Lawrence's Non-Human Analogues."
    Modern Language Notes, 76 (1961), 426–32.